Lombardi's Left Side

Herb Adderley

Dave Robinson

Royce Boyles

PRAISE FOR *LOMBARDI'S LEFT SIDE*

"A powerful book by two great teammates. Herb Adderley and Dave Robinson remind us that racism was not a part of Lombardi's Green Bay. I love both of these guys. We were an exceptional group in a special time and *Lombardi's Left Side* explains it in outstanding fashion."

PAUL HORNUNG
Green Bay Packers 1957–62, 1964–66; Pro Football Hall of Fame 1986

"Every person who cares about the men who played in the National Football League should read *Lombardi's Left Side*. This is probably the most insightful and powerful book ever written about the Vince Lombardi Era.

Herb Adderley, Dave Robinson and Royce Boyles have written a classic that is destined to be relevant for years."

JOE DELAMIELLEURE
Pro Football Hall of Fame 2003
Buffalo Bills 1973–80, '85
Cleveland Browns 1981–84

"Lombardi's Left Side is different from any other book about the Green Bay Packers. This is a history lesson and insight into the fairness of Vince Lombardi and his Dynasty. It happened during a chaotic time in America, and my friend Herb Adderley, Dave Robinson and co-author Royce Boyles have captured it beautifully."

BILL COSBY

"Herb Adderley is unmistakably one of the greatest to ever put on pads. He was also one of the best teammates I ever had. In the early 1970s, while I was battling injuries and the accompanying demons, Herb was a person who in words and other ways helped me keep my chin up. His passion for and commitment to winning, his compassion for his teammates, and his courage were instrumental for me in overcoming my personal problems. Those things were also instrumental in the 1970 and 1971 Dallas Cowboys going to back-to-back Super Bowls.

I would not expect Herb to co-write a book that was not passionate, provocative and challenging. He has not disappointed."

CALVIN HILL
Dallas Cowboys 1969–74
Washington Redskins 1976–77
Cleveland Browns 1978–81

"Just as they played, Herb Adderley and Dave Robinson have written a hard-hitting book. Two great players, who I am proud to call my friends, have produced a great book that tackles some sensitive issues for the first time. *Lombardi's Left Side* will open your eyes to subjects that are nearly unbelievable."

LEM BARNEY
Detroit Lions 1967–78; Pro Football Hall of Fame 1992

"The game of professional football is an interesting dichotomy. It is brutally physical while, at the same time, beautifully graceful. Some of the greats who played this game, our Hall of Fame players, possessed both physicality and grace. Herb Adderley is both physically graceful as well as graceful in spirit. The Hall of Fame cornerback will go down as one of the greatest who ever played his position. He was a shut-down corner who allowed Lombardi to never have to worry about a wide receiver who lined up across from Herb. I have written multiple articles on many blogs concerning the physical and neurological issues that face the NFL Retired Players as well as the despicable lack of support from the Union leadership whose jobs were given on the backs of those who built the league, the players. It was a call to my home one morning, from Herb, a man I had never met, that encouraged me to continue the fight to define who was responsible for the lack of care that some of his great teammates suffered. He cared about his teammates and, in fact, was to do a benefit to help one of his teammates that night. Herb Adderley's courage, as the Class Representative, defied the deceitfulness and the greed of the NFL Players Association leadership. It is not easy standing up for what is right, but I think Herb, who played in a time of racial unrest, applied many lessons learned in his extraordinary life. As a man lucky enough to have played six years in the NFL, I have a great deal of appreciation for the legends who came before me, and no player is held higher than Herbert Anthony Adderley."

TONY DAVIS
NFL Retired

"David Robinson and Herb Adderley were the greatest teammates a professional football player could possibly have. I played behind one and beside the other. The book they have written, *Lombardi's Left Side*, is the best publication with the best information I have read about the Lombardi Packers. Like a velvet hammer, this beautifully written book by Dave, Herb and co-author Royce Boyles reveals important issues from an explosive time in our country's history. I am proud to say I was part of a team that made a difference in a city, a league and a country. *Lombardi's Left Side* tells our story."

TOM BROWN
Green Bay Packers 1964–68

"Everyone is aware of Coach Lombardi's wins on the football field and his historical championships; however, I think one of the most impressive qualities of the teams he fielded was his players' character and the way in which they approached and played the game. Herb Adderley and Dave Robinson were the ultimate team players and two great examples of the importance of leadership and integrity on a team. Both were outstanding athletes and All-Pro defenders, but they were also men of exceedingly high character who were instrumental in Coach Lombardi's teams reaching the highest level of success. *Lombardi's Left Side* tells the story from the perspective of these two players who achieved greatness during one of the more challenging times in our country's history. It's no coincidence that the championship teams that I've been fortunate enough to coach had a core group of high character leadership ... young men just like Herb and Dave. In my experience, it's what separates championship teams from the rest. The lessons in this book carry over into our daily lives as we all strive to become champions in our own right."

Nick Saban
Head Football Coach
University of Alabama

"Every retired NFL player should read *Lombardi's Left Side.*"

Boyd Dowler
Green Bay Packers 1959–69

LOMBARDI'S LEFT SIDE

Herb Adderley

Dave Robinson
Royce Boyles

Foreword by **Bill Cosby**

Requests for permission should be addressed to: Ascend Books, LLC, Attn: Rights and Permission Department, 12710 Pflumm Road, Suite 200, Olathe, KS 66062

All names, logos, and symbols that appear in this book are trademarks of their individual organizations and institutions. This notice is for the protection of trademark rights only, and in no way represents the approval or disapproval of the text of this book by those organizations or institutions.

10 9 8 7 6 5 4 3 2 1

ISBN: print book 978-0-9836952-6-4

ISBN: e-book 978-0-9836952-7-1

Library of Congress Cataloging-in-Publications Data Available Upon Request

Editor: Cindy Ratcliff
Assistant editors: Jeffrey Flanagan and Blake Hughes
Publication Coordinator: Christine Drummond
Dust Jacket Illustration and Book Design: Cheryl Johnson, S & Co. Design, Inc.

All photos courtesy of Herb Adderley and Dave Robinson unless otherwise indicated.

Every reasonable attempt has been made to determine the ownership of copyright. Please notify the publisher of any erroneous credits or omissions, and corrections will be made to subsequent editions/future printings. The goal of the entire staff of Ascend Books is to publish quality works. With that in mind, we are proud to offer this book to our readers. Please note, however, that the story, the experiences and the words are those of the authors alone.

Printed in the United States of America

www.ascendbooks.com

Lombardi's Left Side

FEB   2013

Dedication

Herb Adderley:

To my mother, Reva Adderley, and my grandmother, Elizabeth White, for taking care of me and guiding me on the right road. I will always appreciate and love them for all they did, including introducing me to God.

I am grateful to The Wissahickon Boys and Girls Club and the many people who volunteered to help the kids of Pulaski Town.

I'd like to thank the two people responsible for my football career: My high school coach, Mr. Charles Martin, and Mr. Vince Lombardi. I can honestly say if weren't for Coach Martin in 1955, there is no way I would have played football, because I thought I was a basketball player. He saw something I didn't realize and see in myself. I will always remember Mr. Charles Martin, and his spirit will always live in me.

Vince Lombardi taught me so much more than football. Will, determination, decency and fairness only begin to describe the qualities he instilled in me. The NFL has never seen his equal.

I also dedicate *Lombardi's Left Side* to the player I patterned my game after, who I believe is the greatest cornerback in the history of football: Dick "Night Train" Lane.

This book is also for my daughter, Toni Adderley, and my grandchildren, Justice and Joshua, who mean more to me than I could ever imagine.

Dave Robinson:

To my mother and father, Leslie and Mary Robinson, for instilling qualities of integrity, honesty and work ethic into my life. To my wife, Elaine, and our 50 years together. She was with me for many great times but also sacrificed much for the benefit of my career and our family.

Thanks also to my head coach Rip Engle and the entire Penn State football staff, who showed me the importance of team work.

Royce Boyles:

This book is dedicated to my father and mother, Frank and Stella Boyles, members of America's greatest generation, and who always gave their best effort to family and friends. My classmates and faculty of the 1966 graduating class of Lincoln High School, Wisconsin Rapids, Wisconsin, mean more to me each day. A special thanks to my friends Terry and Pauline Szelagowski, Class of '66, and Scott Keating, Class of '67, an American hero.

To Herb Adderley and Dave Robinson for trusting me to tell their story.

Foreword by Bill Cosby

When I got the call to write this foreword, I jumped 87 feet in the air! For years I have known that my friend Herb Adderley was a special person with remarkable abilities. My admiration for Herbie and his teammate Dave Robinson has only increased with the revelations in *Lombardi's Left Side*. This book is a fascinating examination of two black football players, but it is much more. Co-author Royce Boyles has placed the Lombardi Dynasty in the context of its time to produce a riveting publication. Congratulations to Herb, Dave and Royce for a job well done.

This is the first foreword that I've had an opportunity to write about a person I've known since I was 14. At any given time, I am happy to talk about how close a friend Herb Adderley is to me. I have this picture in my home where I'm 16 and Herb Adderley is 14. The picture was taken in Wissahickon Boys Club. No weights, no steroids, just a kid sleeping, eating and going to school. I want people to see and feel this human being who went on to become an All-American, an All-Pro, an activist and a very, very great human being. The Wissahickon Boys Club was located in Pulaski Town, and I lived in a place called Somerville. I had to take a bus and get off at the corner of Pulaski and Coulter. The bus let you off right in front of the building. You walked straight up those steps and you were in the Wissahickon Boys Club.

There was the Boys Club and various places where one could go: baseball fields, the rec center. We had those pockets that were all black, but they might end as you crossed the street and moved into Polish, Italian, lower-middle class or lower class areas. The Wissahickon Boys Club tried to build minds, too. No shower. You would get on your bus and go home after you played.

Herb was supposed to enter the 10th grade at Germantown High School, where he would probably become All-Public or perhaps All-State in football, basketball, baseball and track and field. However, basketball coach Webb told Herbie the rule was that no 10th-grader could play varsity basketball. It was my senior year athletically but not academically. In other words, I wasn't eligible to play varsity sports. Webb would not let me play because I was failing everything. He said to me, "Unless you pull those grades up, you cannot play." So I made my decision to go about doing whatever I thought was correct in my life.

I was wondering why Herb transferred to Northeast High School, where he became All-Everything in anything he wanted to play. Mr. Webb's Germantown High team was about 70- to 80-percent black, but Coach Webb had rules. In no way was Mr. Webb racist, but he had a way of dealing with things: no 10th-grader could play on the varsity; nor could you play for his team if you were failing your grades.

Two guys on the Wissahickon team joined another team called the Mt. Airy Badgers. Mr. Berry was our coach. This was the world of an all-black team made up of married men and fellows who had graduated from high school or were getting ready to graduate from high school. Herbie and I were the youngest fellows on the team and for the first time we rode someplace farther than Camden. We did these long car rides and we played in Wilmington, Delaware. Mr. Berry could put six people in his car and we would ride.

Some of the guys we played with were married and had jobs. Some of them played for black colleges. It was a wonderful, clean time and I mean that because the guys were married and their wives let them out to play basketball. I don't remember anybody wanting to have a glass of beer. Wives, family, children.

In those days there was no fast food; there were diners. Hamburgers and sandwiches cost 25 cents. Mr. Berry would buy you two hamburgers and a milkshake. I don't think the FDA and the Cattlemen's Association had recognized yet that people would load up on filler and things like that. You got ground beef; you may have gotten beef that was from some part of the cow, but there was no filler. Gasoline was 22 cents a gallon. The racial segregation in Philadelphia was very, very clear. Whether it was the Wissahickon Boys Club or the Mt. Airy Badgers, I don't remember us playing any white teams. When we played with the Mt. Airy Badgers, we would go to the black section, a black gymnasium or black high school on a Saturday night and they would have a basketball game and a dance. This whole evening of a game and a dance cost 25 cents.

The word "Philadelphia" was very important in the advertising. I remember the signs would say, "All the way from Philadelphia," or "The Philadelphia Mt. Airy Badgers." That got people excited.

The Harlem Globetrotters in those days really and truly were the talk and the pride of basketball in the black community. Those men were heroes in the world of professional basketball. It didn't take much for black teenage boys playing basketball to try to emulate them, to take the ball and palm it, to put the ball in one hand and let it slide down the arm and around the back, or to break into a dribbling act of the Harlem Globetrotters. These are things that never reached fruition, but we tried anyway.

We used to have a guy on our team by the name of Bozo Walker, who was a celebrity and tried out for the Harlem Globetrotters. He was one of those guys who had a reputation all around the city. Everybody in the city knew about Bozo Walker. There would be three or four guys people would talk about who didn't make the cut but wowed the playground people, wowed the neighborhood, wowed the rec center people. And if he chose to join the team like the Mt. Airy Badgers, people would say, "Yeah, and Bozo Walker plays for them." Of course Bozo Walker loved to dribble and tried to make a fool out of anybody who would come up and guard him. And Bozo Walker loved to shoot from any place.

Mr. Berry was this wonderful man. I don't remember Mr. Berry getting angry about anything except one time. It was Wilmington, Delaware, and before the game, they put on these hard 78 records. It was wonderful. We got dressed and came out to warm up. I don't think there were more than 85 people in the stands, but here's what happened, man. They put on music over the loudspeaker and the guy put on the Harlem Globetrotters' "Sweet Georgia Brown." And just played it over and over and over and over. Obviously, their team was used to it; we were not. It was the worst warm-up of any basketball team I have ever played on. I don't think we made two baskets in our warm-up.

The spirit of that music entered our bodies and all of us became Goose Tatum, Marcus Haynes and Sweetwater Clifton. Nobody could stop themselves because of the song and the music, which was the exact theme song of the Harlem Globetrotters. We were hitting each other in the head with the ball by mistake and fumbling it all over the place. Mr. Berry sat and watched this basketball team of his fall into a circus team, a sideshow. We just couldn't stop. The person who was enjoying himself the most was Bozo Walker, who decided to just stay at the foul line during the warm-up. You know, you're supposed to catch the ball from the net, you pass it to the fellow and he shoots a layup. Bozo decided to have none of that. He just took the ball and dribbled it between his legs and around his back down the foul line, he would lose the ball, run and get it, come back and do it some more while we were missing shots and hitting each other in the head. In those days we played four quarters, and I think they were eight-minute quarters. We never recovered from that.

I don't remember the score. At halftime we went back in the locker room and Mr. Berry just looked at us and said, "We are not the Harlem Globetrotters. And I don't think the Harlem Globetrotters would appreciate what we just did. So if you could all just settle down and play basketball the way I know you can, this team can be had." This is the time when I am going to say something magical was happening here. And it was happening to benefit the other team. After we went out on the court, Mr. Berry went over to the scorer's table and I believe he asked the guy not to play the theme song.

But the guy played it again, and I think that other team probably won more games than they deserved to win.

You go into the Hall of Fame of your neighborhood before you go into anything. Herb was a big star; I was happy to be performing in places with him. Herbie was something. The people in the neighborhood were getting on the train just to come see Herbie play. Those people will always take with them the total memory that Herb Adderley lived here.

"Herb Adderley played right there and I lived right here."

This brings about a spirit to the neighborhood. It's too easy to say, "If he can do it, you can do it." I don't think it's that clear in the mind of a kid. Except that kids can see and feel good, knowing that Herb Adderley was right there, *right there*. That Herb Adderley played on this court, bounced the ball here, and that I am a part of that spirit. Perhaps to some kids it will make a difference.

I'm sure the same is true of Dave Robinson.

And then there is Vince Lombardi. Oooohhh, the fairness of this Italian.

Even Jim Brown quotes Lombardi. If a man really feels something, he doesn't care what he sees in color, but what he sees in his heart. Lombardi walked not even thinking about color, and I mean that. It's almost a difficult thing to say because it is a cliché. But if it's heart-felt, it's not a cliché.

This book, *Lombardi's Left Side*, is different from any other book about the Green Bay Packers. This is a history lesson and insight into the fairness of Vince Lombardi and his Dynasty. It happened during a chaotic time in America, and my friend Herb Adderley, along with Dave Robinson and author Royce Boyles, have captured it beautifully.

Bill Cosby

Titletown, USA, was born and named on December 31, 1961, when Lombardi's Packers dismantled the New York Giants 37-0 in the NFL Championship game. From left to right, players Tom Bettis, Willie Davis, Hank Gremminger, Ben Agajanian and Herb Adderley celebrate the win. Willie Wood is visible over Herb's shoulder.

Return to Glory

Profound, fundamental changes. Only a few chosen people ever make them.

Vince Lombardi did for football what Abraham Lincoln did for leadership; what Hank Williams Sr. did for country music; what Elvis did for rock-n-roll; what Miles Davis did for jazz; what Michael Jackson did for pop; what Billy Graham did for evangelism; what Nelson Mandela did for commitment; what Rosa Parks did for dignity; and what Muhammad Ali did for boxing and conviction. These people were unique and relevant. Forever relevant. All of them dominated, transcended and changed how we view their realm of influence.

Like the others, Lombardi did not do it alone.

Two of his greatest players were critical elements in winning championships and moving our country forward in a racially explosive time. Two men who were athletic, bright, courageous, disciplined, hungry, confident, proud, spiritual, decent and black, blazed a trail. They played on the left side of the Green Bay Packers' great defenses during the Lombardi Era.

In 1965, All-Pro left cornerback Herb Adderley was the best corner in the game and Dave Robinson was blossoming into a mistake-free All-Pro at left linebacker. By most accounts, Adderley, Robinson and defensive end Willie Davis formed the greatest left side in the history of the National Football League.

It happened in Wisconsin, of all places. At the time, Wisconsinites were predominately white with little exposure to blacks, and the state's citizens had a history lesson unfold before them.

Two great black men shut down the left side of the football field and opened up the right side of our minds.

Tiny Green Bay, Wisconsin, was the location for one of the greatest sports stories in our nation's history. That Lombardi won five World Championships is phenomenal, but with 40 years of reflection, *how* the Dynasty occurred is much more important than we knew back then.

Vincent Thomas Lombardi is arguably the greatest football coach in history. His accomplishments as head coach and general manager of the Green Bay Packers are historic. A bright man who taught chemistry, physics and Latin at the high school level is gaining recognition these many years later as the National Football League's Renaissance man regarding social issues.

In addition to the civil rights movement, the 1960s brought other issues of historic proportion to America in unprecedented doses.

There were the imminent dangers with the Soviet Union because of the nuclear arms race, Cold War and space exploration as well as the quandary young Americans faced with Vietnam and equal rights. America was a complicated place with multiple concerns.

Amidst this, one renowned athlete stood up to racism and the senseless, ill-advised and misdirected Vietnam War. No one paid a bigger professional price for his convictions than Muhammad Ali. With one sweeping statement, Ali crystalized two issues when he said, "I ain't got no quarrel with them Viet Cong. No Viet Cong ever called me nigger."

In the prime of his career, 1967, Ali was stripped of his WBA Heavyweight Champion title and banned from boxing for nearly four years. He was arrested and found guilty on draft evasion charges. At the same time, military and political "leaders" who lied to the American people and the entire world during the Vietnam and Civil Rights years suffered no such consequences.

Courageous people with convictions usually pay a steep price for their values, as Ali did, and there "ain't no" elected politician of the mid-Sixties who is the measure of Muhammad Ali. He will forever be a hero to millions, including Herb Adderley and Dave Robinson.

Herb Adderley with Muhammad Ali

In the midst of the madness, in a Wisconsin hamlet ruled by a complicated man, sanity, decency and order were on display for the entire world to see. A complex man, Vince Lombardi may have been best described by his director of public relations, Chuck Lane: "He was like the facets of a diamond."

The multidimensional man had a great talent for keeping things simple and not outsmarting himself.

In the 1960s, when much of America appeared to be going to hell in a hand basket, others were on a path to a better life.

Herb Adderley was selected as the Packers' No. 1 draft choice in '61 and Dave Robinson was the team's top pick in '63. Adderley and Robinson were the first two black players taken with a Packers' first-round pick.

Following Robinson's selection, the Packers' executive board called Lombardi on the carpet for using first-round draft choices on black players. Robinson explained how the issue was resolved, "He had drafted Herb Adderley in the first round in '61, then Earl Gros, a white running back, in '62, then he had drafted me in '63. They called him in and said, 'Vince, you're wasting draft choices. You don't have to draft black guys in the first round; you did that two out of three years. Black guys are gonna be available in the third round.'"

"Vince said, 'I'm drafting football players. I'm not drafting white or black, I'm just drafting the best players out there. You guys run the business end of the thing, and I'll run the Green Bay Packer football operation.' Case closed."

Lombardi's emphatic pronouncement to the Packers' board occurred in 1963, one year before Congress passed the Civil Rights Act of 1964.

Renaissance was unpretentious and fundamental under Lombardi's direction. Beginning in 1959 when he arrived, Lombardi changed Green Bay's image from a Siberian outpost to a football Mecca. By 1965 players around the National Football League stood in envy of the Packers Dynasty and knew the team was poised to make a run at another championship. The club was basic: no tricks, no gimmicks.

In '65 the Green Bay Packers had something to prove to the league and to their coach. After ruling the football world in '61 and '62, they had gone two years without capturing a title, and the mini championship drought gnawed at the very soul of the Great Coach. General Manager Lombardi bolstered the offense with an injection of talent in '65 by trading for a speed receiver and a kicker.

When Green Bay shipped left linebacker Dan Currie and his bad knee to Los Angeles for wideout Carroll Dale, Robinson was expected to provide an upgrade at the position. Adderley and Willie Davis played on the '61 and '62 championship teams, but '65 marked the first time Lombardi's Left Side won a crown with Robinson as a member.

Davis said he and Currie never completely meshed on the left side, "About half the time, the play would be snapped and Dan would still be hollering, 'Yeah, Willie.' I would say, 'No, Dan, play the play.' With Dave, we had a minimum of communication."

Robinson was moved to the left side in 1965, partly due to a lobbying effort by Willie. The great defensive end got just what he wanted when the switch was made.

Robinson had a specific job to do for both Davis and Adderley. Lionel Aldridge had said Willie had such small legs he could get an off-season job stomping holes in donuts, so Davis needed Robinson to keep tight ends off his legs.

Adderley wanted a clean shot at running backs that were not stopped near the line of scrimmage, and Robinson was the man to make it happen. "I wanted Dave to keep those big guards off me," Adderley said. "I didn't care if it was Jim Brown, Gale Sayers or Leroy Kelly, if I had them one-on-one, they're down."

Arguably the greatest left side in the history of football: Dave Robinson (89), Willie Davis (87) and Herb Adderley (26).

Robinson delivered for both of his teammates.

Davis said, "The greatest years I had and the greatest time I had was playing next to Dave Robinson."

According to Adderley, "His size, speed, quickness and intelligence made Dave Robinson one of the greatest outside linebackers to ever play in the NFL. In my humble opinion, there is no outside linebacker in the Hall of Fame who deserves to be there more than Dave Robinson. He was a great teammate and made the guys around him better, including his Hall of Fame teammates on The Left Side. That would be Willie Davis and me."

Lombardi made four major personnel moves entering the '65 season and put his team on track for three straight championships. Robinson was moved to left linebacker, Tom Brown became the starting strong safety, Carroll Dale started on the left side at wide receiver and Don Chandler solved all of the problems with the kicking game.

In the history of the National Football League, there may never have been a better left side than Adderley, Robinson and Davis. Two are in the Pro Football Hall of Fame and the other should be. All three were originally accomplished offensive players, were shifted from offense to defense, all were acquired by Lombardi, and each is a member of the NFL 1960's All-Decade Team.

The 1965 Green Bay Packer players knew that their jobs and futures were on the line and responded to the coach's whip. Adderley turned in one of the most remarkable regular seasons by any cornerback ever. He did not allow a touchdown pass to be thrown against him. He also intercepted six passes, returned three for scores and led the league in return yards off interceptions.

"Coming in second didn't set well with Lombardi. In 1963 we finished behind the Bears and in '64 behind the Colts," Adderley said. "At the time there was a second-place game in Miami and Lombardi hated playing in it. He officially named it 'The Losers Bowl.' After our second appearance in '64 Coach said that we would never play in the game again. For many of us that meant we were expected to win the NFL Title in 1965."

The team had a singular goal when it gathered for training camp at Sensenbrenner Hall on the campus of St. Norbert College in De Pere, Wisconsin, in 1965.

"Everybody was upset, especially Vince Lombardi," Robinson said. "During one of the first days of practice when everyone was together Lombardi said, 'That thing down in Miami was an abomination. I'm not going down there again; it's a loser's game played by losers.' It was a game for third place and Vince was all about winning."

A couple of other things irked Lombardi when his teams finished outside the winner's circle. He had to coach the western division Pro Bowl squad. Robinson said, "Vince went to the Pro Bowl with all of his tough rules about curfews and so on, and the guys just laughed at him. They stayed up until one o'clock and some of them showed up at practice hung over or drunk. He said he'd never seen such things and wouldn't coach anymore Pro Bowls. He was going to let his assistants go to the game, but he wasn't going."

———————

Before Lombardi was putting together an equal-opportunity team to dominate the century, the newspapers, magazines, radios and what few television sets were in America's homes in the 1950s, carried accounts of the nation's racial troubles.

Reports of violence and confrontations were the face of a struggle. On December 1, 1955, 42-year-old Rosa Parks refused to give up her seat to a white person on a Montgomery, Alabama, bus and the movement was officially underway. The story was prominent news until Montgomery's buses were desegregated 381 days later.

In September 1957 the Arkansas National Guard was needed to protect nine black students who integrated Little Rock Central High School. Adderley would attend college with Ernie Green, one of the Little Rock Nine. In '57, there was a black student-athlete named Elijah Pitts at Philander Smith College, an all-black institution in Little Rock. Coincidentally, four years later, Pitts and Adderley would be two of six rookies to make Green Bay's roster.

The first Freedom Ride left out of Washington, D.C., on May 4, 1961.

James Meredith, a black man who had served honorably for nine years in the United States Air Force, was refused entrance into the University of Mississippi. With a National Guard escort October 1, 1962, he began attending classes. It was the lead story on the news for days.

On June 11, 1963, Alabama Governor George Wallace tried to block integration of the University of Alabama. There was hardly any other news that mattered, until the next day.

On June 12th, civil rights leader Medgar Evers was murdered in the driveway of his Mississippi home.

Ten weeks after the nightmarish June events, Dr. Martin Luther King Jr. delivered the historic "I Have a Dream" speech on August 28th.

With horror, our nation read accounts of a September 15, 1963, bombing that killed four young girls at the Sixteenth Street Baptist Church in Birmingham, Alabama. It was a cowardly Ku Klux Klan attack.

The bodies of three civil rights workers were found in an earthen dam near Philadelphia, Mississippi, on August 4, 1964. They had been murdered six

Federal District Court Judge Frank M. Johnson, Jr. said, "The law is clear that the right to petition one's government for the redress of grievances may be exercised in large groups ..." A group of more than 500 black marchers seeking the right to vote was brutalized on Bloody Sunday in Selma, Alabama, while peacefully exercising their rights. (March 7, 1965)

weeks earlier by the Klan. Grainy black and white film from the recovery scene showed the ugliness of the event.

Repugnant ignorance and brutality were unleashed on blacks who were peacefully marching from Selma to Montgomery, Alabama, in an effort to gain voting rights. Alabama State Troopers armed with tear gas, night sticks and hatred were turned loose on over 500 people at the Edmund Pettus Bridge in Selma on March 7, 1965. The event became known as Bloody Sunday. An outpouring of support for the Civil Rights Movement resulted when television coverage of the vivid brutality spilled from an Alabama bridge into American living rooms.

ABC television interrupted a Nazi war crimes documentary, *Judgement in Nuremberg*, to show footage of violence in Selma, and an unmistakable resemblance was presented to the nation. The comparison between America, land of the free, and Hitler's racial purges was too obvious to be missed. Within 48 hours, demonstrations in support of the marchers were held in 80 cities.

Watts, California, began burning August 11, 1965. Six days, 34 deaths and 1,032 arrests later, the crisis was reduced to a simmer. The Watts riots were sparked by a racial incident.

On April 4, 1968, Dr. Martin Luther King was assassinated in Memphis, Tennessee. News of the event swept the globe and shook America to the core.

By contrast, from 1959 to 1967, blacks and whites shared a locker room, a city and a dream as they played side by side, galvanized a dynasty, and won five championships in tranquil Green Bay. There were many reports of the Packers' victories, and no reports of racial conflict, water cannons, shootings, tear gas, attack dogs or nightsticks.

Hatred, fear and ignorance, necessary ingredients to feed a national paralyzing fight, were not tolerated at 1265 Highland Avenue, Green Bay, Wisconsin.

For 10 years, Green Bay's franchise operated under the Lombardi Civil Rights Act of 1959.

Black players and their families were integral, respected members of the Packers. Green Bay's leader would have it no other way.

More Important Than the Game

Winning was not the only thing.

Something more important than winning football games occurred during the Lombardi Dynasty. Consider this premise if you will: Vince Lombardi was not the major architect of the Packer Dynasty.

Adderley believes God's hand was firmly in Lombardi's life, culminating with historical social change in Green Bay.

"In my opinion, the *master plan* was set for Vincent T. Lombardi to do what he did in Green Bay; what he did for the team, the NFL and the city of Green Bay," Adderley said. "He understood that, and he surrounded himself with the 'chosen few' to help him reach his goals." Adderley does not use the word "chosen" casually. In his written correspondence, Adderley always capitalizes the word when describing the Lombardi people.

The great cornerback is certain Vince Lombardi and his *Chosen* were involved in work that transcended the game.

In the mid-20th century, the Civil Rights battle was our nation's most important and divisive issue. America was locked in a miserable struggle to deliver on its promises to all people. Lombardi and his players conducted a monumental experiment that wasn't bloody and did not pit one American against another. Just the opposite: blacks and whites wore green and gold in harmony to compile the most romantic domination in NFL history.

Lombardi's team rolled up five NFL Championships in seven years, including three in a row. No team has been able to win three straight World titles since the great Packers squads. On seven occasions, teams have won two in a row but have not been able to win the third. In time, some franchise may tie or break that record; maybe.

But there will never be a duplication of how it was done because the circumstances will never be so explosively similar. At the time, Americans were in a racial fight with themselves. Green Bay's head coach and general manager defied mainstream thinking with his use of a large number of black players.

Lombardi and his *Chosen* few won championships partly because of the character of the people, blacks and whites together, refusing to let anything get in the way. The task was daunting and the results were historic.

It is obvious what Lombardi did for the Packers franchise; in all facets of the organization he exhibited a unique ability to understand what needed to be done. With a collection of competent people, he pushed, pulled, tugged and led Green Bay and the NFL into the modern era. He was the epitome of "You'll follow me even if I have to drag you."

The news and sports media focused on Lombardi's winning; the significance of how it was accomplished went virtually unnoticed. Green Bay's power sweep was obvious; sweeping change was not. The game of professional football was forever changed because black players were used in numbers previously unseen in the National Football League. Most of the black players in Green Bay played defense, and arguably the greatest ones were on the left side. In order for the great Italian to have gotten the Packers job, several things had to go wrong for him and right for Packers fans. An examination of some circumstances in the coach's life seems to indicate "all things work together for good."

After five years as an assistant coach with a very strong New York Giants team, the 45-year-old Lombardi was ready to be an NFL head coach and took the challenge of reviving a once proud Green Bay franchise.

Defensive captain Willie Davis said, "I used to go up in his office; many times he would invite you up just to talk about what concerns were for the week and the status of certain things. I remember once when I went in his office and he was telling me he had applied for the Notre Dame opening and never even got a response. He was saying, 'Willie, you came here and I know in your mind after we talked you had something you wanted to prove. I'm going to tell you, I know why you play the way you do every week. Because it's important to you that you meet all the standards that you set for yourself. You know why I know that? Because I lived through the exact same thing. I tell you, there's nothing more important to me than making the Packers winners. It was my one opportunity and finally I got it and now that I got this chance, I'm not going to blow it.'"

Following successful assistant coaching stops at Fordham University and Army, Lombardi had applied for the head coaching job at Notre Dame. He was a devout Catholic who had considered the priesthood seriously enough to take preparatory classes for the seminary. What a college legend he would have been at the football factory in South Bend, Indiana!

The Golden Domers never gave him a response to his job application. Not a letter of rejection, not a placating interview; nothing.

If Lombardi had landed either the Notre Dame or Giants head coaching jobs and been successful, there is no way he would have ended up in Green

Bay. The Pope is about the only Catholic to be held in higher regard than a winning Notre Dame football coach, and that's not a gimme.

Question: How many successful Irish head coaches have voluntarily left Notre Dame to take a better job?

Answer: The next one will be the first.

Lombardi would not have left his beloved home of New York if he had landed the Giants job, either.

Lombardi's time in Green Bay coincided almost precisely with America's most turbulent social upheaval. The Great Coach was in Titletown from 1959 through '68 and historians generally agree America's modern Civil Rights Movement covered the period 1955 to 1968.

As the empowered leader of the Green Bay Packers, Lombardi made far-reaching changes throughout the organization when he took control in 1959. Adderley said, "His level of awareness of racism and discrimination was raised very high. What he accomplished in Green Bay with the team and the city proves that he implemented change for minorities to play in the NFL and live anywhere in Green Bay."

Lombardi's most important decision may have been an innocuous personnel move involving a player whose best days were behind him. What a coincidence: a future Hall of Fame black defensive back of impeccable character just happened to be available at a very reasonable cash price. Green Bay got him for a little money, not a draft choice or a player. Coincidences are for people who believe in coincidences. Others give credit to a master plan.

According to Adderley, "The great Emlen Tunnell, whom Lombardi brought with him from New York to Green Bay, was the first *Chosen* player and it sent a strong message to everyone associated with the Packers. Emlen lived at the Northland Hotel, the only hotel in town that rented to blacks. At that time, the people in Green Bay didn't want him living next door to them; however, the hotel management didn't care because the visiting teams stayed there also."

Lombardi picked up the tab for Tunnell's stay at the Northland. Tunnel served two years in the military and played eleven years with the Giants before joining Lombardi in Green Bay. He was selected to nine Pro Bowls and became the first black player and first defensive back selected to the Pro Football Hall of Fame. By the time he got to Green Bay, Tunnell was 34 years old and his physical abilities had declined, but Lombardi wanted Tunnell's leadership skills on the field and especially in the locker room. Tunnell was a powerful force who knew what it took to be the type of person Lombardi wanted in a Packers uniform. The legendary defensive back showed the young

Packers how to carry themselves as professionals, and his presence in Green Bay meant it was OK for anyone, including blacks, to play in the frozen outpost.

The door was opened wide by Tunnell for black players like Herb Adderley, Dave Robinson, Willie Davis, Willie Wood, Bob Jeter and others who had what it took to be a Lombardi Packer.

Packers' wide receiver Gary Knafelc (Kuh-NAF-ul) had spent five losing seasons in Green Bay before Lombardi took over. "Coach Lombardi knew we were going to have a lot more blacks in, so he brought Emlen Tunnell in to kind of help them along the way," Knafelc said. "Emlen was not only a great football player, but a great human being. He knew the right buttons to push on everybody. He never offended anybody, but he was such a high-caliber guy, everybody looked up to him: black, white, pink or purple."

History has not given Lombardi proper credit for his masterful managing of race relations during a troubled time in America. Without fanfare he met the issue head on. The landscape was rich with racial land mines in the 1950s and '60s, but there was not a hint of difficulty during his watch.

Without flinching, he drafted and traded for black football players in ratios as high as or higher than any team in the league. He was not going to let any issue undermine team unity or keep him from getting excellent players, regardless of color.

Knafelc said, "Before Coach Lombardi came, we would go to Winston-Salem for two weeks; we'd play the Redskins and then play the St. Louis Cardinals. We stayed at the Oaks Motel and at that time, there was segregation, so the blacks could not stay with us."

The inconvenience of segregation bumped into Lombardi during his first pre-season with Green Bay, and he bumped back.

Knafelc said, "When Coach Lombardi came in, we went down there one year and, in fact, that was the year we used to go to the Holiday Inn for our meals and meetings, and the black players weren't supposed to eat with us."

Tunnell took the black players to the back door of the Holiday Inn to eat. According to Knafelc, "A guy from the hotel says, 'You can't do that.' Somebody told that guy, 'Either he eats with us or your repair bill will be quite extensive.'

"Are you serious?"

"We're serious."

Knafelc said, "From then on they ate with us at all of our meetings and the next year we went to the Army camp. We all stayed at Fort Bragg because we could all be together. Lombardi was going to have none of that (segregation) nonsense."

Tunnell's addition served notice: only high quality people of any color would be part of the team's future.

Baltimore Colts Hall of Fame running back Lenny Moore was asked to react to the name of Emlen Tunnell. With a complimentary gasp he said, "Oooooo, what a fantastic human being. He was class all the way down through. A dear friend, I was a great admirer of his for all he was doing and had done throughout the game."

In 1959 the best black player for Lombardi's needs was Tunnell and he just happened to be available. God, what a coincidence.

––––––––––––

Winning was Lombardi's key to social change and vice versa; it was a circular phenomenon. His use of black players helped him win and winning helped guarantee his black players would be accepted by white teammates, the City of Green Bay, fans and the league.

Lombardi made news as a coach, not as a social reformer.

Remember the saying, "You only get one chance to make a first impression?" Those first black Lombardi players needed to be solid citizens as well as game day winners. If some of them had encountered problems with the law or Green Bay residents, it would have been an impediment to the use of African American players. No such problems arose and there was no better person to help show the way than Tunnell.

One of Lombardi's most perceptive players was wide receiver Boyd Dowler. The outstanding pass catcher is one of two men to play every game for Green Bay during Lombardi's reign. He paid close attention to his coach's management of black players. Dowler said, "He didn't back off because a player was African American. I think he was more concerned with whether he felt he could deal with the player; if he dealt with the issue, the team would deal with the issue. I think he felt comfortable enough and confident enough in his own leadership and in the fact that he was the main influence on the Green Bay Packers. He wasn't afraid of it; he didn't recoil with the thought, 'Oh no, no I don't want to get too many African Americans.' I don't think that bothered him one bit because he thought he was beyond that, above that, and he would handle it and he did. He couldn't have handled it any better."

Eventually, history may give Lombardi his rightful credit for expanding opportunities for African Americans in the National Football League. While the United States was trying to find its way to racial equality in a despicable, embarrassing struggle that drew worldwide attention, significant progress was made by the *Chosen* in Green Bay without incident or publicity.

Willie Davis was raised in the South, served in the Army and played two years in Cleveland before being traded to the Packers; thus, he had experienced several different racial environments. He saw real progress in Green Bay.

There is no ambiguity in Davis' mind what Lombardi accomplished. "I tell you right now, Green Bay would be totally, totally misled if they felt for a minute that Lombardi didn't blaze the way, open the way for black players. Not only in Green Bay, but for the rest of the league, because as he took black players and built us into champions, I think the league started to look around and see these black players make a difference in Green Bay. You saw 'em pop up more frequently in other places and, I think to that extent, it was definitely driven by him."

It was during the '60s that Lombardi sculptured his mystique.

The Sixties were both a time and a phenomenon. In addition to racial troubles, it was a time we began to hear "everything is relative;" there was nothing wrong with anything. Change—individually, culturally and politically—was massive, radical and rapid. Authority and rules were questioned and challenged. It was sex, drugs and rock 'n roll; if you remember the Sixties, you weren't there.

Lombardi was an anomaly because he stood for absolutes: rights and wrongs, while being a champion of change. He was a traditional status-quo, conservative Catholic disciplinarian and yet a liberal catalyst for racial progress. He was a highly respected national figure who stood in stark contrast to an America in the process of redefining itself; he knew who he was and what he believed. Vince Lombardi also knew the difference between individual rights and individual behavior. Incumbent with rights are responsibilities. Lombardi was unlike racial bigots of his times: Governors George Wallace of Alabama, Orval Faubus of Arkansas and other politicians, as well as the NFL's last blatant segregationist owner, George Preston Marshall of the Washington Redskins.

Cohesion in Lombardi's locker room was decidedly advanced compared to the racially divided one Adderley would experience with the Dallas Cowboys a decade later.

"Back in the day, there were quotas on how many black players were on an NFL roster, maybe six or seven total," Adderley said. "Lombardi started playing six or seven just on defense. Other teams eventually started doing the same thing and because of that bold move, it opened the door for more black players to earn a spot on an NFL roster. More importantly, black players got a chance to try out for all positions on offense and defense. On our team, Dave Robinson became the first black starting linebacker in the modern era. As a result of Lombardi's boldness, the NFL was established as a fair opportunity employer. The best players at each position made the team because of their skills, not the color of their skin."

Packers' great offensive tackle Forrest Gregg said, "The way I looked at it, and most of the other players did as well, you play the best players you got. They sure were the best players we had."

Much more happened in remote Green Bay, Wisconsin, in the 1960s than winning football games.

In the book *The Lombardi Legacy*, as well as *HBO*'s 2010 Emmy-award-winning documentary, "Lombardi," one of the coach's most courageous decisions was explored: Black defensive end Lionel Aldridge, who joined the team in 1963, was dating and planning to marry a white, Mormon woman named Vicky Wankier. The following is an excerpt from *The Lombardi Legacy* as Vicky Aldridge Nelson explained her situation: "We didn't get married until a couple years later. At that point in time, we decided we were getting married and Lionel went in to meet with Lombardi because the first interracial couple (player) that had ever gotten married in the NFL had been blackballed from any team in the NFL." The player was rumored to be Cookie Gilchrist who later played in the AFL. Vicky confirmed, "Cookie Gilchrist … mmm, hmm. And so Lionel just wanted to find out what was going to happen if we got married, so he went in and met with Lombardi.

"From the rumors that I'd always heard about Lombardi, he was always very non-prejudiced; he had one goal in mind, and that was to win. He was very fair. I had not talked to him up until that point, because, again, I was just engaged. Lionel called me and told me that Lombardi said, 'You know what, I don't care who you marry, as long as you keep the Green Bay Packer team clean, your nose clean, and you play good football. Don't worry about it, the same thing won't happen to you that's happened to Cookie Gilchrist.'"

Lionel's conversation with Lombardi and subsequent support made all the difference. Vicky does not believe the marriage would have occurred had Lombardi been neutral or opposed to the union. She said, "No, no. As much as Lionel and I loved each other, I know Lionel loved his football. I know that would have been a very hard decision for Lionel to have to make between me and football and if I hadn't had the backing of Mr. Lombardi, I don't think I would have survived in the organization, with the wives, with the husbands, with anything. I don't think it would have been possible."

Make no mistake, interracial marriage in 1965 was a very big issue for the National Football League. So much so, pressure was applied on Lombardi to stop the marriage. According to Vicky Aldridge Nelson, the message was delivered in person, "Yes, the commissioner (Pete Rozelle) came into town and tried to stop it. And Mr. Lombardi said (to Rozelle), 'Absolutely not; this is my team. My team is who my team is and nobody can tell me what I can and cannot do.'"

It is not a leap of faith to believe a man of God like Vince Lombardi was needed to take such a noble stand in the turbulent times of the 1960s, when a powerful commissioner was more concerned about the league's perceived image than human rights. Lombardi backed Rozelle down and time has proven the Green Bay coach was right and Rozelle was wrong.

For decades, baseball denied blacks access to the game at the highest level. On April 15, 1947, a singular event changed the game, if not the country. On that day, Jackie Robinson debuted for Branch Rickey's Brooklyn Dodgers, breaking baseball's "color barrier." Fifty years later, April 15, 1997, Major League Baseball Commissioner Allen H. "Bud" Selig retired Robinson's uniform number 42 in perpetuity, thus recognizing baseball's previous shortcomings and celebrating progress regarding equality and opportunity.

The NFL did not have a seminal moment or event opening the human rights doors; however, evidence indicates Lombardi was a courageous, proactive advocate of advancement at the same time iconic Commissioner Pete Rozelle was passive at best. It's one of those little secrets that will seep out in time as we move further away from the Rozelle years. Pete Rozelle did many things well, but not everything. He was commissioner of a league, not life.

Because the NFL had an unwritten quota on black players, a lot a quality talent was readily available for the American Football League in the inaugural 1960 season. One of the major reasons the AFL became competitive with the established NFL so quickly was because of black players. African-Americans like Abner Haynes, Paul Lowe and Lionel Taylor were starters in the inaugural year of the AFL.

In just its fifth year of existence, the new league took a progressive social stance that was fueled by the players. During the 1964 regular season, several black AFL players were refused service by New Orleans businesses, and white cabdrivers refused to carry black passengers. Cookie Gilchrist and other members of the Buffalo Bills led a league boycott and forced the All-Star game out of Tulane Stadium in New Orleans to Jeppesen Stadium in Houston. Gilchrist reportedly had been blackballed from the NFL for marring a white woman.

Conversely, in 1965, when NFL Commissioner Pete Rozelle tried to get Vince Lombardi to stop a mixed racial marriage, Lombardi told the commissioner to run the NFL and he, Lombardi, would run the Packers.

Lionel Aldridge and Vicky Wankier got married, the Packers won three straight World Championships, the Super Bowl Trophy was named after Lombardi and the AFL forced Rozelle into a merger the NFL wanted desperately to avoid. Never underestimate the role of black players in propelling the AFL to legitimacy and Rozelle to the negotiating table.

As Boyd Dowler said, Lombardi didn't recoil when facing racial issues. Perhaps Green Bay's Great Leader knew his purpose in life was to implement the decree, "On earth, God's work must truly be our own."

Hungry for Greatness

You would do well to get to know him, and very few ever really have. In order to appreciate his tenacity, you must understand his constitution.

He is a Green Bay Packer every day. More than that, Herb Adderley is a man of God every hour. People of courage are people of faith and Adderley is overflowing with both.

It's as if God wanted young Herb Adderley in the fold and put him in a triangle of hope from the beginning. In addition to his home, Adderley's three havens as a kid were Enon Baptist Church, the Wissahickon Boys Club and Fitler Elementary School. His triangle of hope had another name: The Hood.

Adderley was born in a section of Northwest Philly known as Germantown. Within Germantown was a small area nicknamed Pulaski Town because a street by the same name ran through the neighborhood. That was the Hood. Go three blocks in any direction from the middle of P-Town and you're not in P-Town anymore.

Two residents of Pulaski Town provided hope for a better life. Basketball took Frank Washington and Zack Clayton to the fantasy world of the Harlem Globetrotters and painted encouraging dreams for parents and kids of P-Town who wanted a better life.

Adderley said, "All of the boys had visions of playing for the Trotters. Zach was also a famous boxing referee. He was the third man in the ring at the Thrilla in Manila between Muhammad Ali and Joe Frazier."

Men who play sports well and care about kids who play the games are heroes of the Hood. In places like P-Town, lifesaving role models are in short supply.

Throughout the ages, parents have been confounded by their kids. Why do some turn out to be good and others bad when raised in the same environment, by the same people, with the same opportunities and temptations? Heartache and joy were a perplexing mix of emotions for Adderley's mother, Reva. She saw one of her sons pursue a path to glory, the other a life of crime.

Adderley's hunger for greatness began practically the day he was born in Philadelphia, Pennsylvania, June 8, 1939.

Adderley discovered early in life, in a tough area of Philly, that he could make courageous decisions and choose right from wrong. "Most of the time I was either in school, church or the boys club," Adderley said.

Al Chandler was born and raised in P-Town, and since the age of five has been Adderley's friend. Even in his youth, Adderley was a magnet; his athletic achievements and personality drew people to him. Four years younger than Adderley, Chandler's best childhood friend was Nelson Adderley, Herb's cousin, and the three were great buddies. "Nelson and I were just like brothers, we were inseparable," said Chandler. "A lot of people wanted to be Herb's friend, but he was careful who he let into his life. I wanted to be just like him. He was so much an inspiration to me and Nelson. We were following Herb all the way; I looked up to Herb like a giant. He was my idol. A lot of people followed this guy, there were a lot of people who wanted to and he wouldn't let them."

The quality of the person, not level of athletic skill, was crucial to being let into the circle of friends.

In order to understand Herb Adderley, it is critical to realize he has always had the ability to make decisions and follow through on them. Some may call it instinct, but he thinks way too much to be accused of operating solely on gut reaction. From the way he chose his friends as a kid, covered receivers in football, or selected issues to support or oppose, decision-making has been a hallmark of Adderley's very being.

If you comprehend that, you have a *chance* to understand him.

Longtime Adderley friend and educator, John Young, said, "As a high school principal, there were many youngsters I tried to get to have the same mentality that Herb had, to make good sound decisions. Think things through and see the whole picture before you start acting or reacting."

Like many inner-city black kids, Adderley came up the hard way, without some basic influences. In the home, it was Adderley's mother and maternal grandmother, Elizabeth White, who raised him and planted his Christian principles. Prayer and Bible study were a routine part of the day. Throughout his life and to this day, Adderley's core values and decency are a reflection of his love of God. Materially, his mother and grandmother didn't have much, but did their best to provide a Christian home and upbringing. In that regard, they had as much as anybody and gave thanks daily.

Ask anyone who knew him as a youngster and they will quickly tell of Adderley's skill in baseball, football, swimming, gymnastics, badminton, track, volleyball, shuffleboard, billiards and his most favorite sport of all: basketball. The kid had game in lots of sports—softball, handball, dodge ball, it didn't matter, he was the one picked first when choosing up sides.

Kids from other neighborhoods would swing by Wissahickon to play with Adderley and his crew. One such youngster from Mary Channing Wister Elementary School in Somerville was named Bill Cosby; yes, *that* Bill Cosby.

From childhood to senior years, the admiration, respect and friendship between Adderley and Cosby has only grown over the decades. Neither has ever forgotten his roots.

Bill Cosby did OK in athletics, running track and playing football at Temple University. He did really OK in life, becoming a megastar entertainer and national treasure to be admired and cherished for the ages.

Adderley's athletic skills turned heads in elementary school and at the Wissahickon Boys Club. There are guys in lots of 'hoods like that and sadly, most of them don't make it out the right way.

Al Chandler said, "We had a few pretty good athletes in our little four- or five-block area, and I don't believe there was anybody who thought they were better than Herb. Several of them could have made it to the pros, but they got in too much trouble and never went on to college or anything."

Adderley is a living example of the axiom, "There but for the grace of God, go I."

With no father figure at home, Adderley needed to learn from those who were older, and he found mentors and organizations that cared about him. "There are too many people to mention who helped me," a grateful Adderley said. Like many inner-city kids, he found safety, guidance and accomplishment at local athletic facilities where good and decent people helped the kids. Nelson Adderley's father, Albert (Herb's uncle), "was just a tremendous supporter of Herb," according to Al Chandler.

Thank God for Wissahickon Boys Club on the corner of Coulter and Pulaski Avenue. More than an athletic club, Wissahickon was a refuge.

Leonard "Bunky" Rhodes was one of the special men who influenced Adderley, Bill Cosby, Al Chandler and other kids from broken homes in the area. "He was eight to ten years older than most of us," said Cosby. "Bunky and his wife, Muriel, showed us what marriage and respect were. They would feed us, wash our uniforms and were an example of goodness. What they showed us was all good."

Rhodes said, "That boys club saved us all. I cannot tell you how important it was to us."

Al Chandler agreed. "The boys club was the anchor of that whole neighborhood. It was the institution that held us together," Chandler said. "If we went there we were OK; there really wasn't anywhere else for the kids to go. It was difficult to get off of the streets and we had a lot of broken homes. When you went to the boys club, they always wanted to know if you'd done your homework and how your grades were. If you were failing, you couldn't go into the boys club; they wouldn't let you in. That was part of the boys club; they would help you with your homework. All you had to do was ask, but most of the kids weren't asking."

Adderley was asking.

"Yes, I did the easy part of my homework at home," Adderley said. "The hard stuff I did at the Boys Club because of the help from people who cared about us."

With school, sports, church and work, young Adderley was a busy kid. He said, "I worked at a grocery store called the Quality Market that was located in the Hood and I also worked at Hassis Bakery to earn money for my clothes and have a little bit of pocket money."

When Adderley, Al Chandler, and their buddies were growing up, places like Quality Market, Hassis Bakery, the local hardware store, drug store, dry cleaners, shoe shops and other businesses provided a few jobs and made the area somewhat functional. There were more bars, four of them, than anything. Today, big box stores and urban flight have gutted places like P-Town of their few small business and working professionals. The Walmarts of the world have long since gobbled up the mom and pop enterprises.

"The bakery was a big deal in our neighborhood," Chandler said. "A lot of the kids used to work at Hassis Bakery. We also used to get broken donuts and pastry the bakery couldn't sell and we'd feed them to the kids for lunch at the boys club when we were counselors."

According to Chandler, "Today, there are no businesses left in the community and there are no professionals living there."

Because of segregation back in the day, black teachers, doctors, dentists and lawyers lived in the neighborhood, providing role models and hope for a better life. Those folks have zip codes in suburbia these days. Individually and for a nation, in some ways segregation was comfortable; integration and change were not.

A mother and grandmother's love can only do so much, and there were problems in the Adderley household.

"My brother Charles was a major distraction for me starting when we were kids," Adderley said. "Before we were teenagers, he tried often to influence me into doing the bad things that he was starting to do. It should be mentioned that my brother and I attended different schools when we were growing up. He hung out with a bad group of guys and I hung out at the Boys Club and with the good guys at school. Charles made the wrong choices his entire life and he paid for it by losing his freedom."

As testimony, Adderley said, "I give all of the credit to God, for being baptized at the age of six, and to my mother and grandmother for teaching us the difference between right and wrong. I listened to them and also had spiritual guidance. Charles didn't listen and he didn't get baptized; the result of him not doing those two lifesaving things turned him into a career criminal. He started out as a juvenile delinquent before he was a teenager, he refused to attend school and he started stealing."

Adderley said, "When he became a teenager, the only school he attended was court-ordered discipline schools. Eventually, he stopped attending school because he got involved with drugs and in order to buy the drugs, he had to start stealing more, including breaking into locked vehicles, private homes, snatching women's purses and just about anything else to get the money to support his drug habit."

When the younger Adderley moved from Fitler Elementary to Roosevelt Junior High, he was the best athlete at his new school and had a growing passion for basketball. Arch rival Fitzsimmons Junior High, in North Philly, was the only team to beat captain Adderley's Roosevelt squad. Better days and better teams were in Adderley's future; Roosevelt and Fitzsimmons players would play together in senior high.

Philadelphia's public school system had what was known as an "A" and "B" system. All of the kids did not start school or graduate at the same time. Adderley graduated from Roosevelt Junior High in January, in the middle of basketball season, and Germantown Senior High's coach would not allow Adderley to join the team in mid-season.

To resolve the problem, it was suggested Adderely use someone else's address to enroll at another high school in order to play immediately. He found a family to accommodate his needs. The owners of a store located across the street from the Wissahickon Boys Club lived in North Philly and registered Adderley for school using their home address. Problem solved. "It took a week to get the paper work done for my transfer. I was a happy kid at Northeast," said Adderley.

His new school reaped instant rewards. Adderley explained, "I was allowed to try out for the Northeast team and not only did I make it, I earned a starting guard spot."

Adderley's compassion for others, blended with his competitive fire, has been a lifelong trait combination. Of becoming a starter he said, "I felt bad about sending someone to the bench, but it wasn't my decision." Adderley's concern for others springs from a heart of gold, but it's coupled with a steel-sharpened mind and an unflinching courage to do what's right. Standing up for the right things, in the face of adversity, is punctuation on Adderley's life.

When Northeast Coach Ike Woolley added Adderley to the squad, a powerhouse basketball team was assembled. There was one glitch.

In the mid 1950s, Philadelphia, and the nation, had a phenomenal athletic story in the form of a seven-foot high school basketball player by the name of Wilt Chamberlain. He was not Adderley's teammate; he played for rival Overbrook High.

Newspapers were the main source of local sports information during those times and high school sports were covered religiously, with "Wilt the Stilt" being the most tantalizing story.

At the time, a young Philadelphia kid by the name of Steve Sabol followed high school sports with a passion. Now the face, voice and president of NFL Films, Steve was a grade-schooler when Chamberlain was dominating Philly high school basketball courts and sports pages with his compelling size, aura and skill. Sabol said, "The papers spent a lot of time covering football and basketball; those were the two sports. The love of sports is part of the culture of this city. Everybody who was good in one sport knew the other guys who were good. Not that they would necessarily meet each other; the only way you would get to know anybody was by competing against them."

From Fitler Elementary to the Green Bay Packers, Adderely was the best athlete on his team and drew some tough assignments. When prep basketball power Northeast squared off with Overbrook, "I had to jump center against Wilt and try to guard him," Adderley said.

Adderley eventually grew to 6'1"; Wilt had him by a foot. Distinguished Philadelphia sports writer Bill Shefski covered a Northeast-Overbrook showdown and ran the headline over his story: "Adderley holds Chamberlain to 48 points."

Adderley said, "Coach Woolley was really upset about the headline because it was embarrassing to me and the team. When he saw Shefski, Coach let him know his feelings."

The writer calmly explained Wilt scored 90 points the previous week against another school, Roxborrow. Shefski told Wooly, "Herb did a lot better."

After the basketball season, "Mr. Walter Sibson, the baseball coach, called me in his office and asked, 'Do you play hardball?' I told him I did."

"What position?"

"Catching is my favorite, but I also play third base and the outfield."

"Will you come out for our team?"

"How can I be on the track team and baseball team with both going on at the same time?"

The schedules were favorable; it was determined there would be only two conflicts when both teams played on the same day. Adderley said, "Both events were scheduled at our field located at 29th and Cambria Streets. I only participated in the running broad jump and high jump in between innings of the baseball game. I wore my track shorts under my baseball uniform and changed clothes between innings so I could compete in both sports. Both times, I ended up second in the high jump and broad jump. We won both meets and I wasn't missed in the 100-yard dash and 440 relay."

Adderley was a tremendous high school athlete; Wilt Chamberlain was incredible. The high school athletic prowess of Wilt Chamberlain defies description, but Adderley tried. "Wilt was the best track and field athlete in the city at the time. I remember a track meet at our field when Wilt entered with his entourage of twenty or more people. He immediately drew more attention than all the other events. Wilt removed his sweat suit, loosened up his seven-foot body and entered the 440-yard dash and won it in 48 seconds; second best time in the city for the event. After the race, he put his sweat suit back on and relaxed for a moment before winning the shot put. It looked like he threw the shot the length of the football field. He won that event too."

In ho-hum style, Chamberlain then blew Adderley away. "I was standing around the high jump pit and watched in awe as Wilt approached the area. He asked the official to raise the bar up to 6'8" and everybody in the area froze and stared at Wilt. He never removed his sweats or cap before he easily did the old western roll clearing the bar by at least five inches. He then rolled out of the pit, dusted the saw dust off his seven-foot frame and coolly left the scene."

When worn together, "cool" and "incredible" are stunning.

Adderley was no slouch at the event as he blazed a high school 9.8 100-yard dash, ran the third leg of the 440-yard relay and won the running broad jump. In the rich history of Philadelphia high school athletics, a precious few players have been four-sport letter winners. Adderley turned the trick in football, basketball, baseball and track.

Adderley said, "Competing against the great Wilt Chamberlain will always rate in the top sporting events of my athletic career."

According to Steve Sabol, "Everybody in Philadelphia knew Herb Adderley. He was a great, great high school football player. He was to football what Wilt Chamberlain was in this city to basketball. As a high school athlete in Philadelphia, Herb Adderley was a cut below Wilt Chamberlain. That's the magnitude of how great Herb was. I knew him and admired him from afar because of who he was."

The whole football thing almost never happened. "I didn't want to play and my mother didn't want me to play, either," said Adderley. "I had never played organized football. In fact, I had never put the equipment on." However, there was this man, perhaps the most important man in Adderley's early life.

Adderley said, "My football career started my second year in high school when the coach, Mr. Charles Martin, started recruiting me to play. He told me

I had a football mentality; while I was a good basketball player, he said I had the potential to be great at football."

After weeks of lobbying, Martin got his man. "Coach Martin told me that I made one of the best decisions of my life when I agreed to play football. That was the beginning of my second year in high school. I missed my first year of football because of the "A" and "B" system; therefore, I only played two years of football."

When Martin asked Adderley what position he wanted to play, the kid said, "Somewhere I can touch the ball. We decided I would play end and I was issued the number 80 jersey."

Because Adderley's decision to play football was made after practice began, he was given a crash course in the passing game. He had two weeks to learn the routes and patterns.

A week before the opening game, during a scrimmage with another school, one of those "spiritual interventions" occurred. The starting halfback hurt his knee.

The high school running tandem of Adderley and future NFL star Angelo Coia sprang to life. "Herb was playing end and somebody got hurt," said Coia. "Our coach, Charlie Martin, brought him over to play running back and he was a natural. In high school you don't know what's going to happen and what guys can do, but when he got to running back it was all over. He was great, just great. He was a stronger inside runner than I was."

Adderley said, "During the second week of practice, Coach Martin asked me if I had ever run with the ball out of the backfield when I was playing two-hand touch in the streets of my neighborhood. When I answered yes, he asked me if I would fill in until (the former starter) got his knee well enough to play. I did."

Adderley was moved to halfback, teaming with his lifetime friend, Angelo Coia.

Going into his first game, Adderley had lots on his mind. "I was really nervous about playing because my mother didn't know that I was playing football. This was going to be my first game, playing a position I had never played. This was going to be hitting against league competition. I was excited."

Coach Charlie Martin had eight plays for Adderley. In reality, Adderley had to learn four plays; he ran the same four to the right and left.

The first-year running back from P-Town would play his initial football game against Overbrook, Chamberlain's old school.

"We had to travel to our practice field via public transportation to change into our football equipment, then board a chartered bus for the ride to the schools we were playing," Adderley said. "We drove from North Philly to Overbrook's field in West Philly for our first game. We rode through beautiful Fairmount Park." The destination was far from beautiful.

"Coach Martin told us that Overbrook didn't have a home field and we would be playing in a roped off area," Adderley said. "That really surprised all of us because we were looking for and expecting to play in a stadium. As I approached the roped off area, I noticed the field was slanted, which meant I would be running up-hill some of the time and also down-hill."

Adderley noticed some other irregularities in the field. "The area was lined with lime and the city workers who lined the field must have drunk a bottle of Thunderbird or Boone's Farm wine. The intervals were not all five yards apart and the lines were not straight. The guys who did the work weren't straight either. Also, there were no goal posts at either end of the lopsided field."

It was a dazzling debut for Adderley, who ran up and downhill, scoring four rushing touchdowns, two for over 50 yards.

Angelo Coia scored three times, and Northeast smashed Overbrook 49–14.

Following the game, Coach Martin said to Adderley, "I thought you never ran with a football."

"That's the truth."

"You just scored four TDs in your first game."

"Coach, I was scared and running downhill most of the day."

Martin had planned to move Adderley back to wide receiver for the season's second contest, which was a home game against Dobbins Tech. He scrapped the idea and gave Adderley another start at running back. "I scored three rushing TDs, caught a pass for another and Angelo ran two in for scores. After that game, Coach decided to leave me at right halfback and Angelo at left for the rest of the season. The original starter never got his job back, and I still feel bad about that because he had college potential."

Adderley's four-touchdown performance earned him a new number, 23, in addition to the starting halfback job.

"Angelo and I ran wild against every team we played, winning by two and three touchdowns a game," Adderley said. "I led the city and state in scoring, and Angelo and I were both named to the All-Public team at the halfback positions." Northeast went undefeated and won the Public League championship.

"We were both very quiet," Coia said. "We got so much publicity and we had a lot in common when we were in school. It was pretty good: when Herb ran the ball I blocked for him, and when I ran the ball he blocked for me."

Herb Adderley

Longtime Philadelphia sports writer Jack Ryan named Adderley and Coia as the greatest high school backfield in the city's history. Who's to argue? Angelo played seven years in the NFL and Adderley became a Hall of Famer. In appropriate homage of their achievements at Northeast High, Adderley and Coia were inducted into the Pennsylvania Sports Hall of Fame. They went in as a tandem.

Following graduation, Coia, who was a year ahead of Adderley, went on to play for the great Al Davis at The Citadel, a military school.

When Adderley entered his senior year at Northeast the spotlight was on him, and much of a promising future depended on his football performance.

He did not disappoint.

"At the beginning of the football season, Coach Martin told me to keep my grades up because I would be getting some scholarship offers," Adderley said. "I did exactly what he told me, no matter what it was. All he had for me was good advice."

Pro Football Hall of Fame writer Ray Didinger said, "Herb was a great high school player at Northeast High. I think he is the best football player ever to come out of Philadelphia—and Philly has produced some really good ones, including Hall of Fame running back Leroy Kelly. I think Herb was the best. His level of excellence, the number of years he sustained it and the championships he won puts him on a level above everybody from Philadelphia."

Steve Sabol was a freshman at Haverford Prep School in Philly when he witnessed the explosive Adderley in an early season game. "In Herb's senior year we opened with Northeast and we were five-touchdown underdogs," Sabol said. "We would always open the season with one of the teams from the public league. Even though we were smaller and all white, we would play those teams before they were in condition and they never took the game seriously. It was a great way for us to start the season."

Sabol said, "For a prep school, we were pretty good. But Northeast, with Herb at halfback, was defending Public League champions. For some reason, Herb was held out of the game. We got ahead of them 19-0, but with about five minutes left in the game, Adderley came in the game. We had to punt, and the first time Herb touched the ball: 70 yards for a touchdown."

For Sabol and his teammates, the Adderley show had just begun, "We got the ball again; we couldn't gain a first down and had to punt. We kicked it out of bounds. On the second play from scrimmage, pitch out to Adderley and he goes another 65 yards for a touchdown. It was 19–14. We got the ball back and made a couple first downs, ran out the clock and won the game. I always said, 'My God, if Herb would have played the whole game we would have gotten beat by fifty points.' Herb was a schoolboy legend."

Adderley's brilliant senior year carried Northeast High to a second consecutive undefeated regular season. He scored 28 touchdowns in eight games, led the city and state in scoring for the second straight year and was a unanimous All-Public League selection.

The dream season was to end with the championship game at Northeast, but a major distraction occurred. "I had a death threat in 1955 the week before we played against Gratz for the Public League high school title," Adderley said. "It scared the hell out of me, my mother and grandmother because whoever did it called our house several times."

Security was tight and safeguards were taken to protect Adderley. "The police were notified and I had protection going to and from school the entire week before the game," he said. "We didn't know where we were going to play until the bus pulled up at Front and Ducannon streets at Olney High School's field. The only people at the game were school officials, teachers, plain-clothes police officers and uniformed officers. No students attended because they didn't know where the game was being played. We won 38–12."

High school football fans in Philly knew Northeast was the best team around, but on paper the successful season was wiped out.

"The second undefeated season was forfeited because we had a second string lineman who was ineligible due to his age," Adderley said. "He played in our first win, a 27–0 rout against Dobbins. He played the last few minutes of that game and never played another minute after that."

Adderley said, "At the end of the year Coach Martin told us that he and athletic director Gus Giegus had to turn the ineligible player in to the school board." The great mentor delivered a painful but principled message.

Adderley said, "I still had a half year of basketball left, so I started playing the week after football ended. We were undefeated when I graduated in January, halfway through the season."

Having carved a remarkable athletic career at Northeast High, a way out of the Hood was waiting for Reva's youngest son. College scholarship offers came rolling in and, once again, Charlie Martin lent his trusted guidance.

"Coach Martin told me that I had to make up my mind which scholarship to accept and I needed to do it soon," Adderley said. "He noticed I wasn't too excited about the colleges that contacted him asking about me, so one day he asked me to stop by his office to hear what was on my mind. He asked me where I wanted to attend college and I told him Michigan State."

It was another role model who influenced Adderley's decision. Much to Martin's surprise, Adderley said, "I watched Michigan State on TV a few times and number 26, Clarence Peaks, is my hero. I want to follow in his footsteps."

Fortunately for Adderley, Martin knew MSU head coach Duffy Dougherty and told the Spartan's head man about the blue chip running back from Philadelphia.

Adderley said, "Duffy requested some film of me to see if I had potential to play Big Ten football at Michigan State. We didn't take film back in the day, which meant I would have to go as a 'walk on' and earn a scholarship."

In the running for Adderley's talents was a dominant black school from the South. Florida A&M was the best football program in the Sunshine State that Caucasians didn't know about. Before integration, where do you think all of that black Florida talent went? Because the University of Florida and Florida State fielded all-white teams in 1957, the Rattlers of A&M were loaded and probably would have smoked any Florida school if a game could have been scheduled.

"The famous coach from A&M, Jake Gaither, made a trip to Philly to recruit me," Adderley said. "I was impressed but not enough to change my mind about going to MSU. Coach Gaither told me I would get caught up in too much competition at MSU and I wouldn't make it." Backing down from a challenge was not in the kid's DNA.

Adderley said, "That was incentive for me to try harder to make the team. I also believed Coach Martin when he said I would be as good as or better than the competition. He never gave me bad advice."

One trip to East Lansing, Michigan, spelled doom for any other school seeking Adderley's services. Upon returning to Northeast High, Adderley met with his trusted advisor, Charlie Martin. "After we shook hands and hugged each other, I took a seat in his office and started talking. I told him the same thing I shared with my mother and grandmother. The highlights of my visit were meeting my idol, Clarence Peaks, and Coach Duffy Daugherty. I told Coach Martin how huge and beautiful the campus was and the size of the stadium compared to our matchbox at 29th and Cambia."

Spartan Stadium had goal posts, a level field, straight lines and seats for 76,000 Big Ten fans. During his visit to the football shrine, Herb allowed himself to dream of one day breaking a long TD run on the stadium floor. He shared his vision with Charles Martin who said, "You will, it's just a matter of time before you get the opportunity to break one."

Always looking out for Adderley's best interest, Martin asked, "Are you *sure* you want to attend MSU?"

"Yes, sir. There is no second choice."

Making the decision was no problem for the seventeen-year-old.

Because of the "A" and "B" system, Adderley graduated the first week in January and Coach Martin revealed a plan. "He suggested the best thing was to get me off the mean streets because of the danger of getting in trouble," Adderley explained. Duffy Daugherty concurred with Martin and the move was on.

Adderley said, "I agreed and was anxious to tell my mother and grandmother about the decision. They were happy and sad about my leaving; sad to see me go but happy I was going to college." During the first week in February, 1957, Herb Adderley left the mean streets of Philadelphia.

The book was closed on an incredible high school sports career in the City of Brotherly Love. Imagine how good a player has to be in order to be selected All-City in one sport in a place the size of Philadelphia. Adderley was All-Public in football, basketball and baseball.

In the history of Philly high school sports, research shows only two players, Lee Elia and Irvin "Bo" Roberson, had won four varsity letters before Adderley did it at Northeast.

Angelo Coia said, "I used to go watch all his games when he played basketball at Northeast. He could have gone to college on a basketball scholarship. He also played baseball and was the best player on the team; everything he did, he did very well."

At the end of his high school career, Adderley was voted the best athlete in Philadelphia. He said, "That award was big because there were some great athletes in all the major sports. The great Wilt Chamberlain won the same award the previous year and that made it even more special, adding my name next to his as 'best athlete' in the city."

As honors and accolades showered Adderley, he was moved to center stage in order to accept awards and speak publicly about his accomplishments. Charles Martin, ever the tutor, guided him. According to Adderley, "Coach Martin said it may be best to 'stand up and be seen, sit down and be appreciated.' I never forgot that and did it as often as possible."

Adderley said, "Nothing would have been possible for me if Coach Martin hadn't convinced me to play football. I listened to him then and continued to listen after I graduated. He continued to give me fatherly advice the way he did the two years I played high school football for him. He told me to keep my grades up to remain eligible and avoid flunking out of school. That frightened me, so I committed myself to make it academically and found the library and spent time in there studying."

Martin helped the first-year collegian work to earn a scholarship. "I lived 45 minutes from campus via public transportation and Coach made sure I had lunch money and tokens to get back and forth to school," Adderley said.

As good as Adderley was, he needed help navigating the mine fields out of the Hood and on to college. Charles Martin helped make it happen.

Like thousands of inner-city kids, Adderley's life could have ended in a heap of unmade dreams on some street named Newhall in Pulaski Town, Pennsylvania. But there was a Charles Martin who cared about Reva's son as a human being, athlete and student.

Ripples of Growth

Adderley's time at Michigan State University was not merely a phase in his life, it was a continuation.

Despite the collegiate environment with its changes and temptations, Herb Adderley remained the same person who came out of P-Town with a set of core values. He made solid decisions as a maturing young man on a college campus and saw a rapidly-changing America.

His friends from childhood and the ones he made at college reflect the wisdom of his choices. People like Al Chandler and Bernie Dobbins from the Hood, in addition to MSU friends John Young, Ernie Green, Carolyn Rush and Gregory Eaton, lived honorable and responsible lives. Early in his collegiate experience, Adderley met a person who describes herself as, "an overly protective woman with a maternal instinct." That's Carolyn Rush, the sister he never had.

In the winter of 1957 Adderley was a teenage student athlete in East Lansing, Michigan, away from home for the first time and trying to permanently escape the mean streets. During that period, two very different people helped teach him the meaning of the Serenity Prayer: "God grant me the serenity to accept the things I cannot change; courage to change the things I can; and wisdom to know the difference."

Adderley said, "My brother Charles was a bigger, stronger, better athlete than me while growing up. That fact caused him to become very jealous of me when he read about my high school career and he was on the cold streets in Philly being a juvenile delinquent. He was one year older than me and very jealous of my accomplishments."

Herb and Charles Adderley, like all of us, came to a fork in the road.

"For the waywardness of the simple will kill them, and the complacency of fools will destroy them ..." *Proverbs 1:32*

"In 1957, he hit a woman in the head, snatched her purse and took off," Herb said. "The woman died a week later. He pleaded guilty to first degree murder and received a life sentence." According to the *Philadelphia Daily News*, the woman was killed for $3.75.

Herb said, "I was seventeen years old, a freshman at MSU when I received the bad and distracting news. I had no choice but remain at MSU and implement my commitment to accomplishing my goals."

"Then you will understand what is right and just and fair—every good path." *Proverbs 2:9*

Adderley dealt with another heart-wrenching development as a freshman. "No one inspired me more than Bernie Dobbins during my college and pro careers," Adderley said. "Bernie was one of my best friends while growing up in P-Town and we worked together at the Quality Market grocery store before he was injured in an auto accident. This happened the same year that I left for MSU. He was involved in a horrible car accident when we were teenagers that left him paralyzed from the neck down with no chance to ever walk again. He was sitting in the back seat of the car driven by a guy who had been drinking and at a high rate of speed he hit a light pole. Bernie was thrown through the back window, landing on the sidewalk after hitting a concrete wall head first."

Rather than a reservoir of defeat, Dobbins was a fountain of motivation.

"He always had a smile on his face and wanted to know what he could do to help me," Adderley said. "He was like that with everyone he knew, and there were a lot of people who knew and cared about him. His inner strength was as strong as anyone I ever knew and he believed he would walk again because of his faith in God."

Bernie Dobbins never took another step and spent the rest of his life on a gurney, in a wheelchair or in bed. He had the type of condition that can make "friends" disappear and run for cover. When one of those "friends" becomes a college football star, first-round NFL draft choice, All-Pro and world champion, that friend can forget lots of people, especially those who are an inconvenience. Herb Adderley is not that kind of friend.

"The bigger Herb became, the smaller he was," said Gregory Eaton. "He always remained true to his friends."

Bernie Dobbins was paralyzed in a car accident and served as inspiration to Herb Adderley and many others.

As a college student back home in P-Town for the summer, Adderley made sure to spend time with his paralyzed buddy. "I had access to a car and I would get another friend to help me lift Bernie out of his wheelchair and place him in the car," Adderley said. "Bernie always had his list of people that he wanted to see, so we took him everywhere he had listed. It always ended up being a minimum of twelve hours."

In order to understand Herb Adderley, it is vital to realize he is intensely devoted. He is steadfast, reliable, loyal, tenacious and trustworthy.

If you understand that, you have a chance to understand him.

Adderley's surrogate sister, Carolyn Rush, said, "Herb never changed, and he wouldn't even know how to change. He is wonderful with his openness, spirituality and his ability to keep a friend for life." The Adderley-Rush friendship has been intact since 1957.

There is another important dimension to Herb Adderley. "Fool me once, shame on you; fool me twice, shame on me," Carolyn said. "He won't let that happen. If you betray his trust, you won't get a chance to do it again. It's like you don't exist."

If you don't understand that, you have no chance to understand him.

Bernie Dobbins had another loyal friend named Andy Pinckney who spent a good deal of time with him. In 1965, Dobbins said to Andy, "You've got to meet Herb."

"Herb who?"

"Herb Adderley."

"You mean the guy who plays for the Packers?"

"Yeah, Herb and I grew up together."

Pinckney planned a little get-together at his apartment in Philadelphia in 1965, and Adderley and Andy have been friends ever since.

A childhood friend of Dobbins and Adderley, Al Chandler said, "When Herb went into the pros, he would go get Bernie and take him to games." Bernie was on a gurney and sometimes they could get him into a wheelchair." Adderley made sure Dobbins was in the care of people like Andy Pinckney and Al Chandler, who watched games from the sidelines wearing passes courtesy of Adderley.

In the 1970s Dobbins was told he had a couple months to live, at which time his bucket list took on added urgency. He wanted to meet a famous baseball player who became paralyzed due to a 1958 automobile accident. His very big wish was to meet National League three-time Most Valuable Player Roy Campanella, who suffered a broken neck when he lost control of his car on an icy street and slammed into a telephone pole.

A retired Adderley and his friend Pinckney put Dobbins in a car and drove four hours from Philly to White Plains, New York. The trio made their way to a very exclusive part of town and saw the name "Calloway" in front of a home. It was the residence of legendary jazz singer and bandleader Cab Calloway. Adderley did the logical thing: he went to the door and rang the doorbell. When the maid appeared, Adderley explained the situation and asked her for directions to Campanella's house. The maid dutifully called Campy's house and got the OK to send the three men over.

When the great Brooklyn Dodgers catcher saw Adderley, he said, "I remember you, I played baseball with your uncle."

Adderley said, "Campy showed us around the house and showed us his trophy room. He had all this magnificent stuff, including his spikes, gloves and three MVP trophies. He asked that he and Bernie have some private time in the trophy room. They stayed in there for two hours until we wondered if they were all right, so we asked. Campy said, 'He's OK, he's got a smile on his face.' After a while longer, Bernie came out of the room, Campy was right behind in his wheel chair and they were both smiling."

Roy Campanella told Adderley, "I'm so glad you brought this young man over."

On the ride home, Dobbins said, "He inspired me so much, I am not going to die and I'm going to walk." With tears in his eyes Adderley couldn't see to drive, so he pulled the car to the shoulder of the road where three grown men cried with happiness.

Bernie Dobbins lived 10 more years.

"Bernie is always remembered in my prayers and I love him," said Adderley. Dobbins lived into the late 1980s.

Pinckney said, "I've met a lot of good people in my life and Bernie is one of the greatest. He was like the goodness of God."

Bernie Dobbins was an exceptional person, not a gifted athlete. So for Adderley in college, he continued to choose his friends based on individual quality and not athletic skill.

———————

When Adderley showed up on the MSU campus, he could have flaunted his three-sport, All-City Philadelphia status, but didn't. Carolyn Rush has been friends with Adderley for 55 years and has become a surrogate sister to him over the years. She learned about his high school athletic greatness while reading the manuscript for this book in December 2011. "Nobody knew," Carolyn said.

Little wonder Adderley was *Chosen* to end up with Lombardi.

One of Adderley's first friends at MSU was John Young, who became lifelong friends even though they came from different backgrounds. "When I looked at Herb, he was a person I felt safe and comfortable with," said Young. "He was always appreciative of things and I think we had some things in common that our parents had given to us."

John's father was a fruit farmer in southwest Michigan who had moved his family from Chicago in order to give his kids an opportunity. Young said, "My dad used the farm to raise his boys; we did most of the work on the farm and he had a job at a plant in South Haven."

Many black families in the area had migrated out of Chicago and Gary, Indiana, to give their children a chance of an improved life. John said, "These were blacks who wanted a better life for their kids. They all had intentions of their kids going to college."

Young lived in a mixed racial environment, whereas Adderley was from a nearly all-black situation. Adderley walked to a city grade school, Young boarded a bus in the country and rode 16 miles to school.

John said, "The backgrounds were different as far as geographical location was concerned, but it was not different as far as philosophy of life. Herb's mother and grandmother had the same philosophy for him that my parents had for me and my brother and sister. And it was one that you would find nationally."

In his succinct style, Adderley said, "One thing for sure we had in common was that we were both black."

Long after the abolition of slavery and before passage of the Civil Rights Act, there was an important period in black American history that has received little publicity. It was a time when blacks could leave their limbs and lives on battle fields for the United States but could not vote for those who sent them off to war or sit at a lunch counter of choice. Segregation was a fact of life in America in the '40s and '50s, but still, black families pursued the unfulfilled promises set forth in the "immortal declaration" of Thomas Jefferson that "all men are created equal."

Those were the times in which Adderley grew up.

A striving black population was a significant component of our country's great generation. Respected black activists were emerging in prominent racial leadership roles in a time before "entitlement shakedown artists" anointed themselves as black leaders.

Black folks knew the deck was stacked against them but taught their children to compete, be tough and never give up. "Our parents were telling us not to get caught up in pity; don't rely on blame; and you have to be twice as good as that white boy," John Young said. "If something would happen to us they would say, 'What did you expect? Do you think somebody's going to be sorry for you? Come up with a plan.' I think today's kids come out of the womb feeling sorry for themselves; we weren't allowed to do that. There was pride; there was a lot of pride."

Vince Lombardi is nearly visible between John Young's words.

Times were tough, but Carolyn Rush said, "We didn't have anything and we didn't care. We just had fun and each other. It only seems awful when you look back. When you're going through a lot of things you don't 'get it' and I guess that's good."

With Jackie Robinson, Larry Doby, Roy Campanella, Hank Aaron and Willie Mays in baseball and Walter Clifton and Walter Dukes in basketball, the Fifties and Sixties provided blacks with a few tremendous role models. Dukes, for instance, earned a law degree after playing two years with the Knicks.

"Those guys carried themselves with pride," Young said. "Today it's almost like some of these black players go out and design ways to be the biggest damn fools they can be. If you go to a club with thousands of dollars of jewelry around your neck, drive a red Hummer and you've got fifteen guys around you talking 'half-assed crazy,' what do you expect? Or you go to a club and you shoot yourself in the leg. It doesn't make sense."

John Young said, "Our families told us 'You don't embarrass your family, you don't embarrass your community, you don't embarrass your race and you don't embarrass yourself.' We didn't go boasting and bragging."

When social change was sweeping America in the late '50s and '60s, blacks were acutely aware of the possibility of progress and improvement for them. They also knew improvements were going to have to be fought for and won. On college campuses like Michigan State University, black students were ultimately more aware of racial issues than their white counterparts.

"Oh yeah, I had an awareness before I went to Michigan State," Young said. "Around the area I lived, the county used to have summer jobs and the white kids got the jobs; black kids didn't get the jobs. It was a given, but because you didn't get a job you didn't go out and tear up something. Just like Herb's mother, my mom and dad taught me if Plan "A" fizzles out, go to Plan "B." It was one of those things that you didn't give up on yourself. Somewhere out there, somebody was going to help you. Someone was going to reach out for you, but you didn't make yourself an unmarketable person."

The civil rights movement was in its infancy when Adderley, Young, Carolyn Rush and Ernie Green began their college experience, but the coalescing of blacks of all ages in America was mature.

"I actually believe between the years of 1955 and 1961 there was a relationship between the black students at Michigan State that never existed on any campus in this country before or since," Young said. "Regardless of ethnic group, economics or whatever, it was a special group. We used to meet at the grill and talk about what was happening. We advised each other what teachers to take and what classes to take. We never had the arguing and fighting and fussing. Part of it was to make sure we got out of school and graduated. We had some kids who were really smart and they would tutor other kids. We all knew our folks sacrificed for us and we were not going to let them down."

Ripples of hope and change were evident for blacks in America during the late 1950s. Young said, "In fact, we went to school with Ernie Green."

Not to be confused with the pro football player named Ernie Green, Ernest Gideon Green is an iconic member of the Little Rock Nine. He was some kind of ripple, destined to be friends with Adderley.

On September 4, 1957, nine black teenagers, including Green, attempted to attend Little Rock Central High School. The event occurred three years after the United States Supreme Court ruled in *Brown v. Board of Education* of Topeka, Kansas, that segregated schools were unconstitutional.

Under the direction of Governor Orval Faubus, the Arkansas National Guard blocked the nine kids from entering the high school, and a mob of hundreds followed the Little Rock Nine, making threats to lynch. President Dwight Eisenhower sent in the 101st Airborne Division of the U.S. Army to help ensure Ernie Green and the other eight students "safe" passage to their classes as they integrated LRCHS. In America's first important test to enact school integration, Green was a major ripple and ranks as a true civil rights pioneer.

Green entered Little Rock Central as a senior, became the first black to graduate from the school in 1958, and accepted a scholarship to Michigan State University. Green was a celebrity before he stepped on campus in East Lansing and was the focus of much press coverage after he arrived. He said, "I wanted to blend in and experience the Michigan State and Big Ten college life. I didn't start out trying to be a political or civil rights leader."

Green was not able to remain anonymous as an MSU freshman and was pleasantly surprised to discover a certain sophomore football player in his dormitory who had a substantial personality and reputation of his own.

"We were in the same dorm, Shaw Hall. He was on one floor and I was on the other," Green said. "Herb was a rock star. Herb Adderley was the man. If you knew Herb Adderley, you were a semi-rock star just by knowing him. His celebrity status on the football field transcended everything else because Michigan State was so oriented toward football."

Athletics have always been a big part of Adderley's life, but never have they defined his entire being. He, like many young African Americans in the late 1950s, was aware of the changing face of America and he chose to be engaged. He did not hide in the mist of sports or behind the myth of celebrity.

"I thought we had a pretty heightened sense of awareness of social issues during that period," Green said. "We were in the fervor of the beginning of all the activism that led up to the end of Dr. King's work. John Young's brother Chuck and I got *The New York Times* partly to keep up with what was going on in the civil rights movement."

In a time of national social change, young black students at Michigan State University created a quasi "think tank" that helped focus on issues affecting people of their heritage.

"The grill was where all the interactions occurred and it was particularly significant for black students," Green said. "Every Friday we had a big social gathering at the grill; sometimes after classes in the afternoon it was also a gathering spot. But Fridays were really the event and Herb was always right there in the middle. He wasn't off to the side where you had to genuflect to see him. With Herb Adderley's star status, he could have really been a prima donna. That he was not. Everybody on campus knew him and gave him wide berth. As Reggie Jackson said, he was the straw that stirred the drink. Herb handled all of his status well and he didn't flaunt it; he took pride in other black students who were on campus and tried to make them feel at ease."

The meetings at the grill were multifaceted and provided a context for social issues, but it was also an attempt to help other students survive the college experience and benefit from it. Green said, "Most of the people that were in our group completed school, did well and accomplished something for themselves and their families."

"Herb was more than a one-dimensional person," Green said. "His approach to life seemed to be to get to know a lot of people and put them at ease. He certainly recognized he had a set of talents that a lot of us did not have and he was going to use those talents to improve conditions for himself, his family and for the broader community."

Adderley, Green and others made significant contributions to social change at Michigan State.

"Ernie and I, along with four other brothers, were the founders of the famous Omega Psi Phi fraternity in 1961," said Adderley. "We celebrated our 50th year on the MSU campus in 2011 thanks to the six founders. We had a three-year struggle to get permission from the administration to add another black fraternity. Alpha Phi Alpha and Kappa Alpha Psi were and still are the other two black fraternities. The reason for turning us down for three years was, 'two black fraternities were enough for the amount of black students enrolled.' We didn't give up and that's why we celebrated our 50th anniversary."

Among the vast array of honors and achievements in his life, Green served as assistant secretary in the Labor Department under President Jimmy

Carter from 1977 to 1981. Receiving praise from a man of Green's stature is to be cherished.

"Clearly, Herb was not just a jock," Green said. "The fact that he was one of the founders of the fraternity shows he was a guy with a vision. I've always been a big Herb Adderley admirer."

Athletically, Adderley was a star at MSU, playing both offense and defense. In 1959, he led the team in rushing yards and pass receptions. As a senior in '60, he served as co-captain, led the team in pass receptions, made the All-Big Ten Conference team and played in the East-West Shrine Game, Coaches' All-American, Hula Bowl and the College All-Star games. Adderley was picked for the All-Michigan State University team in 1970.

His hard-hitting play from a defensive back position is a thing of lore. John Young said, "We were playing Notre Dame at Michigan State (1960) and they had the ball on the one-yard line. They tried four times to dive somebody over the line and each time Herb met him in midair."

MSU football historians regard the goal line stand as the greatest in Spartan history. "George Izo was the quarterback who tried to leap over the top on fourth-and-one," Adderley said. "I met him under his chin and knocked him back to where he started the play." The great stand helped Michigan State beat Notre Dame three years in a row.

Young said, "Herb never, never, ever said anything to me or my brother about that; he would never brag about anything like that."

Just as Clarence Peaks had been his hero, Adderley was making an impression on young players outside of the Midwest. While Number 26 was putting an electric charge into the Spartans and trying to separate himself from this brother's problems, aspiring young defensive backs were copying his playing style. Future NFL Hall of Famer Lem Barney said, "When I was in high school in Mississippi, Adderley was a sophomore at Michigan State and a tremendously great athlete, not just a defensive back. When I got to college in 1963 at Jackson State, I wore the jersey number 26 in honor of Herb. I watched him during my high school and college years and tried to emulate him." Barney and others had no idea the level of desire and concentration Adderley maintained in order to excel and bring pride to his mother, grandmother and himself.

Adderley refused to let his college studies or playing career be affected by his brother's legal predicament. Herb and John Young were very good friends at MSU, but Young graduated and was long gone from East Lansing before he found out about the troubled Charles Adderley.

As for Charles, "I helped get him his freedom in 1972," Adderley said.

According to Carolyn Rush, "Herb got his sentence overturned. He did that for his mother and grandmother."

When Charles Adderley was released from prison, the system kept his number open, knowing he'd be back.

"He spent a lot of time back and forth in prison," Adderley said, "because of violating his lifetime parole, which was a part of his release."

Al Chandler said, "Herb spent a lot of money, spent a lot of time, worried, and did a lot for his brother, and Charles could not have cared less. When he got out, he acted like it was what Herb was supposed to do. He was never appreciative and he never tried to change his life."

Given his freedom and a second chance at life, the elder Adderley returned to the streets of P-Town.

"When he got out he was standing on the corner talking to a bunch of guys," Chandler said. "I knew who he was by reputation, but didn't really know him. One day I saw him on the street and just walked on by. When I got to the middle of the street he hollered, 'Chandler, you're not gonna speak to me?' It was like he never left. He was a personality, but he was a bad penny. He was just a street person and on that street he was a popular guy. He had nothing else to give to anybody. As kids he was a better athlete than Herb, but never developed anything, and Herb developed everything."

Adderley said, "He received a second life term in 2006 for violating his parole for the final time."

On November 11, 2011, the squandered life of Charles Adderley ended in the State Correctional Institution at Rockview, Pennsylvania. He died of a heart attack at age 74.

"Until he died," Chandler said, "Charles was still that same thug he was when he was 19 years old."

Al Chandler has wanted to write a book about the two Adderleys: one chose crime and prison, the other pursued greatness. The title of his book: *Pros and Cons.*

Looking back all these years later it seems the heart, mind and life of Adderley were destined to connect with Vince Lombardi. Two great men of God, highly principled, bright and utterly dedicated to excellence, were a match waiting to happen.

Unlike now when college games, practices and coaches' offices are crawling with representatives of teams and scouting combines, Adderley said, "I had no contact with any scouts during my four years at MSU." The thought of playing pro ball occurred to him only after Duffy Daugherty told Herb some scouts had shown an interest.

Green Bay's talent scout, Jack Vainisi, convinced Lombardi to draft the best athlete available for the '61 season, and that was MSU's Number 26. If Adderley had gone to an all-black school like Florida A&M, even the great Vainisi may not have found him.

On December 27, 1960, one month to the day following Jack Vainisi's death, Vince Lombardi made Herb Adderley the first black player selected with a Packers' first-round choice.

CHOSEN.

Fortunately for Green Bay, the Detroit Lions did not have a selection in the first round, so Adderley didn't end up with the pro team located 55 miles from East Lansing.

A remarkable series of events unfolded in late 1960 that culminated with Adderley becoming a Green Bay Packer.

"I was in San Francisco representing MSU for the East against the West in the college Shrine Game," Adderley said. "We stayed at St. Mary's College in Santa Clara, California, and it was there I received a telegram from the Packers notifying me I was their No. 1 draft choice." It read:

Dear Herb,
I want to be the first one to officially notify you that you were the
GB Packers #1 draft choice. I am looking forward to meeting you
and welcoming you as a member of the GB Packers.
Sincerely yours,
Coach Lombardi

The upstart American Football League, Canadian Football League and Green Bay Packers descended on St. Mary's in an attempt to sign the talented Spartan. Adderley said, "There were three men, Al Dorrow of the New York Titans, Lou Agase of the Toronto Argonauts and Bill Austin of the Packers. They all had contracts and bonus checks for me. I spoke to each of them separately in my dorm room. Dorrow started off with a $2,000 signing bonus but dropped out when I got up to $4,000."

Agase may have felt he had an advantage because he had been the defensive line coach at Michigan State before taking the Argos job.

"I somehow ended up in the parking lot outside of the dorm with Agase and Austin. The bidding went up to $5,500 and I verbally agreed to sign

Agase's contract. He reached into his coat pocket to get the contract for me to sign and it was not there. He had left it in his hotel room."

Who, or what power, caused that to happen?

"Agase went back to his room to get the contract and while he was gone, spiritual intervention took over and directed me to sign with the Packers," Adderley said. "Austin pulled the contract out of his pocket and I signed it on the hood of a 1957 Ford in the parking lot at St. Mary's College."

For the Packers to land their number one pick in '61:

The cost of the bonus: $5,500.

The cost of a one-year, no cut contract: $15,000

The cost of God's intercession: priceless.

"I believe spiritual intervention had something to do with Agase forgetting to bring the contract with him," Adderley said. "When he returned to the parking lot and I told him I changed my mind and signed with the Packers, he was furious. He started cursing at me and Austin and threatening Bill. Austin never said a word, and I walked back in the dorm with a check and $15,000 contract. I don't know what happened between Agase and Austin." Apparently nothing.

Agase was understandably furious because he wanted, and tried earlier, to sign Adderley in the worst way. The Argos representative had failed in a seedy attempt following the college season.

"Agase tried to bribe me a week after my final game at MSU when my eligibility had run out," Adderley said. "He placed four thousand dollars, cash, on my dorm room desk as a signing bonus if I signed to play for him and the Toronto team. I told him I was going to wait for the NFL draft, even though I could have used the money."

Thou shalt not bribe.

In 1995 Adderley was named recipient of Michigan State's Outstanding Alumni Award, and guess who was in attendance at the ceremony?

"I was invited back to MSU by head football coach Nick Saban to receive the award, and Lou Agase was sitting in the audience," Adderley said. "I hadn't seen him since the signing in the parking lot at St. Mary's College in 1960. When I started to tell the story about how he tried to bribe me, he got up and walked out. There is no doubt in my mind I did the right thing by not accepting the bribe money and signing with the Packers. Spiritual intervention had a lot to do with my spur-of-the-moment decision."

Here endeth our lesson.

Adderley respectfully declined an effort to induct him into the MSU Hall of Fame. Gregory Easton said, "Herb would not go in because other worthy players like Clarence Peaks and Jim Ellis had not been enshrined. That's the type of guy Herb is."

Pro Football Hall of Fame writer Ray Didinger said, "In my opinion, Herb Adderley was the most complete NFL cornerback I ever saw. He could do everything. Some people call my radio show and say Deion Sanders is the best. Deion is in the Hall of Fame and deservedly so, but the next guy he hits will be the first. Herb could cover, hit, run and return kicks. There wasn't anything he couldn't do."

When opponents went into the area of Green Bay's number 26, he often made the spectacular happen. His average yards per return on an interception stands at a nifty 21.8 yards.

Pity the quarterback who had to run a play to his right, which was Lombardi's Left Side of the Packer defense. Quarterbacks who faced Green Bay were forced to decide when to tempt suicide. The Packers' left corner was a man with unique athletic ability, an unshakable nerve and unwillingness to back down.

When Adderley played left corner for the Cowboys, his teammate on the right side was Hall of Fame cornerback Mel Renfro. Odd as it may seem, Adderley and Renfro didn't receive recognition on any Cowboys official "greatest list" even though both are enshrined in Canton.

Adderley and almost anybody would have been outstanding; when coupled with Jeter in Green Bay and Renfro in Dallas, the corners were truly great.

"Herb was a great athlete; he's a Hall of Fame athlete, but how did he get there? He knows it was a God-given gift and he made it come forth," said John Young.

"I do know that so many good things have happened for me that I can't take credit for," Adderley said. "I still believe spiritual intervention took over and made decisions for me. It helped me be in the right place at the right time too many times to remember. Again, thank God for making everything possible for me. I was lucky to live in-between the boys club and the church. I always thanked my parents, because if not for them, I wouldn't be alive. I never forgot my grandmother, either, because without her, it would have been very, very difficult for my mother to raise my brother and me."

Greatness united with gratitude is among the most appealing combinations in all of sports.

A Promise Kept

If not for a promise made to his dying father, Dave Robinson could easily have been another Billy Fleetwood. Another statistic.

Instead, as a high school freshman, he chose a path of sports and academics that ended with scholarship offers from every single school in the Ivy League, setting him on course for athletic and social achievements in college and professional football. Through football, Dave Robinson helped change the world around him. A lifelong criminal, Billy Fleetwood ended up serving life in prison for murder. Life can be a fine line sometimes.

The two were once the best of friends, growing up in Mount Laurel, New Jersey, before Billy turned to crime and a string of bad decisions that forfeited his freedom. And Dave knows damn well that could have been him, too, if not for some sage advice from a strong man on his deathbed.

Leslie Robinson was dying. But he was proud, being a father to each of his eight children until the very end, particularly his youngest, Dave, in whom he saw both intelligence and athletic ability. He made Dave promise him to use sports to stay busy, to stay positive and to keep out of the trouble he saw coming if he continued to run with troublemakers like Billy Fleetwood.

The day his father died was the first day of Robinson's basketball tryouts. He made the team and started filling his after-school schedule with sports practices and games instead of idle time on the streets. And he began to walk that path.

Though clearly bright enough for a rewarding career in engineering, his chosen field, Dave's athletic prowess was nurtured during a stellar football career at Penn State, leading him to the Green Bay Packers, where, ultimately, his relationship with Vince Lombardi brought out his potential far beyond the game of football. In the end, it was just as much about Robinson's character as his football prowess during those turbulent but successful years, and his contributions to Lombardi's innovative, "color-blind" system culminated in a record three consecutive NFL Championships from 1965-67.

The descendant of African slaves who settled in New Jersey after the Civil War ended, Dave was an echo of his color-barrier-breaking namesake and hero from a generation before, Jackie Robinson. Heavily recruited to be the first black football player at the University of West Virginia, he instead suited up for the Nittany Lions, where, despite death threats, he was the first black to play at the Gator Bowl — in the deep south of Jacksonville, Florida. He was also the team's MVP of the game.

As the Green Bay Packers' No. 1 pick in 1963, Robinson entered the league when racial and social norms were starting to be questioned, and he took the opportunity provided by Lombardi's "color blind" approach to change the way black players were forever viewed, particularly at the linebacker position he helped revolutionize.

At the time, it was galling to some in the NFL that a black player would be taken in the first round (not Lombardi, who smartly made Herb Adderley his first-round choice two years earlier). When Robinson was selected 11th in the 1963 draft, the final pick in the first round, it surprised even him, who figured he'd be drafted in the middle rounds as a tight end or maybe defensive end, both of which he played his last two years at Penn State.

But once a need arose for the Packers during training camp and he was moved to linebacker, another barrier was there to be broken. A black linebacker? Hadn't been done before in the NFL, but Lombardi couldn't have cared less about that — he needed another player and Robinson turned out to be that and more, forever destroying any stereotypes with his prototypical mix of brains and brawn (6'3", 245 lbs.), redefining the outside linebacker position.

His accomplished career includes one of the most memorable plays in NFL Championship Game history, when his instinctive blitz against the Dallas Cowboys' Don Meredith in the final seconds of the '66 title game forced a game-ending interception, clinching the Packers' second straight NFL title and punching their ticket to the new "Super Bowl," and immortality.

Inducted into the Green Bay Packers Hall of Fame in 1982 and the College Football Hall of Fame in 1997, Dave Robinson has yet to be inducted into the Pro Football Hall of Fame in Canton, Ohio — a mistake hopefully to be corrected.

Richard David Robinson's story began May 3, 1941, in a comfortable but bustling home in Mount Laurel Township, New Jersey. One of eight children born to Mary Elizabeth and Leslie Robinson, Dave was truly the baby in a strapping group of good athletes — boys and girls.

Robinson's next-oldest sibling, Frank, was three years older than he. The next was Henrietta (Retta), who was six years older, while the oldest were more like parental figures, if they hadn't already left the house. The family was blue-collar and hard-working — Mary was a housekeeper; Leslie worked as a young man for the Works Progress Administration (WPA), later for years at the Campbell Soup Company and for the township. A larger-than-life figure and former Marine boxer, his health failed him at a young age, though, and he died while Dave was a freshman in high school, but not before instilling in his son the values that would shape his remarkable success.

Growing up, Robinson never knew anything about his father's side of the family—it was never discussed. But he learned a bit about his mother's side and how her grandparents descended from African slaves.

Mary told her youngest child many stories of the family's history in America and their rise through tragic beginnings. Of course he didn't know it at the time, but Robinson's own life and journey in some ways would later complete that success story. They were stories he now wishes he remembered in more detail.

"She knew the actual boat my ancestors came over on and the name of the captain of that boat that landed in Annapolis, when they were sold off as slaves," he said. "It was a Dutch ship that came in from Dutch Guyana. They used to farm slaves there, and then the Dutch would bring them to America—the same way you would cattle today."

By the early 1800s, the family was living in New Jersey, where an unforeseen, impending interracial pregnancy caused some maneuvering that ended up in their freedom, as they were used as part of a cover story.

"The master's daughter got pregnant by a slave, so (the owners) gave them their freedom and sent them to Delaware to a little town called Townsend, and she went with them," Robinson said. "They told all their friends down in Virginia she was going north to visit her aunt, and the slaves were just going with her. When the baby was born, they kept the baby as their own and she returned to the plantation. No one except the insiders knew."

Ever since, Robinson says, the racial mixture in his family has enjoyed some variety.

"Some people in my family, you couldn't tell if they were white or black," he said.

When slave hunters came to Delaware, though, the family was forced to return to New Jersey—a risky proposition because even government papers that showed you were a full citizen meant little for free blacks near the Mason-Dixon line.

"If a slave hunter came to town and you showed him your papers that said you were free, all he'd do is tear the paper up: now you have no proof," Robinson said. "Then they'd take you back down south and sell you back into slavery again. No. 1, slaves couldn't read; you only had the master's word that paper said you were free. No. 2, slaves were branded or marked. That's why my mother never let us have tattoos or anything."

The family, with the help of the Underground Railroad, ended up staying in an encampment in a wooded area, waiting to be sent to Philadelphia or Morristown on their way to Canada, and safety. Then all of a sudden, the war ended. They were free. But now, they needed to find a home, and they didn't need to look far.

"The Underground Railroad stopped like that, and they were left in this encampment," Robinson said. "Families in the area when the war ended in April, 1865 simply stayed where they were."

Not wanting to go back to Virginia, newly freed blacks in the area started a town of their own, called "Lawnside," which Robinson said was the first all-black town in the state. He still has relatives who call it home.

"For years, when I was a kid, it was all black," he said. "The mayor was black, and still is black, police chief, the judges—everything was black in town. Now it's probably gotta be 70–30 or 60–40 black and white."

It was at Lawnside where the family picked its European-sounding surname, "Robinson."

Options were a bit limited at the time, as Robinson explains.

"(Slaves) didn't have any last names. He was 'John, Joe, Jack,' whatever, so they took the name of the plantation owners," he said. "Robinson being a Swedish name, he must have been from a Swedish-owned plantation."

Years later, life was anything but easy for young Mary Gaines. She was in eighth grade and living in a little nearby town called Mount Laurel when her father was stabbed in the heart with an ice pick during a bar fight. Her schooling days—and her childhood—were quickly over. As the oldest child, Mary was now needed to help support the family, so her mother sent her to become a domestic maid, cleaning homes in the area while helping to raise her younger siblings.

In 1924, when she was 21, she met Leslie, and the two were married later that year. Robinson doesn't know how they met. She was still supporting the family but wanted to get out on her own, which caused some problems with her mother, who was against a marriage. An independent woman, Mary soon took matters into her own hands, later saying she allowed herself to get pregnant as an excuse to get away.

"Whether she did, I don't know, but either way, my sister was born," Robinson said. "My grandmother never forgave my father for taking my mother away. Never did."

Leslie Robinson was a tough-minded working man who was pulled out of school after sixth grade by his father, and never went back. Their discussion was apparently a simple one.

"He said, 'Well, have you learned to read and write?'" Robinson said. "'Yes, sure,' all proud. 'Can you add and subtract?' 'Sure.' 'How much is such-and-such? ... Let me see you write your name ... That's enough schooling.' And Leslie went to work in the fields as a laborer. He was a butcher for a while, he did everything—whatever it took to raise a family in those days."

As a young man, Leslie Robinson worked in the WPA, and was proud of his service and the results. It was a tough job but an honest living, and he impressed upon his youngest son the importance of hard work and having something to show for your efforts.

"He was so proud of the work he did on Route 70," Robinson said, noting his dad used to take the long way to Atlantic City just to take the kids down the highway. "All the way down he told the stories about working for the WPA. It really impressed me as a child and even today how important it is to put people to work, and how proud these people were to work. He was so proud. 'We worked right here. This happened right here.'"

In a time of racial strife, it was also with the integrated WPA where Leslie worked—and worked well—alongside whites, foreshadowing a path his youngest son would take on football fields, campuses and cities across the country a generation later.

The youngest of the family, Dave Robinson is just happy to be around, though it was through a brother's sad fate he arrived.

In 1940, Mary was pregnant with her eighth child when doctors detected in her a heart murmur they feared could potentially threaten her health. This should be her last child, they said.

"They were going to wait until the baby was five days old, let (Mary) get her strength back, and then they were going to tie her tubes," Robinson said.

But by the time Morris Robinson was born, he was already dying. A hole in his heart was something doctors could not repair, and he lived for only three days. Grieving family brought him home for the first and last time, burying his tiny body in the church cemetery, in a small box, as Robinson remembers hearing.

"All the kids got to see their brother, then they took him out and they just buried him," he said. "No casket, no service, no nothing. I can remember going to his grave a lot when I was a kid."

Still in the hospital, Mary's doctors still wanted to schedule her surgery, but she refused, saying she was going to "go home and get another boy to replace the one she lost." Thankfully for Dave, she did just that.

"She went home, put my dad on his job, he did his thing, and for the first time, she followed all the doctor's orders," Robinson said. "When I was born at 10 pounds, she said that's why I was so big, because she did everything according to the book. So I just got snuck in under the wire. I'm on 70 years and counting. I figure I'm living on borrowed time."

One advantage of being the baby of the family was having older siblings around to help take care of him. One older sister had a boy of a similar age who grew up with Robinson, adding another close playmate.

"Our family came in groups," Robinson said. "(My parents) took a hiatus for about four or five years. When I was born, my one brother was the youngest in that (first) group of four, and he was 12."

The age difference helped Robinson bond more closely with his "younger" set of siblings, particularly during the summers, when Leslie would get tickets to vacation in Atlantic City.

"The older ones didn't go with us because they had their life at home, so the ones that would go were up to about the brother that's 10 years older than me," he said. "We'd bundle in the car, mom and dad and about four or five kids, and then take off."

Family trips were the exception, though, as life was fast-paced enough around the large household, with Mary's cooking being the staple of home life. The family dining table was the mainstay back then, and with the big Robinson boys, it was well-used. "Four on this side, four on this side, mom on one end, dad on the other end," he said. "Ten people. And no McDonald's around the corner, either, as I remind my son … My dad couldn't put 10 people in the car and go anyway," laughed Robinson.

Rural 1950s New Jersey was a world away from today's reality for most kids, punctuated by two-mile walks to church, or five-mile walks to school. It was a world of imagination and ideas for young Dave, a bright boy as well as a good athlete. Television was not yet part of the Robinson household, and the world extended only as far as the family car, city bus or soles of your shoes would take you.

But stepping out of Mount Laurel, he quickly learned your destinations were limited by your skin color.

———

It was on those family trips to Atlantic City when Dave began to see the realities of life outside his small, mostly black town. In those days just before the Civil Rights movement, segregation was still the status quo, and nothing embodied that like the "Steel Pier."

"There's two big piers there, the Million-Dollar Pier and the Steel Pier," he said. "Million Dollar Pier, you had integrated bathing at the beach. North toward the Steel Pier, the beach was all white, and that was the way.

"We could never get up past the Steel Pier."

He and a friend once wandered to the nearby Claridge Hotel, where they were chased away. No blacks allowed.

And Robinson hasn't forgotten the sting, either. The place is a casino now, and even when he later settled nearby, he refused to visit.

"My wife wanted to go, and I said, 'I wouldn't give them a penny,'" Robinson said. "She said, 'That's a long time ago,' and I said, 'Yeah, it was only yesterday in my mind, though.' I remember it like it was yesterday."

Robinson was no stranger to segregation. His school at Mount Laurel was only for blacks, and it was there, in that small, three-room building, that he began to show his instinct and intellect when he started picking up on the teacher's lessons for older students.

"When I was in first grade, I could hear her teaching the second-graders," he said. "And if you were sharp and didn't just sit there and play around, you could get ahead."

Back home, Robinson's world out of school provided far more chances to interact with his white neighbors, like the Butterworths, with their boys Everett and Carl.

Just like in any American backyard, the four boys tried to figure out sides for two-on-two football games—a tall order for the Butterworth boys, considering the future talent they were up against.

"We found out we could kick their asses," Robinson chuckled. "So then Carl and I would play against Frank and Everett, and that evened it up a little bit."

When it came time to go back to school, the boys met up in the morning and walked down the road to catch the bus.

It had the same stop, but two different destinations.

"The bus would stop at the black school, where I got off, and Carl went to the white school," he said. "Then at night, we came home on the same bus and we walked home, best of friends."

Robinson was "pissed" about the whole thing but didn't know what to do. Their families talked about it and didn't know what to do, either. It didn't seem to make any sense.

"We didn't enjoy it, and we wanted to know why, because there's no such thing as 'Separate but Equal,'" he said. "The white school definitely had the better situation, and I wondered why."

Desegregation came to New Jersey in 1948, and it came with its own set of challenges. Black students were put under a microscope, and for young

Dave, his moment came in the second grade. It would not be the last time he had to prove himself to a "white" world. His former teacher, now teaching at the white school, came to talk to Mary and Dave about his joining her classroom that fall.

"(She said) 'Already, there's some rumblings that the black students won't keep up to the white students,'" Robinson said. "'I know Dave is sharp enough to do it, so whenever I have a question, you had better raise your hand and have the right answer!'

"I'm seven years old. You talk about pressure! Hell, man, stoppin' the Cowboys on the three-yard-line, that's nothin'," laughed Robinson.

Robinson did raise his hand a lot that year with a lot of right answers, and it was soon obvious he was an exceptional student as well as a talented athlete. The academic success emboldened him, and he would soon be heavily recruited by schools across the country as much for his brains as his brawn. His tremendous athletic potential nearly went untapped, though.

A large-framed, natural athlete, Robinson followed in the footsteps of his older brothers, whom he tried to emulate right up until when he was a freshman at Moorestown High School, where, naturally, he wanted to play on the football team. But first he'd have to get past the toughest defender he'd ever had to elude.

His mother.

Mary Robinson was no stranger to sports, rooting for Jackie Robinson's Brooklyn Dodgers and the bruising Marion Motley's Cleveland Browns, but at that point, it had been brought too close to home. She had seen Dave's brothers come home injured too many times and was not going to let it happen to her baby. She refused to sign his permission slip, no matter how he pleaded.

Finally, it took intervention by his father—gravely ill at the time—to change her mind, after Dave came home from school one day, nearly in tears from frustration.

"He said, 'What's wrong?' and I told him, 'Mom refused to sign my permission slip to play football.'" Robinson said. "He was bedridden, so she came in to talk to him and he said, 'Well, it's not fair not to let Dave play. The other four boys all played.'"

He was right. The other boys did play football, but they had also gotten hurt, one suffering a broken arm. Quite reluctantly, she gave in, and in one stroke of a pen launched a ground-breaking journey.

———

Football was far from Robinson's only sport of dominance, though. The winner of 12 letters in track, baseball, basketball and football, and before there was Dave Robinson the Nittany Lion All-American or Green Bay Packer All-Pro, there was Dave Robinson the two-time undefeated state champion basketball player. It was on the hardwood, in the crucible of highly competitive New Jersey state tournament basketball, where he first touched the greatness he would later achieve in the professional ranks.

A wiry 6'3" center who could "jump out of the gym" with a 42-inch vertical leap, Robinson was a key member of legendary Moorestown High School teams that posted combined marks of 44–0 in 1958 and 1959, winning consecutive New Jersey State Championships. One of his favorite moments was dominating a much taller opponent during a key game in one of the title runs.

Robinson's Moorestown, New Jersey, high school basketball team reeled off 44 straight wins and captured two consecutive state championships in 1958 and '59. Dave is number 24, leaping for a rebound.

"It was the state semifinals (against) some big 6'9" German immigrant from Lakewood," Robinson said. "He was just killing people, just out-jumping all the kids in high school, no problem, and they threw the ball up and I got the tap, and I could see I had him shaken. Then he got the ball up in the corner and was driving to the bucket and I went up and blocked his shot, and the kid ended up with like, four points for the game. After that, he was a basket case. We had a great team."

It was during his sophomore season that Robinson learned that even for sports "stars," life still had certain racial realities.

The issue at the high school was that some white fans worried about too many black players on the starting five. To try to sooth some racial nerves, the team's coach, Pete Monska, had a standard practice of starting only one or two black players, but as Robinson's game improved, it was obvious he should start.

Monska intended to make a move. Of course, that meant a majority of starters would be black. This was big news. The school board called the coach in for a meeting.

"They said, 'We always had a couple black guys on the starting team, but never have had three before,'" Robinson said. "And he said, 'I don't think I'll start three this week.' He started four," laughed Robinson.

Monska and his wrecking crew never looked back and never apologized for how dominant they were, regularly having to schedule scrimmages against college freshman teams from nearby, such as St. Joseph's and Temple, because there was no challenge in going against fellow high-schoolers.

"We beat everybody by 20–30 points," Robinson said. "In fact, we went to Temple and beat the freshman team so badly that their coach came in our locker room later and said, 'I got six scholarships here (laughs) if anybody wants to come to Temple.' And that's when Temple was in the NCAA finals and lost to Kentucky." We were ranked by *Scholastic* magazine No. 3 in the nation. And we said, 'Who the hell is No. 1 and 2?'"

These days, Robinson chuckles at the notion he could have made it in the NBA had he chosen basketball instead, but no one can question his success in high school, something that definitely caught the attention of universities and colleges and ended up helping his eventual football career.

"I was only 6'3", so I'd have to have been a forward," Robinson said. "I think I would have done very well in the Ivy League, though. The Ivy League wanted me to play basketball, big-time."

In fact, Robinson was wanted as not only an All-State basketball and football (second team) player, but a baseball player, too. A centerfielder, he also pitched occasionally as the No. 3 starter, with a fairly impressive variety in his arsenal for a high-schooler.

"I didn't have a curveball, but I had a hard one that spun like a curveball. It just didn't break like one. I guess they'd call it a slider today," Robinson said. "It came in spinnin' and the first one would zip by their nose. They didn't dig in too much after that. They were awful loose in the box (because) they saw it spinnin' but it wasn't breakin'."

The forkball, or split-fingered fastball, was his specialty, because with his large hands, he could throw the pitch without difficulty.

"You throw with the ball between your fingers, and it comes in like a knuckleball," Robinson said. "It comes in really slow and breaks like a screwball. It's hard to hit, and you throw it to left-handers. Most high school kids couldn't throw that pitch."

He was encouraged by his baseball coach, who played minor league ball, and went as far as attending tryouts with the Philadelphia Phillies and Milwaukee Braves, though nothing ever came of it.

"The Phillies were easy because the Phillies' scout was from my hometown, and he arranged that; and then I got a thing with the Milwaukee Braves," he said. "I went up and had a tryout, but I didn't want to go play. Never talked any money. My mother was just adamant about me not playing baseball. I was going to go to college."

In the end, it was football that turned out to be the best sport for Robinson and his build. In the mold of his older brothers, and his father, who was a powerful athlete in his own right and enjoyed success as a boxer.

In fact, if not for a rival who would one day become heavyweight champion, Leslie Robinson might have been a contender himself. But he lost his big fight and his big chance. And he never forgot the man who crushed his dream.

Back in the 1920s, Leslie was a promising young heavyweight who competed while serving in the Marine Corps in New Jersey. He wasn't the only promising fighter at the gym, though. Another young heavyweight by the name of Arnold Cream was being groomed by ring owners for a shot at the heavyweight title.

A box-off was held between the two, and Cream won convincingly, literally knocking Robinson from the ring. From that point, their careers went on very different paths: Robinson, a club fighter for a few more years; Cream taking his game, and a new name, "Jersey Joe Walcott," to legendary status when he finally claimed that heavyweight title in 1951.

Years, later, when Robinson's freshman football team matched up against rival Woodrow Wilson High School, an opportunity presented itself for a little family revenge, and Leslie Robinson snapped at the chance like a lightning left jab, looking for some payback.

He found out Cream's son played halfback for Wilson, and wanted Dave to send a personal message, so he sat him down for a talk. It wasn't any Knute Rockne speech, just straight and to the point, the kind of conversation he was used to having with his father.

"He said, 'I want to see you take him out for me.' I said, 'Yeah, I'd take him out, anyway,'" laughed Robinson.

The training was serious, though. Before the game, Leslie Robinson showed his son how to prepare for breakfast what he used to eat before fights.

"He took a boneless roast and sliced a piece off to make like a steak and pan-fried it, then put water on it to take the grease off and gave me that with eggs," Robinson said. "He said, 'Steak and eggs. This is what you eat before a big game. This helps you.' First time I ever had steak and eggs."

On game day, it wasn't until the second half when Robinson finally found the perfect opportunity to deliver a smashing hit. Vincent Cream got the ball and headed his way.

"He was getting ready to run the sweep and he went to hurdle me and I caught him on the rise, standing there," Robinson said. "He hit the ground and he's laying there. There are about 800 people at the game and 799 of them went, 'Ooh,' and one guy went, 'Yeah! That's my boy!'" laughed Robinson.

Ironically, when Jersey Joe later ran for sheriff of Camden, New Jersey, Robinson helped campaign for him, later asking the champ about the old boxing match with his father, but to no avail. The champ remembered the gym, but not his opponent that day.

"My dad sure didn't forget it!" Robinson laughed. "But 'Jersey Joe' was a great guy, and I got along fine with him.

"It's just so funny, how sports are."

––––––––––––

Sadly, father-and-son moments between Leslie and Dave Robinson would be few from that point. The family has a history of heart trouble, and Leslie's health quickly faded throughout Dave's freshman year of high school. Still, he always did what he could to see his son play football that fall, with older son Byron picking him up and parking the car on a hill overlooking the field.

One morning during a doctor's visit, Leslie was told to get to the hospital right away for tests. Instead, he got a ride to Dave's football game that day and was there when Mary finally tracked him down, pleading with him to go.

"My dad said, 'Well, it's like the third quarter. When the game's over, I'll go to the hospital,'" Robinson said

After the game, he went to Mount Holly Hospital, never to return home.

For Dave's sister Retta Robinson and the rest of the family, it was a difficult holiday season. "He went from the football practice field to the hospital just before Thanksgiving and he died the Monday after Thanksgiving," she said. The elder Robinson did have the chance to listen to his sons play on the same team together before he died, though, against rival Mount Holly. With one game left in the freshman season, Dave was promoted to varsity for the Thanksgiving Day game, where he would suit up with his older brother Frank, a senior.

"It was the biggest thrill of my life," Robinson said.

The brothers played next to each other on the line for a half dozen plays, and later went back to the hospital to visit their ailing father, who listened to the game on the radio.

"I told him I played in the game, and he was all excited," Robinson said.

Retta said for her father, listening to that game, with Frank and Dave playing together, meant everything to him.

"Back here that game has the same significance as Army-Navy," she said. "My dad never came out of the hospital, but he was very proud."

Leslie Robinson was most pleased with his youngest son's success in sports because he knew it provided a way to keep some bad influences from creeping into his young life, influences he would not be around to counteract or counsel his son about. Influences like Billy Fleetwood.

One late fall day, with football season over, he asked his son about his future plans, noting that basketball season was coming up and the coaches wanted him to try out. He knew he was dying, and soon would not be around to counsel and keep watch over his youngest child.

"He said, 'Listen, your mother worries about you after school, hanging out with Billy,'" Robinson said. "'She knows where you are when you're playing sports, and I really wish you'd consider going out for basketball.' And I said, 'Well, I have to let them know by Monday.'"

Monday came, with the first basketball practice of the season scheduled for 3 p.m. Around 11 a.m., Robinson was called out of class. His father had passed away.

There, he decided to commit to playing on the team and to fulfill his father's final wish.

In doing so—just as Leslie Robinson hoped—basketball soon gave him plenty to focus on during those long northeast winters, and he filled a busy sports schedule throughout his high school years. In the end, he didn't have time to get in trouble with people like Billy Fleetwood.

"When basketball season was over in March, baseball practice had already started in January indoors," Robinson said. "I also high-jumped and threw the shot put and what-not (in spring). My mother was happy because she knew where I was every day. The big thing was I never came home after school—maybe five times during my four years in high school. I'd start Labor Day with football, and football went to Thanksgiving, basketball season started, like in October, so early November they start practicing, so I'd go right to basketball."

Robinson credited his father's common-sense advice for keeping him on a straight path that eventually led him to success.

"He only went to sixth grade, but he was a very intensely intelligent man and he saw what I didn't see about coming home after school, and that's what he told me and that was key," he said. "I followed my daddy. I just really admired him a lot, and I listened to whatever he said."

Robinson said even at the end, when his father was too weak to rise from bed, he still maintained control and respect in the household. When a younger nephew accused Dave of hitting him, Robinson's mother punished Dave by letting the nephew hit him back, which he didn't appreciate, and he let his mother know it with a verbal barrage.

"He knocked the shit of me," laughed Robinson, "and I was mad and I was storming and crying and screaming at my mother. My dad called me in there and he said, 'Listen, I don't believe what your mother did was right, but you don't ever raise your voice to your mother.' And I firmly believe that. And so many things like that, in life, he taught me. He was a strong man, a very strong man."

Lesson learned.

The paths of Dave Robinson and the ill-fated Billy Fleetwood began to separate, never to cross again.

"He went to jail, I went on to Penn State," Robinson said.

———————

As good an athlete as he was—and Robinson is in the Green Bay Packers and College Football halls of fame (and should be in Pro Football Hall of Fame)—he may not even have been the best footballer in his family. That distinction, he says, belongs to older brother Byron, a guard in high school who graduated in 1949 when Dave was eight, long before the integration of black players in the college ranks. Therefore, there was little attempt by colleges to attract black players.

"He didn't have any scholarship offers, (but) the coaches who saw us both play said he was the best Robinson ballplayer they ever had," he said. "My dad couldn't afford to send him to the store, let alone send him to college, though, so he never went to college."

Robinson said he has a hard time these days explaining to his own son how things were then.

"In 1949, they just weren't going around scouting black people for scholarships," he said. "None of these southern schools were taking black ballplayers, and northern schools only carried one or two. If you had four on a team, you had a lot of blacks on your team. Most of the old-timers, Fritz Pollard, Paul Robeson and those guys who played football in the '20s and '30s, they all had to work their way through college."

Byron Robinson was no walk-on. He could have been a dominating college lineman and perhaps an NFL legend in his own right.

"He was a great football player," Robinson said. "Just a great waste of talent."

Byron Robinson may not have blazed the trail into football greatness, but he was crucial in holding the family together after his father's death, taking on that paternal role for his younger siblings.

"Byron got us going and went to work to help support the family, and that's what was expected of him," Robinson said. "He was single then, while my other brothers were all married and gone off. If I needed something and I would have gone to my father for it, I went to Byron. He almost acted like a second father."

Frank, three years older than Dave, was another talented guard who did attend college, at Maryland State, but ended up choosing a career in the ministry over a free agent contract with the Detroit Lions in 1960. He was another who could have played in the NFL, Robinson said.

"You had to go both ways in those days, and Roger Brown, who was drafted by the Lions, he couldn't play offense, so my brother used to play all the offense," he said. "When they went down to scout Roger as a defensive tackle, they also saw my brother playing offensive guard, so they wanted my brother to come as a free agent."

But had Frank left for camp, he would miss his timeline for being ordained as a minister that summer; he'd have to wait until the off-season. He stuck to his higher calling, though he did later question the timing.

"He said he wanted to go with the Lord. I said, 'The Lord don't pay that well,'" Robinson laughed.

Robinson credits Frank for encouraging him to further his football career.

"He said, 'If you have a chance to go pro, do it, because you'll never forgive yourself. If you don't make it, you come home, but at least you gave it a try. I always regret never giving it a shot.'" Robinson said. "Because people like Roger came back and Johnny Sample, and they said (to Frank), 'You're good enough to play on (Detroit).' But he never went back." Dave had no huge ambitions for football, either, despite his size and considerable athletic pedigree. A thinking man first, his instincts were to use his considerable intellect to earn a living, not his body, banging into people on a football field. Once letters started pouring in from schools, though, it was clear that he was going to get a chance at the best of both worlds.

Retta Robinson said it was a chance none of his older brothers had—in part due to his unusual intellect, but also the changing times.

"(Before), the opportunities were not there. Period," she said. "By the time Dave got there it opened up some ... Frank's scholarship was a partial; Dave received a full scholarship. Changes were being made gradually, not in great leaps and bounds."

Academic achievement is what really put Dave above the rest, Retta said.

"Dave was kind of phenomenal," she said. "They sat up and took notice because of his SAT scores; he did very well. (Before), blacks were not encouraged to take the SATs because it didn't matter. People don't realize there were a lot of subtle obstacles; subtle discrimination. It wasn't blatant like it was in Mississippi and Alabama but it was still there."

Retta said her father made sure his children knew the importance of higher education, and that was ingrained in Dave's thinking.

"My dad had said the time was coming when a man would not be able to get a job digging ditches if he didn't have a college education," she said. "We could not afford college tuitions—that's why when Dave and Frank had summer jobs, to start football practice (was a big deal). Other men in the neighborhood would say to my dad, 'That's kind of stupid, you could use the money those boys are making.' My dad's answer was, 'That's all right, there may come a time when, with their playing sports, they might be able to support me when I can't support myself.' He looked forward to that." Money was never far from Leslie Robinson's mind, and for good reason. Raising eight children is no easy task financially, so during the summers, kids who worked chipped in for room and board.

"If you made $100, you gave dad $50; if you made $25, you gave dad $12.50," Dave said. "One week everybody chipped in, and my dad said, 'Wow, I have $110, $120. If I could make this every week, we could live like kings.'"

That's all Robinson needed to hear, and something clicked in his mind. He knew what he wanted to do, he just needed to figure out how to get there.

"I decided I was going to get a job making $100 a week, $5,200 a year after taxes, and that's what I wanted to go to school for," he said. "That's all I wanted. Football was just a way for me to get that job; it was never the end product.

"I never wanted to play pro football."

———————————

Getting a free ride to college was great, but Robinson was more focused on what he wanted to do for a career afterward. He said a national push toward math and science at that time seemed to ensure a career as an engineer of some sort.

"I graduated from high school in 1959 and Sputnik was just launched, so at that time the Russians were ahead of us," he said. "Any kid who could add two and two and get anything between 3.8 and 4.2, they said, 'You go be an engineer,'" laughed Robinson

When he took his entrance tests for Penn State, Robinson scored a 98 percent on the math, prompting the counselor to suggest engineering as a career, something he didn't like the sound of until some motherly advice put things in perspective.

"My mother knew that all the engineers she cleaned homes for had very nice houses," he said. "So she told me she wanted me to be an engineer. So I went to school to major in engineering."

One small detail: Robinson knew little about what engineers actually did. "I knew math was big, 'cause they liked that math," he said. "And I knew they made more than $100 a week, so that's what I was going to do."

Once he got into his coursework and began succeeding, Robinson started to narrow his sights on a career path, focusing on getting a job as a municipal engineer, working with construction and sewage issues.

"I was a trash man during the summer when I worked for the city and I noticed one of the things was the township engineer," he said. "I thought I could get a job as a township engineer in my hometown, and my wife and I would settle down and have a good living."

Mechanical engineering was Robinson's first career choice, but when he hurt his shoulder and was laid up for six weeks, he couldn't draw during the design course, so he switched to civil engineering.

"I would have been a metallurgic engineer, or mechanical," he said. "I wanted to come up with a new propulsion system, whatever it was going to be. I was going to get some kind of propulsion system other than a gas-powered engine."

Ultimately, Robinson realized he needed to go to college to find that $100-a-week job. And the better he got at football, the better chances he wouldn't have to pay his way to a good academic school. With this new outlook, he applied more of himself on the field, as well as in the classroom. "I couldn't go to school unless I got a scholarship, and I was going to use that," he said.

Robinson's college recruiting process was a unique one. All 26 schools he applied for accepted him, including the entire Ivy League, who envied his balanced resume. He could afford to be picky, and he was.

"They were starving for good ballplayers, but most of the good ballplayers couldn't pass the exams to get in," Robinson said. "I had very high SAT scores and a high IQ, so to get a ballplayer who had the high grades and was also a good athlete, all the Ivy schools came down like a ton of bricks on you."

Like a good engineer thoroughly testing a design, Robinson went to visit them all.

On a trip from Philadelphia to Ithaca, New York, Robinson got his first experience on an airplane, and before taking off saw a few things that did anything but ease his mind about either the trip or the new life he was getting into.

"I'll never forget, my mother takes me to the airplane and I'm in there sitting by myself in the plane, looking at this old Delta DC-3," he said. "It's at night and the (engine) fires and I see fire coming out, and I'm thinking, 'Aw, shit,'" he laughed, "because you could see the fire coming out of those plane engines at night, the props … The plane is shaking and all that."

He survived his subsequent flight to continue his whirlwind tour at Colgate, where officials offered him the prestigious "War Memorial Scholarship," an academic honor offered to only one student a year. If that student turns it down, it remains vacant, as it did that year. It was an impressive offer from an excellent university, but Robinson didn't want to settle on the gridiron.

"They played lousy football," he laughed.

Another tempting opportunity arose when a black man who had become a successful businessman thanks to Columbia University offered a job to Robinson if he attended his alma mater, located in New York City.

"Columbia's so big, he just walked into the classrooms and had gotten his education for free that way; taken the courses he wanted do," Robinson said. "So he felt he owed the university, and he was going to take care of me. He basically said, 'I'll adopt you as my son and pay your mother to work for me,' because he couldn't pay me; that was illegal. This guy had a black cosmetics company and he was going to take me under his wing because he didn't have any children."

But Columbia wasn't Robinson's thing, either.

"It was a lousy football team, lousy coach, lousy part of town," he said. Outside the Ivy League, Rutgers, in his home state of New Jersey, was a strong possibility, but inexplicably, head coach John Stegman turned Robinson off during an interview and school officials didn't exactly roll out the red carpet when he visited campus during the annual Rutgers-Columbia game.

"It's a big, big game (and) Rutgers didn't even invite me to the game, which was *at* Rutgers. Columbia invited me to sit on the Columbia side of the field," he said. "Rutgers just treated me like garbage … and that was my state university; I wanted to go."

Robinson continued to narrow his list. A couple Pac-10 schools called but were never considered, as staying near home was foremost on his mind. "Having lost my father my freshman year, I wasn't sure about my mother's health and I wanted to be close enough where if I had to get home in a hurry, I could do it," he said.

"If I wanted to play big-time football and be on the East Coast, the only ones that were left were either Pittsburgh or Penn State or Syracuse, but Syracuse didn't recruit black ballplayers all that much. There weren't a lot of scholarships out there for you in those days if you were black."

Robinson ruled out Pittsburgh after hearing rumors the school decided not to recruit black players to avoid possibly being excluded from bowl games—normally played in the South—or at the very least, being hurt by unfair officiating. Whatever the reason, Pittsburgh clearly had no interest in him.

"I can't tell you how many Pittsburgh alumni who turned my name in to the university (to be recruited) all say they heard Pittsburgh contacted me but I had no interest in going," Robinson said. "They never contacted me." Racial barriers were just part of life back then, Robinson said. You overcome them or you don't.

"This is the hand you were dealt," he said. "You really, really can't sit here today and realize what it was like in 1958, 1959 or even '63 when I got to Green Bay. Whole different world.

West Virginia heavily recruited Robinson and pulled out all the stops to bring him to Morgantown, West Virginia. Officials were trying to racially integrate their teams, meaning some black football player was going to be the first.

The Mountaineers and head coach Pappy Lewis wanted Robinson to be that man, but after some time in town, he wasn't so sure the fit would be such a good one.

"They had had these articles about Pappy Lewis' lily-white team, how they didn't have any blacks then, and how West Virginia had a strong racial history because West Virginia left Virginia rather than leave the union," Robinson said. "Why they didn't have any black football players was highly unusual."

When Robinson visited the campus, he was offered "the moon" by boosters, from free clothing to jobs for his mother. Coaches had a black student show him around the area and tried to encourage the locals to make a good impression on their prized recruit wherever they went.

"They'd gone around to all the places around campus and told them they were bringing this black recruit in this week, and everybody opened their doors to me," Robinson said. "I went anywhere (I) wanted to go."

Was it the right fit, though? Lewis tried to convince him he could be a "big frog in a little pond" by being the Mountaineers' first black football player. He didn't know the ambitious Robinson, though.

"He said, 'If you go to Penn State, they have a lot of blacks — the Lenny Moores, the Rosie Griers and all those guys — you'll just be a little frog in a big pond,'" Robinson said. "But I was thinking all the time, 'I'm gonna be a big frog in a big pond,'" he laughed

Progressive as he was, becoming the Jackie Robinson of Appalachia wasn't exactly what he had in mind, and his suspicions were confirmed the first time he returned as an opposing ballplayer the next year with Penn State's freshman squad.

"The worst experience of my life," he said. "They called me everything in the world. The fans, there were only about 30 in the stands because it was a freshman football game, and the players, the guys who would have been my teammates, they called me all sorts of stuff … And I just wore their asses out."

As Robinson looked across the field, he noticed there still were no blacks on the West Virginia sideline.

Finally, it looked like Robinson would choose the Ivy League's University of Pennsylvania, where they wanted him to play basketball and football, and the financial deal was also a good one. He even had his room and roommate picked out.

"At Penn State, you had room, board, tuition and fees and $15 a month spending money, for incidentals," Robinson said. "In the Ivy League, you get the room, board, tuition and fees … (then) they took the average expenses of the money spent by the average student at Pennsylvania, which was $2,300 a semester, to give me. I was only a 35-cent bus ride from home. You're talking about $2,300; I could help my mother out. I was all ready to go."

Like a last-second Hail Mary, Penn State, which, for some reason, had stopped recruiting him months before, called to ask if he'd committed to a school. Robinson said he hadn't and agreed to meet with Penn State guards coach and longtime assistant Sever Toretti, who came to the family home for a visit, a stack of films under an arm. The dance was on.

"I knew they were a big school," he said. "He started wooing my mother with his charm and everything else."

Robinson had come up on Penn State's recruiting radar earlier because one of his high school assistants was a former captain for the Nittany Lions, and asked his former coach, Rip Engel, to take a look .

"They sent the local scout from the South Jersey area to look at me and show films and what-not, and that's how they got interested in me," he said. "He came down during basketball season and saw me playing basketball. So it was just a fluke that I even got to Penn State."

Flukier yet is how they stopped recruiting him, and it wasn't until he arrived on campus in the fall of 1959 that he figured out what happened—a comic mistake that could have changed his life.

"The first class I go to, there's another kid right beside me named David Robinson, a white kid from Philadelphia, on the smaller side," Robinson said. "He says, 'Are you Dave Robinson the football player?' I said, 'Yeah.'"

The "other" Robinson said when he arrived for orientation, he was invited to attend the football dinner, and caused quite a stir by his appearance, as he told the story to Robinson.

"We come down off the elevator, and of course, there's Coach (Rip) Engel and Coach (Joe) Paterno and all these guys waiting, and they see me come off and they're shocked,'" he said.

The coaches must have thought their recruiters had gone mad. At that point, the school stopped sending letters of interest and forgot about him until it was nearly too late. But for Robinson, the timing was perfect. Penn State was an excellent academic school offering a full scholarship to play football for one of the best programs in the nation, just a few hours' drive from home. He didn't need any more convincing. He was going to "Happy Valley" to make his mark, and find a way to get that $100-a-week job, one way or another.

"I was determined not to have to go to school where my mother had to pay one penny," he said. "In fact, when I went to school, all my family would send me money from home, and I took all the money and put it back in the envelope and sent it home. I said, 'Hey, I want to make it on my own or I'm not going to make it at all.'"

And the Barriers Fall

Everything seemed to fall into place for Dave Robinson at Penn State, both on the field and off.

The football program was a winning one under Engle's leadership, with a bright young assistant named Joe Paterno ready in the wings. Grades were no trouble for the heady Robinson, and socially, he was finding plenty of good, clean college fun.

One of Robinson's close friends at Penn State was basketball player Al Chandler, the childhood friend of Herb Adderley's from Philadelphia. The two would see each other around campus, at parties and at the student union, and before long became good friends.

"We had a very close group," Robinson said. "All the black students hung out together, and Al was one of the guys, very likable."

Chandler had never met Robinson before going to college, but had heard about him, more from his basketball exploits than football, and was taken aback by his down-to-earth nature.

"Dave's a super, super guy, one of the nicest people I ever met," Chandler said. "First of all, athletically, he was the star, he was the guy on campus. And after sports, I mean, he was just a nice guy to be around. Everybody just liked Dave. It seems like we've been friends ever since we met."

That was likely from playing cards at the Penn State student union. "He competed playing cards like he did playing football," Chandler said. "In fact, he broke a few chairs being so dramatic in there. He hated to lose at anything."

Robinson said bridge and a popular offspring, bid whist, were the big games at the union.

"There would always be a lot of guys playing," he said. "The bridge games were kind of a select group, but every black student on campus was about playing bid whist. I was a bid whist man." Robinson's competitive nature always seemed to rise to the occasion, no matter the situation, Chandler said.

"We left this party, and I don't know how we got into the conversation about who was the fastest, and I said, 'Dave, I could beat you,'" Al said. "And he said, 'OK, let's race from here to College Avenue.' And it was like one or two o'clock in the morning and we're on the street, racing."

The two took off down the street, with Chandler slowly taking the lead before Robinson reached out and horse-collared him, throwing him to the ground.

"(He) kept on going to the corner and said, 'I won,'" Chandler said. "I said, 'Dave, you didn't win, you threw me down (laughing).' It wasn't like he was trying to hurt me, but he wasn't gonna lose to me, you know. I laughed like hell when he threw me down, and I think it's so funny that he wasn't gonna let me beat him."

Perhaps Robinson's drive to be the best stemmed from the fact he knew a lot of attention and pressure were on him to succeed. He was the only black player on Penn State's traveling football team, so he was easy to spot, for better and for worse.

"Among the black students, that made me a very big man on campus," Robinson said. "And we had a lot of people who were friendly, and I knew a lot of people."

Despite who you knew, though, being black had its disadvantages then, particularly when it came time to find housing. Both Robinson and Chandler chose to avoid the hassle by living on campus.

"There were black fraternity houses, so a lot of guys joined a fraternity just to get housing so they weren't trying to look around for an apartment," Robinson said.

The predominantly white town simply wasn't ready to handle the needs of black students, either, all the way down to getting haircuts.

"When I got to Green Bay, I wasn't devastated by not being able to get a haircut, because we couldn't get a haircut at State College," Robinson said. "There was one barbershop in Tyrone, Pennsylvania, and we went there—twenty or thirty miles away—because the guy in Tyrone was black but he could pass for white, and he would cut your hair. Then we had a couple guys who came to the university whose fathers were barbers or had some barbering skills, so this guy would come to your room, and you could get your hair cut that way."

At Penn State in the early 1960s, the students were more open about new ideas and the mingling of blacks and whites, culturally and otherwise, which made things easier.

"There was interracial dating when I was there, and there was nothing said about it," he said. "It's probably a lot more prevalent today than back then, but when it occurred, it wasn't an unusual situation, like, 'Oh, so-and-so's dating a white girl.' It wasn't a big thing."

At parties where alcohol was served, Robinson was present, but never imbibed.

"I didn't drink in college at all," he said. "Actually, they wanted me to drink beer to gain weight. I didn't start drinking until I got to Green Bay. Two years of Vince Lombardi, I became a drunk," he said, laughing.

After Robinson and Adderley's pro careers ended, Chandler reconnected with both of them, with mixed results, as one might expect when long-time friends and pranksters are involved.

"I would see Herb when he came home, and he would tell me, 'Oh, you should see Dave, he's blown up to 300 pounds,'" Chandler said. "And obviously, Herb was going back and telling Dave the same thing about me." The jig was up when Robinson and Chandler finally saw each other at Adderley's wedding.

"Dave was standing outside, and he just grabbed me and picked me up and held me up in the air," Chandler said. "He said, 'You don't weigh 300 pounds.' But Herb had never told either one of us the truth, that neither one of us had blown up to 300 pounds," he laughed.

"I used to go and see them play … but I didn't get a chance to get to a lot of their games, and I just missed them, really totally, through their pro careers, because they were gone. Now I talk to Herb, we email each other like three or four times a day, and when I started seeing Dave again, it was like we never lost contact."

––––––––––––––

Robinson got off to a good start with the Nittany Lions, playing guard and defensive end on a winning team. When Penn State was invited to the 1961 Gator Bowl, played in the Deep South of Jacksonville, Florida, it would be the first time a black player appeared.

But it almost didn't happen.

From the beginning of the bid acceptance, team officials were besieged by threats and hate mail and tried to find a way out. The team held a vote on whether to go, and everyone except Robinson voted "yes." Engle and Paterno pulled him aside to find out why.

"They said, 'We understand your problems, and if we go, we're all going to stay together. You'll be with us,'" Robinson said.

What the coaches didn't know was the reason he didn't want to go to the bowl game is he already lined up a job working at the post office during his break. He needed the money.

"They thought I didn't want to because I didn't want to go down South," he chuckled. "I wanted to work. I was naïve to some of those things."
Once Robinson got to the Sunshine State to prepare for the game, though, he found out exactly what was going on. Quickly.

"We go down there and we can't stay in Jacksonville because Jacksonville's got a non-integrated living law," he said. "I couldn't live in the white hotels; they couldn't live in the black hotels."

The team then headed to the friendlier confines of St. Augustine, where Robinson was briefed about his altered living arrangements.

"All year long I roomed with Dick Anderson, but this game, I didn't room with him," Robinson said. "They said, 'This kid's coming down from Pittsburgh on Thursday, and you'll have a roommate.'"

When Thursday came and the player didn't show up at the train station, Robinson got a hold of him back in Pittsburgh and asked why he didn't make the trip.

"He said, 'Are you kidding me?'" Robinson said. "'I'm catching hell in *Pittsburgh*! Why would I get on a train and ride 19 hours just to have someone screw with me some more?' I said, 'You got a point, you got a point.'"

So Robinson stayed alone, and after practice he'd walk across the tracks to a hamburger shop run by a Philly native who was happy to see him. The feeling was mutual.

"I remember the big old hamburgers with about ten pounds of meat were a quarter, and 12-ounce sodas were a dime," he said. "I'd sit back, and we'd sit down and talk and I had a great time."

The rest of the team went downtown, though, to a predominantly white area Robinson tried to avoid. Finally, teammate Bob Hart convinced him to go.

"I said, 'Bob, this is St. Augustine and I'm black. They don't want me down there; I'll get embarrassed,'" Robinson said. "He said, 'No, they'd love it. You see the little kids, and they're getting autographs after practice and everything, they love that in this town, go on.'"

The two found a restaurant, sat down and ordered food without any issue. Or so they thought.

"I sit there and Bob said, 'See, no problem—the waitress didn't say nothing,'" Robinson said. "(Later), she comes up, gives him his hamburger and a Coke and I said, 'Miss, I ordered a Coke.' And she says, 'Oh, sorry.' I look, and she's waiting at the end of the counter with my Coke in a to-go cup," Robinson said, laughing. "So I took the check over and I paid it and went to walk out the door and the waitress said, 'You're forgetting your Coke.' And I said, 'You couldn't pay me to drink that Coke.'"

Robinson walked out, Hart hurrying right behind, voicing his disbelief.

"I said, 'Bob, I told you it was gonna happen,'" Robinson said. "'You owe me a dollar for the Coke, though.'"

The night before the game, Robinson found out from fans that he wasn't just going to be the only black player on the field, he would be the first ever to play in the Gator Bowl. The news was anything but comforting.

"We were sitting in a club and a guy comes up and says, 'Hey, Robinson, you're the guy who's going to integrate the Gator Bowl tomorrow, right?'"

Robinson said. "I said, 'No, I'll be the only black on the field; not the first black.' He came back with a copy of the *Pittsburgh Courier*, a popular black paper in those days, and sure enough, it read, 'Robinson to Integrate Gator Bowl Tomorrow.' I said, 'Jee-sus Chrrr-ist!'"

Curfew was at 11 o'clock for players, but Robinson was in bed by nine, staring at the ceiling and thinking about what could happen.

"I couldn't sleep," he said. "I was a nervous wreck."

For Retta Robinson and the rest of his family members, things were much less tense, though, and people were in a celebratory mood and brimming with pride about Robinson's impending breakthrough.

"At the time I had an account at a men's store in Philadelphia, and when I opened the account they asked, 'Who are you shopping for?'" she said. "I told him it was for my brother. My mother said, 'My baby is going to play in the Gator Bowl and when he steps on the street or wherever, I want him to look as nice as anybody else.'"

On the morning of the game, coach Rip Engle had some surprising news for Robinson when he got to the stadium. A late lineup change. "I had been hurt and missed several games in the middle of the season, and he says 'Jim Schwab played very well and he's a senior and this is his only chance to show up on TV, so we're going to start Jimmy for this game,'" he said. "'Then, after the first series, you can go in and play with the first team. We'll go to other bowl games next year and you'll get a chance to be introduced on TV.'"

Robinson was disappointed—mainly because he told his friends he would be introduced—but told Engle he understood. If only he did.

After the game, a 30–15 victory, Penn State officials came into the locker room with a stack of letters they'd saved up, warnings and threats about Robinson's safety. They had been screening his mail to let him focus on the game.

"One of them said, 'If you introduce that black bear, if he comes running out before the game, I'm a marksman, I was in the military, and I'll shoot him on the 50-yard line on national TV,' and all sorts of things," Robinson said. "So they took him seriously, and they didn't start me. And there was more: They talked about, 'After we kick your ass, you take that black so-and-so and your 'n'-loving asses back to Pennsylvania.' All kinds of shit. My wife kept all those letters."

*Nittany Lion Dave
Robinson with Penn State
Head Coach Rip Engle.*

College football wasn't all about battling racism and personal threats, though. For Robinson, it increasingly become about having the chance to match up with other great players of the era and seeing how he stacked up. Playing professional football wasn't on his mind at the beginning of his college career, but after holding his own against some of the most highly touted talent in the nation, he started to believe he could.

"That's why I wanted to go to Penn State," he said. "I wanted to know how good I really was, and Penn State was the nearest school with big-time football."

One of the greatest players Robinson sparred with was the late Hall-of-Famer John Mackey of Syracuse, who matched up with him on both sides of the ball during four years of hand-to-hand combat.

"We played on top of each other all day long," Robinson said. "I had to block him, he had to block me."

Outside of playing against each other for their respective schools, the two easterners would be frequently paired as roommates during regional all-star games early on in their careers, and became good friends. Another Syracuse great and college football icon, running back Ernie Davis, was another tough adversary for three years in college and played "as advertised," Robinson said.

But realizing that he was good enough to play with the very best really never clicked until his battles with the legendary Mike Ditka of Pittsburgh, who proved to be the measuring stick Robinson needed to set his sights on a pro career.

"My sophomore year, I went one-on-one with Mike Ditka, and we put Mike out of the game," Robinson said. "We had a good day against Mike. He was a dominant defensive end in college."

Ditka, then an offensive and defensive end, was also an All-American and future NFL Rookie of the Year with a big motor and a mean streak, giving opponents fits on both sides of the ball. On defense, he was known for his uncanny ability to read and chase down a sweep from the backside with reckless abandon.

"The left defensive end is very seldom blocked on the sweep because they can't get there, but Ditka got there; he would catch guys," Robinson said. "Just chase 'em down."

It's a strength Penn State coaches decided to turn into a vulnerability, and altered a left sweep play to take advantage of Ditka's aggressiveness.

As the backside guard, Robinson would generally pull left on the play, helping to lead the runner. This time, he would instead pull right and cut off Ditka, who would surely be roaring around the backside in hot pursuit. The perfectly designed play fell apart—though to greater effect on the target—

when left guard Joe Blanstein botched the call and also pulled right, unintentionally catching Ditka with a move Robinson still chuckles about.

"He wheeled, I wheeled, and Ditka came in and we high-lowed him," Robinson said. "He was surprised, because he was coming hard down there. He left the game for awhile.

"I see him a lot but I never talk to him about that."

Ironically, Packers fans may have Ditka to thank for Robinson deciding to go pro.

"My next year, Mike Ditka was NFL Rookie of the Year, and I said, 'If that's the best they got, I can play this game,'" he said. "That's when I really

A consensus All-American tight end at Penn State, Lombardi ultimately decided Dave Robinson would be a linebacker in the pros.

thought about going to pro ball. Now Mike was good, don't get me wrong, but I just said, 'If he's … one of the best of the best, I can handle those guys.' And I got great confidence. Half the letters I'd gotten from teams I didn't fill out before, I'd just throw them in a box. That's when I started filling them out and sending them back in."

When a lesser-talented Penn State end was drafted that spring by the San Diego Chargers of the American Football League (AFL), Robinson was sure he could make it in the pros. Still, he focused on his academics and didn't pay much attention until his senior year, when he got a call from the NFL's defending World Champions, the Green Bay Packers, looking to replace their great tight end, Ron Kramer. And they wanted to use their first pick of the 1963 draft on him to do just that.

Robinson doesn't remember getting any attention from Green Bay before the draft, but apparently he had some inside help in catching the attention of the man in charge.

"Joe Paterno worked for Green Bay as a scout, and later, Joe Paterno told me he's the one who told Vince to draft me," he said. "(Penn State) sent some film, and Vince drafted me. Joe and Vince were like that. Joe knew Vince from when he was in high school, when he played against Vince's high school team, St. Cecelia, and Joe was a quarterback from Brooklyn. They're both from New York. He followed Vince's career. Joe Paterno loved Vince."

Today, a top draft pick like Robinson would be the subject of months of speculation and mock drafts and be a household name for millions of even casual football fans. On draft day, he'd likely be one of the two dozen or so athletes sequestered in waiting rooms, waiting to hear his name called and walk across the dais to applause and a handshake with the commissioner, or on a live camera at his house, waiting for that phone call and tears of joy and hugs from relatives and friends.

Things have changed in 60-some years.

On the morning of draft day, Robinson got a call from a Packers official asking if there were any teams he really wanted to play for.

"I said, 'Well, I've always been a New York Giants fan,' and I chuckled." Robinson said. "He said, 'Well, if the Giants don't draft you and we did, would you sign with us?' I said, 'I don't care where I play; I'll just play anywhere.'" Later that day, Robinson was coming home after visiting some friends when he heard he had a message.

"Penn State had phones in the hall; they didn't have them in the room, so I had to make this collect call to see who this is, and he said, 'This is Dick Voris. We just drafted you in Green Bay,'" Robinson said. "He said I wouldn't have any problems and, 'We'll be in touch with you,' because Vince was with the team, getting ready for the championship game."

The NFL had moved their draft date to December 7, before the season had even ended, just to prevent other leagues from poaching players.

"The Canadian Football League (CFL) was drafting early, after Thanksgiving, and then all the guys who they drafted, they'd tell them—especially black guys —'You're not going to be drafted by the NFL anyway,' and get you to sign a contract," Robinson said. "That's how 'Jete' (former Packers defensive back Bob Jeter) got messed up, going to Canada for two years. They told Jete he wasn't going to be drafted. And when he was drafted by Green Bay in the third round, he couldn't go; he had already signed with Vancouver in the CFL. And then he played his option out."

Robinson never met Lombardi during the drafting process and only spoke with him very briefly on the phone, but the man left quite an impression, as he would continue to in the future.

"Dick Voris talked all the time, because Vince was worried about the championship," he said. "Vince's whole concern was beating the Giants. He hated the Giants, of course."

For the Robinson family—with so many talented athletes who were driven with love by a father who was now no longer there—Dave's first-round pick was bittersweet, said Retta Robinson, who was out for a drive when she heard her little brother was drafted to play professional football, and in the first round, by the World Champions.

"It's a three-and-a-half mile drive from Moorestown to Mt. Laurel, where we lived," she said. "I think the newscaster's name was Bill Campbell and his comment was, 'Oh boy, look at this, the rich get richer: the Green Bay Packers signed Dave "Lefty" Robinson, a first-round draft choice.' I was so shocked I almost drove into the ditch."

The moment was also bittersweet for the family, though, because they couldn't share the joy with the patriarch and role model who helped lead his son down the positive path he'd ultimately chosen.

"It was happiness and sadness that my dad was not alive to sit down in front of the television set and watch his son play," she said. "My mom was able to, and if at all possible she would be in the stands watching him in person in high school, college and the pros. We were all very, very proud because one of ours made it. That just didn't happen, you know, a poor country boy making it."

With the help of friends and family, Robinson had plenty of support as he started a new career.

"We were convinced he could do it; that's the way we were raised," Retta said. "If you wanted something bad enough and worked hard enough, you could accomplish it, and that's what he did. As a family we were encouraging."

Just as Robinson was settling in to thoughts of playing for the two-time defending World Champions, he got a call from someone who could also be very encouraging and persuasive: Al Davis.

An assistant coach and personnel man with the AFL's San Diego Chargers, Davis told Robinson the team had just selected him in the third round of the AFL draft, and he wanted to talk contract and money. The young league was in the midst of a bidding war with the NFL, and players drafted by both leagues could stand to gain handsomely by playing one side off the other, and many did.

Robinson talked it over with his longtime girlfriend and future wife, and for her, the decision was easy.

"She said, 'You bullshit the people all you want, we're going to go to San Diego. I can't stand cold weather!'" Robinson chuckled. "'Fine with me,' I said, 'As long as I get the money.'"

The wheels began turning again, though, as Robinson studied the NFL's retirement plan. It would be a tough sell for Davis and the AFC, but he was willing to listen.

"I really thought I'd go in the NFL, play five years if I could, and then get out, have a pension and go to work and support my family," he said. "That's all I wanted to do."

Davis worked for Sid Gilman in San Diego and, quite simply, his job was to sign Robinson. He put on the hard sell and might have convinced Robinson if not for the AFL's tenuous financial structure.

"Al Davis came to New Jersey and spent quite a bit of time with me and my girlfriend, Elaine—my future wife," Robinson said. "She told Al Davis right to his face that she did not want to go to Green Bay, she wanted to go to San Diego—she did not like cold weather, so Al just kind of laughed. A great guy. I loved him."

If Davis wasn't working on Robinson, his associate Mr. Locasale was.

"They would double-team me; if Al had something to do, then Locasale would talk to me," he said. "He came all the way from San Diego to see me. He came to Jersey and spent a lot of time talking, took Elaine out to dinner one night and everything. We went to dinner, and the waitress came to me and asked, 'How do you want your steak?' I said, 'Cooked,' Robinson laughed. "In my house, you didn't say, 'Mom, bring me a medium-rare,' it was just cooked or it was raw."

Later, she asked if he wanted a shrimp cocktail, which didn't sound appetizing.

"I said, 'No, I don't drink,'" Robinson laughed.

When the negotiations finally got down to numbers, the deal reached $30,000 for two years and a bonus. Then he got a call. Davis was on the line. He didn't have good news.

"I was the No. 3 draft choice for San Diego, and they signed the first-round and second-round (picks), Rufus Guthrie and a kid from Syracuse (guard Walt Sweeney), and they were out of money," Robinson said.

Davis was in damage control mode. Working more on behalf of the AFL than the Chargers, he proposed a new deal.

"Davis said, 'It would be a big coup for the AFL if Green Bay's first-round pick would come to the AFL,'" he said. "So if you sign with us, we're going to immediately send you to a team that has money, which is Buffalo. So I called Elaine, 'Baby, San Diego is out of the picture; it's either Green Bay or Buffalo.' She had never been to Green Bay, but she had been to Buffalo, and she said, 'Buffalo—no way!' She knew Buffalo was cold. So she told me, 'You go where you want to go.'"

———————————

When the decision had to be finalized, it happened on the top of a taxi cab, of all places, right outside the Gator Bowl, where Robinson had just been named MVP. The Packers weren't taking any chances on losing their top pick.

"I came off the field. We just won the game and (Dick Voris) called me over (and) I signed on the top of a taxi cab, and everybody was there taking pictures," he said. "He had a check for me for $15,000, and he took the contract to New York and had Vince sign it, and then he sent me back a copy. I also took the check and put it in the mail to my bank."

For Robinson, the biggest thrill of getting that first professional paycheck was finally being able to buy nice Christmas gifts for the most important women in his life: his mother, girlfriend and sister.

"I always wanted to buy Christmas gifts for (them), and so I went to the local bank to negotiate — everybody knew I had been drafted and everything--and I told 'em the whole thing, 'I'll have money, but I don't have any money now,'" Robinson said. "My local bank gave me a 60-day demand note for $300, and so I had money to buy my mother and my sister and everybody gifts and I went to Hawaii with some pocket change."

Perhaps it was a good move for the Packers to sign Robinson when and how they did, because lurking in the Penn State locker room after the game was none other than Al Davis, who was told by Robinson about his just having signed with the Packers for $45,000 over three years.

"Al said, 'You know, the way you acted, I thought you already signed with the Packers,'" Robinson said. "Because a lot of people were doing that illegally. He said, 'Otherwise, I think we would offer you more than the $45,000; we'd have gone to $48,000.' I said, 'Al, if you thought I signed before the game, you really don't know me.' And he said, 'I guess not.' And that's all he said. I would never do something like that because I would have been jeopardizing Penn State, myself and the whole nine yards."

So Green Bay it was, and playing for the World Champions. Retta Robinson said once her little brother knew he was going to play for the Packers, he was excited as could be and couldn't wait to get home after his first trip to "Titletown" to tell everyone about it.

"He got a car, a Bonneville convertible, and drove all the way home from Green Bay to Mount Laurel without license plates and never got stopped," she said. "He said the cops followed them for about five miles on the Pennsylvania Turnpike but they passed him and let him go. In Green Bay he didn't have everything you needed to get license plates, but he had the paperwork."

Surveying his new workplace in the middle of winter, Robinson, a hearty northeast native, remembers one thing in particular that caught him off-guard about his new home on the "frozen tundra."

"*Huge* mounds of snow," he said. "I couldn't believe it. Huge snowbanks. And I said, 'Wow, these people really love this town because they all have the Green Bay footballs on their antennas.' And a guy said, 'No, that's because when you come to a corner, you can't see the cars coming, so you've got to look for the antennas instead.'"

As he drove by Lambeau Field (City Stadium then), parts of the road were bordered by five-foot drifts.

"I've never seen so much snow in my life," Robinson said.

When he reached the team offices at the Downtown Motel, he was taken aback by how second-rate the whole operation looked.

"You had to go around to the back and up to the steps," Robinson said. "I said, 'World Champions—they got a shitty office. This is really a small town. This is terrible.'"

Once inside, the office was actually "kind of nice," though. That is, until he heard the booming voice of one Vincent Thomas Lombardi.

"I sat down in a chair, and I'm sitting there facing the secretary, and I hear Vince in the background screaming on the phone about something—he's always yelling and screaming about something—and then he came up to me, he says, 'Are you Robinson?' I turned around and looked and I saw him, this little shitty guy," said Robinson, laughing, "a little squatty guy. I thought, 'What the hell?' He was only around 5'10". Shit, I could take this guy, easy. He's not one of the 'Seven Rocks of Granite.'

"I soon found out it was a little different."

Oddly enough, the two had common tastes in automobiles. Right away, Lombardi arranged for Robinson to get a car at Brown County Motors, a favorite spot of his to send players and coaches.

"I had a Bonneville convertible, and Vince was driving a Bonneville convertible," he said. "Mine was blue—I can't remember what color his was—and Elijah Pitts had one that was red. It was kind of funny, everybody said,

'Oh, I see. Vince and the No. 1 have the same car.'"

When it came to football, though, car allegiance certainly meant nothing to Lombardi. Only winning, and lots of it. Thankfully for Robinson, the coach saw in him a spark of greatness in his talent, as well as a bold, bright intellect. The two would develop a unique coach/player relationship, but it would take some time to earn Lombardi's respect, something that became immediately apparent to Robinson during his first practice with the team, following the Packers' humiliating loss to the 1963 College All-Stars, led by Robinson himself.

"Vince Lombardi came in and he is pissed. *Pissed*," Robinson said. "I sit midway in the meeting room—the black guys kind of lumped together—and Vince came in. I'm sitting there waiting to see what this guy has to say and he's real livid and he's screamin' and hollerin' … he's stopping the camera and chewing guys out."

As the action moved through perhaps Robinson's finest play of the game, shedding All-Pro tight end Ron Kramer to plant running back Tom Moore two yards behind the line, the camera stops and Lombardi speaks. Robinson thinks he's about to earn some praise from the old man.

"'Do you see that? Do you see that?' (Lombardi said)," Robinson remembered. "And I'm thinking, 'Hey, I'm about to get a little praise here.' He says, 'Kramer, that guy's a rookie! He probably won't even make the team he's going to, and look what he did to you on that play,'" Robinson said, laughing.

What Lombardi apparently didn't know is it was his own first-round pick who made that play. He was just wearing jersey No. 86, not his soon-to-be-familiar 89.

"Willie Wood pulled me over and said, 'Don't buy a house,'" Robinson chuckled.

While the College All-Star game may not have endeared Robinson to Lombardi, the experience did give him a chance to see how versatile his first-round pick was. The first week of camp, Robinson played defensive end; the second week he played tight end; and the last week, linebacker.

"They had me at defensive end and Lionel Aldridge was playing offensive guard, and Lionel stunk at guard, so Vince moved him to defensive end, and he showed real promise," he said. "Well, he had Willie Davis and he picked up Urban Henry from the Rams, who was a starting end. Lionel was going to be a backup and they didn't want to stockpile me behind them; that would have been four defensive ends with only a 38-man roster."

The Packers then moved Robinson to tight end to evaluate him as a possible backup to Kramer. Again, the numbers didn't look good.

"So (fellow rookie) Marvin (Fleming) started looking good at tight end, so you figured they weren't going to cut Marvin, either," he said. "So now you've got Ron Kramer, (backup) Gary Knafelc, Marv Fleming and Dave Robinson —you're not going to have four tight ends, so they moved me to linebacker, and they needed a linebacker bad."

Ultimately, that was the chance to show his skills, where his speed, size and smarts could help shut down an entire side of the field, from rushing the passer to dropping into coverage. At that point, Robinson said he just "settled in" to his new position, eventually redefining it over the next decade.

And, of course, he likes to joke with his friend Fleming about how he opened up a roster spot for him by being good enough to switch to defense.

The friendly banter goes all the way back to the 1963 Hula Bowl, when they played tight end on opposing teams.

"My team won, and I was MVP. I had 165 yards in receptions," Robinson said. "I always tell Marvin, any time he gets going, 'Don't you understand? If I wasn't versatile to play either linebacker or tight end, you would have been cut, and I would have been tight end.'" (laughs)

Robinson said while he conceded he could have made "a lot more money" playing tight end in the NFL than playing defense, he believes he could have fared pretty well no matter where he lined up.

"I played defensive end in practice a couple times. I had no trouble rushing the passer at all from the left side; Lionel (Aldridge) played the right," Robinson said. "When (Green Bay Head Coach Dan) Devine was there, I played some defensive end, and I didn't have any trouble. I could have played other positions, but I was happy where I was, don't get me wrong."

Perhaps Robinson could have helped revolutionize the tight end position like the men he ended up trying to chase down and smack forearms with: Mackey and Ditka.

"When I played tight end, I hit, too," Robinson said. "When I was at Penn State, we ran more than we passed, and they used to say, 'Dave Robinson out there is like having a third tackle.' In fact, Dan Radakovich, the assistant coach at Penn State, when he went to Pittsburgh (Steelers), he tried to trade for me. They needed a guard real bad, and he'd seen me (when) I played guard my sophomore year at Penn State. But the trade fell through."

Lombardi appreciated Robinson's talent and refusal to back down from a challenge. One day, he sat him down and told him why he switched his position.

"He said, '(Defensive coordinator) Phil (Bengtson) and I had always felt you'd be a great linebacker; we weren't sure if you could play defensive end or right end," Robinson said. "The problem is that there are no black linebackers in the National Football League, and you'll be the first one. And our focus this year is on winning the third consecutive World Championship, and we don't need any distractions. So if anyone comes to you and talks about being the first black linebacker, I don't want you to answer them, and want you to tell them to see me.' And that's what I did. (I) never saw a word in print about it."

———

Lombardi was very sensitive to racial issues and was aggressive in stamping them out, but once the black players went home from work, in Green Bay, they were often strangers in a generally friendly but strange land. The situation wasn't necessarily menacing, but there was a constant racial tension all the same in the small, blue-collar, nearly all-white city.

When Elaine Robinson was pregnant with twin boys during Robinson's rookie year, she stayed home in New Jersey. In fact, none of the married black players' wives lived in Titletown that year.

"(Players) brought their wives up, but they wouldn't stay in Green Bay. Green Bay was a rough town," Robinson said. "In fact, in '63, Elijah Pitts brought Ruth up there with him, and at the end of training camp, she said she couldn't take it and took a job as a substitute teacher back in Arkansas, and took (son) Ronnie. Willie Wood brought his wife a couple years before, and she said she couldn't take it in Green Bay and went back. It was a rough situation."

That decision ended up with Robinson moving into Pitts' house in Green Bay as a roommate that year, but Elaine was determined to join him the following season.

"She said, 'I don't care. A wife's place is with her husband,'" Robinson said. "So when I went to camp in July, we packed up the car, the twins, and (ourselves). We put a U-Haul on the back and we took off for Wisconsin."

To help his young sons get through the long drive, Robinson, ever the engineer, rigged his Bonneville convertible's back seat with a bed board, a piece of four-by-eight wood, and constructed a play and rest area.

"We put this two-by-four on top and put mattresses so the kids could crawl around like a playpen, and when it was time to feed, she'd bring one up front and feed him and put him in the back," he said. "They had pillows back there and they slept back there, all the way. I drove all night long to get to Green Bay, Wisconsin."

With Elaine in town, Ruth Pitts came up in 1964, giving each other a close friend and needed confidant.

"They hung together," Robinson said. "They were the first two black wives, really, to come to Green Bay. Even Ruth and Elaine were uncomfortable, but they had each other to bond with."

Robinson said it was difficult for the black players to understand what their wives or girlfriends faced during the day, or at the games.

"We're gone all day; we didn't see each other," he said. "We got up, went to breakfast, practice, lunch, practice, and then after dinner, and meetings after dinner. We got to go home at nine o'clock and had to be back here by eleven.

That's all they saw us, just two hours a day, or less than that because you had travel time in there. That's all they saw us. And most of the time, she's alone with those kids, all by themselves."

Elaine would have "gone crazy" if not for Ruth's presence, Robinson said, and vice-versa. Perhaps misery loves company, but the tough times helped the two forge a strong bond. They needed each other—and probably a good sense of humor—to laugh off some of the things that happened.

"When they walked down the street—and they're 21, 22—the only black women you saw in Green Bay were go-go dancers, or they were hookin'," he said. "So guys would come up to them, 'Where are you dancing, dear?' And they'd be drunk. And women don't appreciate that. And they weren't necessarily people from Green Bay, it was these farmers coming in because Green Bay was the Mecca, the guy's first time in the big city, and 'Hey, here's a hooker, hit on her.'"

When the families went downtown with the children, they always attracted a curious crowd.

"People came up to them; they wanted to play with their hair. They had never seen hair like that," Robinson said. "And it was all sorts of things—little things—but it pissed the women off. People didn't mean it maliciously, half of them, but it would be very offensive. And having never dealt with black people, people didn't understand what it was like."

Robinson went through similar incidents when looking at houses in the area.

"My landlord once told me, 'It's not much of a house, but probably a lot better than the one you've got at home,'" he said. "Then I showed him a picture of my house back home and he said, 'Whoa, you live there?' I told him, 'Hey, my friends and I wouldn't even live in your home, let alone something like this.' But people—they really did—all they saw were those pictures on TV, with black people in tenements, and in the ghetto. They were just uninformed and didn't know."

Sometimes the ignorance could even reach near-comical proportions. In 1967, the Robinsons moved into a three-bedroom house on the Fox River that Willie Wood, another black player, used to rent from an older lady. Once they got to know her, she admitted—not without some shame—how the place became available to the players in the first place.

"She had the house and she got into an argument with the next-door neighbors (so) she said, 'I'll fix you—I'll rent to blacks!'" Robinson chuckled.

"And after we got in, she got to know Elaine and what-not, and she became one of our best friends, Inez Barrett. She used to baby-sit Richard and David during the games. She owned the Carleton Inn, and they'd spend Saturday Night at the Carleton Inn and watch the game with her, and Sunday after the game, we'd go pick 'em up."

Robinson said both sides ultimately came away with a little better understanding of the other.

"Her son and I became good friends, and her husband, but it was just that way," he said. "She always used to say, 'I'd never been around blacks, never seen any blacks in my life. I didn't know what to expect.' Until she did, then she kind of felt bad, and went back and tried to make amends for it, which wasn't necessary. She was a nice lady."

Such racial tolerance, or willingness to learn from mistakes, was not the case with some of the white players' wives, particularly some from the Deep South, who could be rude to the wives and the husbands alike.

"A lot of the southern wives really resented me," Robinson said. "Some of them … they levitated more toward Marvin than me as far as doing things, because Marvin was no threat to 'em. They were really offended there was a black No.1 (pick). The wives kept a lot of shit going and would tell their husbands, the husbands would tell Vince, and Vince would call Willie Davis, and Willie would call us and say, 'Hey, man, we gotta report to such-and-such and cool it.'"

Davis, the well-respected, preacher-like clubhouse leader, served as the liaison between the black players and Lombardi, who was more than willing to cede some authority to make sure his communications and team chemistry were solid.

"If any issues came up with the black ballplayers, Vince went to Willie," Robinson said. "Speeds Bar was one of the places that was off-limits for blacks when Vince came. Let's say there's something going on, (if) Vince wanted to stop the guys from going to Speeds, Vince would go to Willie Davis, and Willie Davis would get all the black players together playing cards and say, 'Hey, man, coach is a little worried about something going on at Speeds, and word's out that you guys are porking all these white women in here. Be cool, you can do what you want to do, but don't be too obvious inside the bar.' Stuff like that. Willie gave me what Vince wanted me to know, and then Elijah (Pitts) told me what was really going on. Marvin and the 'Train' (Lionel) and I, we didn't know anything. We couldn't help each other."

Davis's role was an unofficial but important position Lombardi established when he was hired in 1959, starting with the acquisition of Emlen Tunnell, who helped convince Robinson to sign with the Packers. It was advice that earned Robinson an extra $9,000, too, as it turned out.

"In the beginning, San Diego was offering me $42,000 (over three years), all guaranteed, and Vince would only give me $12,000 a year—12, 12 and 12— if I wanted a guaranteed, no-cut," he said. "But he said if I didn't take a no-cut, he'd give me 15-15-15. I was really toying with it, and Em Tunnell said, 'Hey, Vince Lombardi is a big egotist. If you're the worst football player in America, he won't cut you and tell the rest of the league, I've made a mistake. Take the money.'

"That's why I signed."

Dave Robinson, left, with former high school football teammate Hank David at the Belmont Hotel, 1967.

Building a Dynasty

The most important unknown person from the Lombardi era was Jack Vainisi.

Vainisi spent 10 years as a talent scout building a roster that allowed a coach from New York to become a legend.

There are 10 players and one coach in the Pro Football Hall of Fame who were acquired by Jack Vainisi. The same can be said of twenty-eight members of the Packers Hall of Fame. Without contributions of the great talent scout, there would be no Lombardi Avenue in Green Bay.

Jack Vainisi began collecting players for the Packers in 1950, before the team had a general manager. He scouted, evaluated, drafted and signed a tremendous core group of players who were in Green Bay when Lombardi arrived from the New York Giants in 1959.

Future Hall of Famers Ray Nitschke, Forrest Gregg, Jim Ringo, Jim Taylor, Paul Hornung and Bart Starr were waiting when Lombardi was hired. "The two trades with Cleveland made our team," said Paul Hornung. "We got Hall of Fame defensive tackle Henry Jordan one year and defensive end Willie Davis the next." Jordan was acquired in a trade from Cleveland in '59 and was enshrined at Canton in 1995. The other two Hall of Famers eventually obtained by Vainisi were Willie Wood and Herb Adderley. One month to the day after the great scout died, Green Bay selected Adderley in the first round, based on Vainisi's recommendation. Ten players and Lombardi are in the big Hall of Fame; Jack should be there too.

Also on the roster in "Lombardi's Waiting Room" in '59 were Dan Currie, Bobby Dillon, Boyd Dowler, Bill Forester, Hank Gremminger, Dave "Hawg" Hanner, Billy Howton, Gary Knafelc, Jerry Kramer, Ron Kramer, Norm Masters, Max McGee, Bob Skoronski, Johnny Symank and Jesse Whittenton. Jack Vainisi mined gems; Lombardi polished them.

Green Bay Packer history would be anemic if the names listed in the above two paragraphs were removed. The hallowed Packers Hall of Fame would echo with emptiness and the stadium rim would be nearly naked of great names. Without Vainisi, not only might there be echoes and nakedness, there might be a team named the Milwaukee Packers. Or, God forbid, the Minnesota Packers. The Gopher State was looking for a team in the late 1950s and joined the NFL in 1961. The difference between football greatness and façade is 260 miles: the distance between Green Bay, Wisconsin and Minneapolis, Minnesota.

Vainisi may have put more great players in the National Football League than anyone in history. The list of great players accumulated by Chuck Noll for the 1970s Pittsburgh Steelers may rival or possibly surpass Vainisi's efforts, but it's hard to find anything else that does.

Three different head coaches bungled the Packer's bevy of talent before Lombardi took command. The great *Green Bay Press-Gazette* sports writer, Art Daley, said, "Before Lombardi got here, Green Bay had two teams: one at the stadium and one at the train station." Daley meant there was little stability and continuity because players were coming and going constantly.

Many of the ones who stayed were not completely dedicated to professional conduct. Longtime Packer receiver and great storyteller, Gary Knafelc spent five years in Green Bay before Lombardi's arrival and experienced some wacky episodes with his rowdy teammates. Beginning in 1950, the Packers ended their season with West Coast games against San Francisco and Los Angeles.

One such three-day train ride occurred in 1954, when rookie Knafelc and his Packer mates were sequestered for the California trip.

Dick Afflis played guard at Green Bay from 1951-54. He eventually became one of pro wrestling's early popular stars with a beer-drinking image that held wide appeal in Wisconsin. Dick "The Bruiser" is center stage in a classic story.

Put a football team on a train for three days and hope for the best. Mix in a healthy dose of ego, an equal supply of beer and one effective agitator, and all the hope in the world is useless.

"All there was to do was play cards and drink beer," said Knafelc, "As a matter of fact, whenever the train stopped, coach Liz Blackbourn had us all go outside and run around the train. That's how stupid he was. So, here we are the last day sitting in the bar car. Dick Afflis and Jerry Hellvin, a tackle from Tulane, were sitting right across from me and Dave "Hawg" Hanner. They're sitting there, loaded. I didn't drink.

"Afflis thought he was tough; he was the only guy who lifted weights. He had a 32-inch waist and a 57-inch chest. Hanner started baiting Afflis and got Dick to say he was the toughest guy in the league. Hellvin said, 'Bullshit, I'm the strongest guy in the National Football League.' Afflis grabbed a beer can— that's when they were made out of real metal, not aluminum. He just crushed it. Hellvin did the same thing. Afflis took a can the long way and crushed it; Hellvin did too. Afflis' face was beet red; he took a can and put it between his forearm and bicep, inside of his elbow. He flexed his arm and crushed it."

The act was duplicated by Hellvin. Knafelc said, "Afflis took another can and smashed it, bottom first, right over his nose. *Smash.* Cuts on both cheeks, bleeding. Afflis looked at Hellvin and asked, 'What do you think about that?' Hellvin said, 'You win.'

"You damn right."

"Afflis got up, he could hardly walk out," Knafelc said. "That's the kind of guys we had."

The tough guys from Green Bay were shut out 35–0 by San Francisco and closed out the season by dropping a 35–27 decision to the Rams.

It's hard not to wonder what would have happened if Lombardi had found one of his players drunk on a team plane flying to the West Coast. The player may have been ordered to run around the plane. Being ordered to do so by Lombardi, he might have done it.

Jack Vainisi
Photo courtesy of Fritz Van

As much as anyone, Jack Vainisi was responsible for the Packers hiring Lombardi as head coach and general manager. No small achievement, Vainisi survived the triple debacle regimes of head coaches Gene Ronzani, Liz Blackbourn and Ray "Scooter" McLean. Lombardi's hiring in 1959 meant Green Bay had four coaches in one decade, the first and only time it happened in the team's history. San Francisco 49ers quarterback John Brodie entered the NFL in 1957 and simply described the Packers of those times as "crummy."

Green Bay's franchise was a mess from top to bottom before Lombardi grabbed the organization by the throat. A cumbersome, inept board of directors had crippled the franchise and was in dire need of restructuring.

Jerry Vainisi, younger brother of Jack, served as a Packer ball boy before and during Lombardi's early years in Green Bay. An accomplished football man in his own right, Jerry was named general manager of the Chicago Bears in 1972 and later served the Detroit Lions in a similar capacity. Jerry was at the helm when Chicago won Super Bowl XX and later drafted Barry Sanders for the Lions.

According to Jerry Vainisi, "When Jack negotiated with Vince about coming to Green Bay, Vince told Jack, 'I don't want anybody else above me in the organization saying that I have to keep a player or get rid of a player. I want to be able to control who comes and goes. In all other aspects of the club, you (Jack) will be the general manager.' The relationship worked really well."

Jack's other brother, Dr. Samuel Vainisi, said, "I remember Jack telling Lombardi when Lombardi got here, 'You run the show; take everything.' The board of directors was so huge and they were so disorganized. Somebody had to take over; that was one of Jack's frustrations. There were just too many people with their fingers in the pot that didn't know a damn thing about football."

A longtime member of the Packers Board of Directors said Lombardi would not have taken the Green Bay job if not for Jack Vainisi. Before Lombardi accepted the dual responsibilities of head coach and general manager, he insisted on defining his authority. At a 1986 Packers game in Green Bay, Jack's brothers, Dr. Sam and Jerry, learned how Lombardi crafted his deal. The Vanisi brothers were watching a game from the press box when longtime executive committee member Jerry Atkinson approached them and said, "Sam, I'd like to talk with you and your brother during halftime."

The three got together for a sandwich at the half and, according to Dr. Sam, Atkinson said, "This never came out, but when Lombardi came to Green Bay, he said, 'I don't want to deal with any of you guys. Get my contract and I will sign it with Jack Vainisi, but he's the only one I want to talk to.'"

Dr. Vainisi explained, "Jerry Atkinson said, 'I wanted you to know he wouldn't deal with anybody but your brother.' Lombardi and Jack were really very close. It's just a shame that Jack passed away because they would have been a great team together. The two of them hit it off very well; he was thrilled to have Lombardi."

On more than one occasion, Marie Lombardi told Dr. Sam, "My husband loves your brother." A Vainisi draft choice and Packer great, Ron Kramer confirmed the admiration, saying, "It was incredible how much Lombardi liked Jack."

Dr. Sam Vainisi stated emphatically, "What a lot of people don't realize, Lombardi would not have been here if it hadn't been for Jack. Jack was the one that went out and talked with Lombardi. I'm almost positive it was Paul Brown who suggested Jack go talk to him. Jack was really desperate looking for a coach."

Following a meeting between Lombardi and Vainisi, Jack made a very strong recommendation to Packers President Dominick Olejniczak. Dr. Vainisi said, "When Jack came back he said, 'Ole, we gotta get this guy. Make this man an offer.' And Lombardi came here."

At 45 years of age, Lombardi was relatively old when he got his first head coaching job in Green Bay. He had a clear idea of what he wanted to do both on the field and in the front office to resurrect the long-suffering franchise.

Shyness was not a problem Lombardi had to conquer.

Just so everybody understood who was in charge once he took the job, Lombardi flexed his authority early and often. Knafelc spent five seasons in Green Bay before Lombardi took over and recalled a team meeting at which Olejniczak made an unwelcome appearance.

Gary said, "When Lombardi came here, he was in charge of the Green Bay Packers, which meant he was in charge of every phase of the Green Bay Packers, and no one ever questioned his authority. So when anyone walked into his meeting while he was talking to his players, they were intruding, and for him, that was unacceptable. Olejniczak and Art Daley of the *Green Bay Press-Gazette* walked in one time—just opened the door and walked right in. He stopped our meeting, turned around and said, 'Get out. Don't you ever come into my group when I'm talking to my men.' They never came back again."

Pat Peppler, player personnel director for Lombardi from 1963–68 said, "He took all his chances right away. It was before I was there, but I heard the story that Olejniczak came down to the practice field with a list of things the board of directors said were wrong in the 1959 intra-squad game. Reportedly, Vince took the paper, crumpled it up and threw it away and said, 'I'll coach the goddamned team.' You're never stronger than you are the first day on the job."

Lombardi made decisions of genius. He took a job with a franchise that had hit rock bottom, had lots of talent and was desperate enough to hand him control. Upon closer examination, Adderley's contention of a *Chosen* collection of people seems valid. Jack Vainisi was just 23 years old when he got the scouting job in 1950 and may have accumulated more talent than any scout in NFL history.

Jerry Vainisi offered insights into older brother Jack's achievements in Green Bay, "I always have believed he was under-appreciated. People in football back in that era knew how good he was, but Vince was such a dominant figure that everybody took a back seat to Vince, including my brother. Lombardi did come in and turn around a 1-10-1 team, but I always thought Jack came up a little bit short on the credit he should have received."

In a 1968 conversation with Jerry Vainisi, Lombardi himself echoed the sentiments saying, "Jack has never gotten the credit he deserved."

At the NFL level, Lombardi's favorite trading partner upon arrival in Green Bay was Paul Brown of the Cleveland Browns. Henry Jordan, Willie Davis, Bill Quinlan and Lew Carpenter were acquired from Cleveland in Lombardi's first two years. "Vince robbed Paul Brown," said Paul Hornung.

A working relationship had been established between the Packers and Browns before Lombardi took over.

Jerry Vainisi explained the arrangement, "When I was named general manager of the Bears in '83, Paul Brown called me. At that time he would have been with the Bengals. He said, 'Jerry, your brother Jack and I always used to have an understanding if either of us had a player we thought could play, but we didn't want him to be in our division, we would trade them to each other.' He asked me if I would be interested in continuing that same relationship. I said, 'In a heartbeat.' I think because of the relationship between my brother and Paul Brown, those early trades would have been more my brother than Vince."

In 1959, Henry Jordan was acquired from the Browns, Fuzzy Thurston from the Colts, and both played all nine years Lombardi coached the Packers. It was, however, another personnel move that influenced the Packers organization positively to a degree that may not be measurable even these many years later.

A black player, defensive back Emlen Tunnell was obtained from New York in a straight cash deal. In 1948, he became the first African-American to play for the Giants. Simply stated, Tunnell was and is NFL royalty. He displayed excellence both on and off the football field and was a perfect choice to help Lombardi change the losing culture that gripped Green Bay's suffering franchise. Tunnell was a winner and had been part of championship teams in New York during Lombardi's time as an assistant coach. The great defensive back was a natural leader who knew how to carry himself as a professional, and his presence in the locker room showed the young Packers what they needed to become.

Tunnell played 14 years in the NFL, the first 11 years with the New York Giants and the last three in Green Bay. He was a nine-time Pro-Bowl selection and ended his career with a record 79 interceptions. Lombardi once told Dave Anderson of *The New York Times* that Emlen was, "a pastor, a cheerleader and a coach, as well as a player."

It was no small matter in Lombardi's mind when it came time for Emlen Tunnell to end his career in Green Bay. He had earned the right to be treated with dignity and respect. It was such a delicate issue that Lombardi solicited the help of two great Baltimore Colts who held Tunnell in high regard.

Lenny Moore said, "Vince came to me and Jim Parker at the Pro Bowl after the '61 season and said, 'I see you guys seem to be pretty friendly with each other.' I said, 'Oh, yeah, Em is my man, he's a good guy. What's going on?' Lombardi said, 'I would like to see if you could kind of help me out, I'm struggling with this situation. I'm going to have to tell Emlen that maybe he needs to hang it up football-wise. I don't know how I'm going to tell him that it's all over. I know you guys are friends and maybe you can encourage him a little bit. Whatever you can do, I certainly would appreciate.' Would you figure Vince Lombardi would do that?"

Moore said, "I'm thinking to myself, 'That's a deal that's up to Emlen.' But I admired the feelings Vince showed me and the respect he showed for Emlen. What he was showing was his love for Emlen and how difficult it was going to be to tell Emlen it was all over." Lombardi was also showing respect for a black man he no longer "needed."

By trusting opposing players with his concerns, Lombardi displayed his admiration for, and trust in, two rival players who could have used the information to create turmoil between Tunnell and Green Bay's head coach, and thus help the Colts. Lenny Moore said, "I was shocked that he would come to me and Parker and make that statement." All parties involved were above such behavior.

Tunnell was the first African-American and first defensive player elected to the Pro Football Hall of Fame. He told the *Des Moines Register* he was the "first black everything: player, scout, talent scout, assistant coach and first full-time black assistant coach in the whole league."

As great as the Lombardi Dynasty was, it may have been even better had Jack Vainisi not died prematurely. He contracted a serious medical condition in July of 1947 while serving with the United States Army in Japan, causing damage to his heart. Vainisi was a relentless worker with significant health issues. Those factors, combined with a less than stellar effort to care for his physical condition, hastened his death.

At age 33 he fell victim to a fatal heart attack in his home bathroom on November 27, 1960.

Lombardi wondered if he contributed to Vainisi's death with his hard-driving managerial style and conveyed his concern to Jackie Vainisi, Jack's widow. Jerry said, "Because of the intensity and pressure Lombardi put on Jack. I don't know if it was a telephone call, or at the wake, or funeral, but Lombardi asked her if she thought he had killed him. Jackie said, 'No. This is what he wanted to do, loved to do, and knew there were certain risks involved with it.'"

Art Daley attended several of the NFL drafts, which were held in Chicago. During his first year covering the event, he noticed the Packer personnel had index cards with information about individual college players. Daley saw some of the cards had stickers on them and was curious what the stickers meant. He was told it indicated the players were "Negro."

Adderley said, "Jack Vainisi recommended me to be drafted as a running back, but Hornung was established as an All-Pro and MVP. Lombardi told me that he drafted me as the best athlete in the draft, but he wasn't sure where I was going to play on offense."

In 1960 the Packers traded for Willie Davis, signed Willie Wood as a free agent, and late in the same year, selected Adderley number one. In no small measure, the historic addition of three great black Hall of Fame players were vital ingredients that transformed an improving team into a dynasty.

Lombardi's disdain for losing is evident in one of his more remarkable achievements. In just his second year at the helm in Green Bay, he guided his club to the NFL Championship game against Philadelphia. It is the only meaningful playoff game Lombardi ever lost and occurred two years after he inherited a pitiful 1-10-1 Packers squad.

Dave Robinson said, "Lombardi was very firm that you either win a game or you lose it. In the five years I played under Lombardi, he never spoke about the loss to the Eagles. They went from the outhouse to the penthouse real quick, in two short years. You'd think he'd be proud of it, but as I understand it, he never showed film of that game to the team."

Willie Davis concurred, "That may very well be true. I don't remember ever seeing the Philadelphia game. I think Coach Lombardi made it a point to try to get that game out of our systems, from him and us."

When asked if Lombardi showed him the Eagles game, Boyd Dowler said, "Never."

Becoming Titletown

In the 1960s, teams did not fly their first-round draft choices into town for press conferences and other sorts of hoopla.

Most players saw their new cities for the first time when they reported to camp.

On the morning of Saturday, August 5, 1961, following the Friday night College All-Star Game in Chicago, Adderley began his journey to Green Bay and NFL immortality. What was waiting for the young man from Philadelphia in the remote reaches of Wisconsin defied his most ambitious visions. God generously blessed Adderley with skills and talents, but Adderley could never have imagined the growth, friendships, triumphs and memories he was about to experience. The best nine years of his life were about to unfold and challenge his sense of wonder. Even the hopes and dreams of the ultra-achiever from P-Town would be one step behind the events. And Herb Adderley was seldom a step behind anything.

He played in more College All-Star games than any man in history. Adderley was a member of the collegiate team in '61, played in the game five times after the Packers won world titles under Lombardi, and was a member of the Cowboys club in the '72 game. Seven times he played in the charity game at Soldier Field.

"The first thing I noticed about Titletown was a sign posted on Highway 57 stating the population was 68,000, so I knew it was a very small town compared to Philly," Adderley said. "However, there were more people there than in East Lansing, so I didn't have to worry about getting the small town blues, because I learned how to avoid it during my four years in East Lansing."

Uncertainties abound in the world of an NFL rookie and any form of familiarity is appreciated. Adderley said, "The only assurance I had from the Packers was the no-cut contract I negotiated in the parking lot at St. Mary's College in Santa Clara, California." At his first day of practice, Adderley saw a new old friend on a coat hook. "My jersey, with the number 26, was hanging in my locker the first day of practice without me asking for it." Thank you equipment man Dad Braisher.

There are two ridiculously obscure facts about Adderley. Drafted in the first round as a running back, he never had a carry from scrimmage and he played cornerback in two games during his rookie year without ever practicing with the defense.

Boyd Dowler said, "We drafted Herb in the first round and when he came in, he was actually my backup at wide receiver."

The Packers were deep at running back with Pro-Bowlers Taylor and Hornung, plus halfback Tom Moore, but the MSU rookie turned heads with his natural ability. Hall of Fame halfback Hornung said of Adderley, "He was the best. Adderley was our best athlete. He could do anything; he could run, he could catch. That was the only guy I ever worried about playing my position. When they switched him to defense I was pretty happy, because I knew how good he was. I could tell he was a sensational athlete. He was cocky; he was a cocky bastard, which was good. We had a very confident group."

Adderley said, "Lombardi had the most difficult training camp in the NFL because it was all about getting in physical shape and football shape. We did a lot of running, including the hated grass drill."

There were two signature exercises in Packers camp as conducted by Lombardi: the nutcracker and grass drills. "We worked out in the morning session with shorts on and had to run a couple of laps before practice started," Adderley said. "After that, we did stretching exercises and then the grass drill. Coach had us run in place, then hit the ground when the whistle blew. When he blew the whistle a second time, we would get up and run in place until he blew the whistle again, then hit the ground again. This was repeated until we lost count as to how many we ended up doing. After we regained our breath and balance, we broke up into different groups and worked on techniques. The morning sessions were conditioning sessions more than anything else."

Adderley said, "I had to learn the terminology on the offensive side of the ball first in order to learn and know my assignments, then run the plays that were called in the huddle. Lombardi didn't tolerate mistakes or accept excuses.

"Because most of the teams had only six or less black players, we had to be mistake-free, hustle all of the time, give one-hundred percent effort every time that we stepped on the practice field and during games."

The rookie also got his first glimpse of Lombardi's dedication to building a team and challenging the status quo. Green Bay's coach was entering his third year at the helm and had taken steps to combat the effects of segregation on his ball club. "We played the Redskins in an exhibition game in 1961 in Columbus, Georgia," Adderley said. "We stayed on a United States army base, Fort Benning, because black folks couldn't stay at the hotels."

Adderley played little except for special teams during his first year in Green Bay. The Packers were in excellent shape at cornerback and Lombardi did not like starting rookies. "My first year I didn't know where I was going to play," Adderley said. Jesse Whittenton on the right corner and Hank Gremminger on the left provided great play for Lombardi on the '61 championship team. It was 1963 before a first-year man, defensive end Lionel Aldridge, started a season opener for the great coach. You can win a lot of bets with that piece of trivia.

Adderley's few plays from scrimmage came in game three of the pre-season against the Bears at Milwaukee County Stadium in the annual Midwest Shrine Game. "Sometime during the game I was hit by the Bears' great linebacker Bill George and I dislocated my collar bone," Adderley said. "I did not play in another preseason game after that. Dr. James Nellen performed the procedure to put my collar bone back in place at St Vincent's the next day."

During his three-day convalescence, Adderley was surprised when his coach popped in for a visit. "Lombardi came over to visit me and I almost fell out of the bed when he walked into my room," he said.

Lombardi said, "Thank God it wasn't your shoulder because your career could be over." The Old Man assured Adderley the collarbone would heal with no problems.

Adderley said, "Lombardi also told me not to worry about anything because I was going to be a member of the Packers team but he didn't know what position. His final statement to me was, 'You're too good of an athlete to sit on the bench.' He shook my hand and said he would see me at practice in a few days."

The injury had a direct impact on Adderley as he was shut down as a running back for the remainder of the year. He said, "I really believe Lombardi did not play me as a running back in '61 because of my injury in the Bears game."

When training camp ended and players left the confines of Sensenbrenner Hall, the scramble was on to adjust to the city and find housing.

Lombardi worked hard to help the black players find descent accommodations, but the process took some time. It was not illegal for landlords to refuse to rent to blacks in 1961 because the Civil Rights Act, which was also known as the Fair Housing Act, did not go into effect until 1968.

Even white Packer families had some problems in the early Lombardi years, as Olive Jordan Frey explained. Olive was married to Hall of Fame defensive tackle Henry Jordan until his untimely death in 1977. "When we first went up there in 1959, it was very difficult for anybody to find an apartment because the previous generation of Packers had been a little bit rowdy; a lot rowdy," Olive said. "Nobody wanted to rent to them because the apartments were torn apart. I often thought to myself, if it was difficult for us, what was it possibly like for the black guys?"

In Adderley's rookie year he lived in a place known as the "little shack down by the tracks." He said, "All of the black guys had trouble finding housing in Green Bay because no one wanted to rent to us in '61. Willie Davis, Elijah Pitts and I shared a one-bedroom converted shack on Velp Avenue just outside of Green Bay. The property was owned by Packer Hall of Famer Tony Canadeo's brother, Savy, who was in the exterminating business and his office had rat and roach spray stored there. Willie had access to the one bedroom and Pitts and I would flip a coin to see who would sleep on the couch in the living room. The loser had to sleep on a U.S. Army cot in the kitchen. Whenever I had friends visiting I would get them a room at the Downtowner Hotel because it was too embarrassing to show them where I was living. Homeless shelters in Green Bay were better and had better furniture."

Lombardi often told his players they were professionals and should conduct themselves as such. He used his will and determination to help change a city and allow his players to find respectable housing commensurate with their standing in the community.

Willie Davis said, "I've said kind of quietly to myself that in many ways, what Coach Lombardi did in Green Bay, all the way from helping us find a place to live, he understood what our problem was and he wanted to make a difference. I remember he called up and said, 'We're gonna find you guys a place.'"

With the help of local businessman Paul Mazzoleni, a service station owner, improved housing was secured. Davis said, "He actually was the one who helped us. Lombardi was very bothered, he said, 'It's just a shame that the people want and expect you to come and play, and the next minute they almost don't care enough to find a place for you.'"

The push for improvement started paying real dividends in Adderely's second year. "In '62 we had a few choices of decent houses to live in because of Lombardi making a major move. I lived in an apartment on Lori Lane on the west side near Mason Street, and a block from Premontre High School. In '63 and '64, Willie Wood and I had a nice two-bedroom house four blocks from Lambeau. We had a large yard and a garage. It was a very nice house, thanks to Lombardi."

Assimilation and acceptance of black Packer players into the city of Green Bay also took time; it was a process, not an event.

"I remember some of the first times I was in downtown Green Bay; people would come up and ask if they could touch me, because they'd never seen a black person," Adderley said. "They knew we were Packers so they would call out all of the guys' names until they announced the correct one." A favorite tactic was for fans to ask, "Are you Willie?" With both Davis and Wood having the same first name, the white folks were just playing the odds.

Adderley's adjustment to Green Bay was much easier than other African-Americans who attended all-black schools. He said, "It was easy establishing a friendship with white folks because of my high school coach Charles Martin and his wife, Lillian. They treated me like I was their son and they will always be my all-time best white friends. I also had quite a few white friends during my four years at Michigan State, so there were no adjustments."

Defensive tackle Henry Jordan and his wife, Olive, moved to Green Bay in 1959 when Lombardi acquired Jordan from the Cleveland Browns. Henry and Olive saw an influx of black players added mostly to the defense. Notable African-American players in the early years included Emlen Tunnell, 1959; Willie Wood and Willie Davis, 1960; Herb Adderley, 1961; Dave Robinson, Lionel Aldridge and Marv Fleming, 1963. According to Olive Jordan, the inclusion of black players was a non-issue. She said, "There was nothing to handle, they were teammates."

One of Olive's dearest friends is Adderley. She said, "Herb does not offer friendship easily; I saw that in his first year. I am very pleased and proud me and Henry were friends he included on his list."

Aside from the Packer family, white people in the greater Green Bay area also developed friendships with African-American players. Longtime season ticket holders Al and Nancy Volpintesta from Appleton were probably the first Caucasians to genuinely befriend the Civil Rights Era black Packer players.

"The first player we met was Nate Borden," said Al Volpintesta. "We met him in Lombardi's first year, 1959. After a game, we saw him leaning against a wall in a bar across from the Northland Hotel and we felt sorry for him because he looked so pitiful."

Nancy said, "No one was talking to him and we went over. We just put ourselves out there to Nate and a solid friendship began building from the first meeting in the Mayfair Lounge. He introduced us to a lot of the ball players including Emlen Tunnell."

Al and Nancy quickly earned the seal of approval from Green Bay's black elder statesman, who told other players, "These people are not phonies. They're not just talking to you because you're a football player; you are their friend."

The Volpintestas and Adderley instantly became friends when he joined the team. "I do not remember where or the date I met Al and Nancy," Adderley said. "The great Emlem Tunnell introduced me to them and if they were friends of Tunnells, they were friends of mine."

Nancy's first impression of Adderley has lasted for 50 years. She said, "Herb Adderley is a gentleman and a humble, gifted football player. He was a celebrity who didn't act like one. Sometimes when he would come off the field he would wave at us in the stands because he knew where we sat. After every single game we would go to the locker room at the north end of the stadium, wait for Herb to come join us, then go out."

Not only would they go out, Al and Nancy entered the inner circle. Adderley said, "They were welcomed to our Packers-only gatherings after home games and I got them tickets for the three Milwaukee games. We became very dear friends and we still are the best of friends. We had a lot of unforgettable fun together during my nine years in Green Bay."

Al and Nancy Volpintesta forged close friendships with many Green Bay football players, including Herb Adderley.

Al and Nancy's key to cherished relationships with the black players was simple. She said, "They trusted us."

Like every first-year Lombardi player before him, Adderley spent the season learning how to get over being a rookie. Years later, running back Donny Anderson said, "The biggest thing with Lombardi and rookies, you just didn't play football, you played special teams. You were not counted on. Through his experience, rookies just made too many mistakes."

Lombardi put Adderley on every special team he had and maybe a couple others besides. Adderley said, "I practiced running back kickoffs my rookie year. I also practiced running down from the end position on the kickoff team. I played on both punting teams, including being one of the first guys down field after the punt."

With the addition of the Cowboys in 1960 and the Vikings in '61, the NFL expanded rosters to help bolster talent for the entire league. Therefore, Lombardi added six rookies to a very strong 1961 Packers team: Adderley, Ron Kostelnik, Elijah Pitts, Nelson Toburen, Lee Folkins and Ben Davidson.

For years, Adderley and either Tom Moore or Pitts lined up side-by-side to return kickoffs. "I would always say to whoever was back there with me, 'Let's get the offense good field position,'" Adderley said.

Who knows what moment was the greatest in Adderley's career. A nomination for the honor occurred in his first year when Green Bay's head coach was forced to play the rookie from Michigan State in Detroit. Adderley had never practiced a down with the defense, but on November 23, 1961, he was pressed into action against a very strong Detroit Lions team just 55 miles from his college campus.

Adderley said, "I played the corner the second half against the Lions my rookie year. In Detroit, old Briggs Stadium, Thanksgiving Day in 1961 was the game that Hank Gremminger got injured. At halftime, Lombardi told us there was an emergency because of Hank's injury and that we had to replace him with the best athlete on the team."

Ever the master of handling ball players, Lombardi broke the news to Adderley about 15 seconds before the Packers left the locker room for the second half. Adderley said, "He walked over to me, placed his hand on my shoulder and said, 'Herbie, do the best that you can,' and walked away. He didn't tell me until we were ready to go back on the field; He didn't want me to have time to think about it. I was in a state of shock and very nervous after being notified that I had to play the left corner the second half on national TV on Thanksgiving Day. I had gotten tickets for friends from MSU and—most importantly—my teammates were watching me along with Lombardi. I didn't have time to think about what was happening, so I did what he asked of me, and did the best that I could do. I still get goose bumps when I think about the situation. It was my first time playing the position; I had never had any practice before replacing Hank at the left corner in the second half in '61."

Lombardi's decision was rewarded in spectacular fashion as Adderley used his marvelous athletic skills to seal a win. Green Bay held a slim 14–9 lead late in the game and Lions quarterback Jim Ninowski took aim at the new guy on the corner. Mistake.

One of the interested observers was Green Bay's offensive tackle Forrest Gregg, who said, "Gremminger got hurt and Herb had to go in and man, all eyes were on him. We were watching him; the Detroit Lions were watching him and trying to take advantage of him. They threw an 'out pattern' over on Herb's side; he was in good coverage position on the receiver. Boy, Herb all of sudden changed directions, came in front of that receiver, intercepted that ball. That was the difference in that ball game."

Adderley did none of the things Lombardi feared of a rookie. With time running down and Detroit tacklers closing in, Adderley had a chance to try for superhero status — or goat horns. Instead of risking a fumble, he returned the ball nine yards to the two before stepping out of bounds. Versatile Paul Hornung kicked a 9-yard field goal to wrap up a 17–9 win and give Green Bay a 9–2 record and a clear path to a divisional championship.

"The best I could do was not have a TD pass caught on me," Adderley said. "I had an interception for my first regular season pick and it set up the winning points to beat the Lions."

As a rookie, Adderley never practiced with the defense, but played in two games as a defensive back and intercepted a pass in each contest. In the 1961 Championship Game, he picked off Y. A. Tittle (14) late in the 37-0 win on the day Green Bay, Wisconsin, became Titletown, USA. Also pictured are Willie Davis (87), Willie Wood (24), Henry Jordan (74) and Del Shofner (85).

The rookie cornerback made a splendid debut; however, it didn't win him a starting job or more playing time. Lombardi would not let him sniff the corner in games or practice until the last two minutes of the last game of the season, a 37–0 rout of the Giants in the NFL Championship game. Green Bay's great coach let Adderley play mop-up for the last two minutes of the title game and Number 26 was exceptional once again.

Adderley said, "My thoughts were the same as they were in Detroit at halftime when Lombardi informed me that I was going to play the second half at the left corner. I was shocked when I heard him yelling my name to replace Grimminger with less than two minutes to play. I ran on the field and did the same thing that I did in Detroit: intercept a pass. That move by Lombardi did get me to thinking that I may end up playing the left corner in '62 because he told me that I was too good of an athlete to be sitting on the bench."

Green Bay officially became Titletown on December 31, 1961, with the championship win over New York and the victor's crown sat well on the head of the rookie from P-Town. He said, "When the game was over, I felt like a champion because I played on all of the special teams and contributed to the team that way."

Adderley also felt like a responsible young man with a playoff check and a wish list. "The money meant a lot because I never had that much," Adderley said. "Between my bonus money and first year salary I bought a house for my mother and grandmother in a much better and safer neighborhood. I put some of it in the bank, I updated my wardrobe and I had a few dollars left for pocket money. I bought a used car, a '58 Buick, and I did not buy a new car until 1963."

Adderley's official stat line for his rookie year included 18 kickoff returns for 478 yards and a 26.6-yard average.

What was supposed to have been five months away from Philadelphia turned into nearly a year's absence. Following the season, Adderley spent the busiest off-season of his life as the Cold War whisked him off to military service. America in the early 1960s was in the midst of a military build-up due to the crisis in Berlin, Germany, and Adderley made a quick transition from active world champion to active private E-2, United States Army. "I had less than a week to report to Ft. Leonard Wood in Missouri after the '61 season," Adderley said. "Lombardi arranged for Elijah Pitts and I to join the U. S. Army Reserves based in Milwaukee. I didn't have enough time to drive to Philly, so I drove to Lansing, Michigan, to leave my 1958 Buick Limited with a friend. I left the next day for military duty and headed out for twelve weeks of basic training."

With the help of his old buddy, Retired Colonel O.C. "Ockie" Krueger, from his days as an assistant coach at Army, Lombardi was able to slip many of his players into the reserves and thus avoid a two-year hitch of active duty.

"I went to Fort Leonard Wood and didn't even know Pitts was there," Adderley said. "One day I was out just relaxing and jogging and I saw him raking leaves. I asked him, 'What are you doing here?' He asked me the same thing."

After basic training Adderley was shipped off to Fort Sill, Oklahoma, where he was assigned to an artillery unit. "I had to buy a watch for the first time because I was on a strict time schedule every day for six months," Adderley said. In spite of the tight schedule, he found time to think of a way to keep athletics in his life. "I saw a way out of afternoon work by trying out for, and making, the baseball team. Playing catcher and batting cleanup was a lot easier than loading up 105 missiles in cannons, so I had no second thoughts about playing a little hard ball."

When Adderley's six-month military obligation had been met, he wanted to pick up his car and visit his mother and grandmother back in Philly. Vince Lombardi had other plans. Adderley said, "Because of playing in the NFL, I qualified for an early release, which was granted a few days before training camp opened. I had less than a week off before having to report to training camp."

For the first time in a year, Adderley was free from the confines of either an army base or a Lombardi compound. Free as a bird, he was driving back to Philly, listening to the radio and answering to no one. Tranquility had a very short shelf life in Lombardi's world.

"I heard on the car radio that I had been released from the army, nobody knew my whereabouts and I was being fined one hundred dollars a day for missing practice," Adderley said.

The only possible rational thought popped into his mind.

"Oh shit."

Adderley said, "I continued driving to Philly and when I arrived home my mother gave me a hug and said, 'Willie Wood called and said you better call Lombardi sooner than soon to explain where you are.' I called Willie first."

After getting the low-down from Wood, Adderley called his head coach and said, "I haven't seen my parents since the beginning of the season and it was essential to see them." Lombardi allowed his second-year man and first-year cornerback to spend a day or two at home in order to live the philosophy: God, family and the Green Bay Packers.

According to Adderley, "He said, 'OK, but you better get your ass in training camp ASAP because the left corner is yours and you need all the work you can get.' I stayed home for a couple of days before driving to Green Bay and my career as the left corner started the first at camp. 1962 was a very important year for me and, in my opinion, it was the second best year for me in the NFL.

Removing All Doubt

Vince Lombardi's best team, and arguably the greatest team in Green Bay Packers' history, was the 1962 squad.

The offense was primed and set with excellence everywhere. Bart Starr was at quarterback with Taylor and Hornung in the backfield. Max McGee, Boyd Dowler and tight end Ron Kramer supplied outstanding targets for Starr. The offensive line was mature and well-honed with three years' experience in Lombardi's system under the direction of assistant coach Bill Austin. Skoronski, Thurston, Ringo, Kramer and Gregg will forever be famous in Packers' history.

Name recognition of the defensive players is another matter. Even hard-core Green Bay fans are hard pressed to name the defensive starters of the greatest team in franchise history. The defense was simply superb. On three occasions it shut out the opposition. Four more times it allowed seven points or less. Assistant coach Phil Bengtson's unit led the league with fewest points allowed: 10.6 a game. In 1962 the Packers won their games by an average of 19.1 points a game. That's a great team and great defense.

One major personnel change was made to the defense in '62.

Adderley said, "I was notified when I reported to training camp that I was going to be the starting left corner. The best thing that happened for me was being switched to defense by Lombardi." Adderley responded by being named All-Pro in his first year as a starter at a very hot spot.

The athletically gifted second-year man from Michigan State had impressed Coach Lombardi with his natural skill and performance when pressed into emergency duty against the Lions in the '61 Thanksgiving Day game. Adderley had something else in his favor in 1962: he had gotten over being a rookie.

Adderley said Lombardi told him years later, "It scares me to think how stubborn I was to move you to defense."

When Adderley reported to training camp, it was a cram course in how to play the corner taught by assistant coach Norb Hecker. "On the field before practice and after practice he showed me how to use the sideline and hash marks to anticipate and eliminate pass routes the receivers can run from their alignment," Adderley said. "He showed me which patterns could be run once the receiver comes off of the line of scrimmage; he helped me with my stance, showed me how to push off either leg when closing in on the receiver or a ball that's hanging in the air."

Hecker poured it in and Adderley poured it on. "We worked on this stuff every day before and after practice. When the pre-season games started I tried to implement everything Norb taught me, and we watched the films after the games."

Instantly, Number 26 was a big hit on the left corner.

"He was good the minute he walked over there," flanker Boyd Dowler said. "Herb was a tough guy; he'd tackle you, he could cover and run. He liked the competitive part of defense as far as hitting people. Instinctively he fit on that side of the ball. He had more of a defensive temperament than an offensive temperament and Lombardi knew that and moved him to defense. Lombardi watched him for a year and moved him over."

When a head coach tinkers with talent, he's screwing around; when he knows what he's doing, he's managing. In one of his finest moves, Lombardi put Adderley on the left corner permanently and shifted Hank Gremminger to safety. According to right cornerback Jesse Whittenton, it was terrific. "Oh God, I think so," he said. "Herb had great moves; he was so damn fast and quick. He was good from the beginning, no doubt about it, and Hank was a good safety."

Lombardi built a world championship team by integrating his club without incident. He needed high-quality people to help him, and Hank Gremminger deserves credit for moving to a new position when a black player replaced him on the corner. Hank and others cooperated with the process for the benefit of the team.

"Hank offered his help, especially with the receivers during the film sessions, and he would school me on their moves when they ran certain key pass routes," Adderley said. "He was a great teammate, an excellent d-back and a friend of mine."

Adderley had his sports heroes, and early in training camp he decided to duplicate the play of one of the all-time greats. Steve Sabol of NFL Films said, "The only cornerback who I think is in Herb's category is Dick 'Night Train' Lane. Herb never made a tackle below the jaw line. He was a devastating tackler."

Sabol had it exactly right. Adderley's play on the corner was shaped by a comment from his coach. "Vince Lombardi called 'Night Train' the greatest cornerback he had ever seen," Adderley said. "After hearing that statement from one of the greatest coaches ever, I decided to pattern my game after Night Train Lane. I watched film of him every chance I got. He was the best corner in the NFL and I wanted to get the same type of respect.

Herb Adderley patterned his game after the man who is considered the greatest cornerback in pro football history, Dick "Night Train" Lane (81).

Photo courtesy of *Pro Football Hall of Fame*

He defined how to play the position during his illustrious fourteen-year career. He was known as a headhunter. His facemask and clothesline tackles were so vicious that the NFL outlawed those types of tackles. He was also known for stripping the ball from the receiver and recovering the fumble."

Few could argue that Adderley mirrored Lane's style precisely. "You could say that we were punishing, aggressive tacklers playing a violent game," Adderley said. "Hard hits would have receivers looking around and sometimes dropping balls that they should have caught; it's called intimidation. The next time we faced the same receiver, they knew what was coming if they caught the ball."

Dowler was very familiar with both Night Train and Adderley. "I lined up against Herb for years. I went running out there for years and had him cover me in practice. They were both physical, Night Train was a little bigger.

I know one thing, I never got anything done against Night Train; nothing." Adderley put a lot of receivers in the same category.

"Herb covered me every day in practice. We got along great; it was very competitive and we only had a couple dust-ups in all the years," Dowler said. "You could tell right away when we went one-on-one that he was really good. It didn't take a genius to figure that out."

Boyd added, "When they moved Adderley over on defense, I'd come back from running a route. I'd walk by Lombardi and say, 'He's really quick, he's a struggle; he's tough to beat.'"

Training camps were brutal in Green Bay from 1959–67 in part due to grass drills and the infamous nutcracker, a violent tackling drill that tests strength and fortitude; these were two of Lombardi's favorites. However, one group got a pass on the hamburger drill. "The offensive linemen, defensive linemen and linebackers were the guys involved in the tough nutcracker drills," Adderley explained. "The d-backs were doing other non-contact maneuvers. The d-backs didn't have a lot of contact during training camp because there were only six of us and Lombardi didn't want to lose any of us because of an injury. We always had it easier than the other guys because of the injury factor."

Not to be confused with Adderley's MSU classmate and civil rights leader Ernest Gideon Green, the Packers drafted running back Ernie Green from the University of Louisville in 1962. Adderley said, "Ernie Green and I became friends during training camp and suddenly he was traded to the Browns." If Adderley is right, Lombardi made a decision to trade Green based on race.

"It was known by all of us that Ernie Green (a black player) was more fundamentally sound than Elijah Pitts because Ernie had coaching at a major college. In my opinion, Lombardi traded Green because he knew Green had the skills to play in the NFL (without being cut as a result of quotas). Lombardi liked Elijah Pitts and knew Elijah would have been caught up in the quota with another NFL team and would be sent packing back to Conway, Arkansas. Coach was willing to keep Pitts as a third string back behind Hornung and Moore (if that meant him making into the NFL)."

Adderley remained friends with the second Ernie Green who blessed his life. "Every time we played the Browns we would have a warm greeting before and after the game," Adderley said.

NFL games played before the regular season used to be known as exhibition games because the league took its game around the country in an attempt to generate interest in the brand. The contests were also used to evaluate cities for potential expansion franchises.

Vince Lombardi may well have reshaped the NFL based on two racial incidents he encountered in the South during the '62 exhibition season.

"We had a game in Jacksonville, Florida, against the Cardinals, and the black players were stopped at the door of the hotel by a black bell hop who said out loud, 'Black folks are not allowed in the hotel.' Everyone was shocked and pissed off, especially Lombardi," Adderley said. "We had to wait for a black cab driver to come from across town to pick us up and take us back to the black section to stay at a black-owned motel. Lombardi had enough of that shit and called Pete Rozelle and told him the Packers would never play a game where the black players couldn't stay in the same hotel. It blows my mind thinking about how Lombardi hated racism and discrimination in the '60s and I had to deal with it ten years later with the Cowboys."

The second incident involved the league's top bigot, Washington Redskins owner George Preston Marshall.

From 1940–1963, the Packers played the Washington Redskins in pre-season every year, except 1941 and 1950. The longtime agreement between those two clubs came to an end over a racial incident directly involving Green Bay's head coach and general manager. It's important to remember Lombardi, being Italian, was of Mediterranean skin and had coarse hair. Additionally, during training camp, he was out in the sun with his ball club conducting two-a-day practices, therefore, developing a deep tan. The '62 game was scheduled in Columbus, Georgia, and the Packers went to North Carolina to spend time during the week before the contest. At the time, Marshall owned the Redskins.

Marshall was an acknowledged racist and integrated his team only after being threatened by the United States government. In 1962, Interior Secretary Stewart Udall gave the team an ultimatum to either sign a black player or be evicted from the new District of Columbia Stadium.

During the Packers' stay in North Carolina, Lombardi and his wife, Marie, went to a restaurant for dinner and encountered a situation that set in motion a string of events that ended the Green Bay-Washington pre-season agreement.

Dave Robinson recalled how a maitre d' refused to seat the Lombardis. "I wasn't there, but paraphrasing, he said, 'We don't allow blacks in this restaurant.' Vince said, 'I'm not black; I'm Vince Lombardi.' The maitre d' said, 'I don't care who the hell you are, you're not bringing that blond woman in this restaurant to have dinner.'"

Having been refused service, Lombardi called Marshall and told him of the incident, at which time Marshall laughed at Lombardi. It took a year, but

Green Bay's general manager settled the matter with Marshall the following exhibition season.

By spending the entire training camp with the defense, Adderley found a home and became close friends with his fellow "Class of '61" rookies Ron Kostelnik and Nelson Toburen.

Adderley said, "I was learning a new position as best I could and improved a little bit each game. After the College All-Star game and five exhibition games, I was ready for the season to start."

The team and Adderley were spectacular. In the first three games Adderley intercepted three passes, the team shut out two opponents and held the other to a meaningless fourth-quarter touchdown in a 34–7 route.

Adderley broke the mold of Lombardi players. Until Adderley arrived, there was no Packer who was electric, who had scary moves and speed. Like all of Lombardi's men, Adderley was fundamentally sound, but he had that extra gear and those abilities that made him one of the first "shut-down" corners in the game. That means being able to shut down the run and the pass. A total cornerback package was wrapped in a number 26 uniform.

The '62 season came down to the Packers and Lions and two of the most memorable games in a long-term rivalry.

Across Lake Michigan, the Detroit Lions were really good except at the most important position: quarterback. There is no telling how good the receiving corps of Gail Cogdill, Terry Barr and tight end Jim Gibbons could have been with an accomplished signal caller.

Dowler said, "In those early years the Lions were easily the second best team in the league. They were really, really good, especially on defense."

Detroit fans have a right to be sick these 50 years later about what happened in '62. Their team lost three games by a combined total of eight points and sent seven players to the Pro Bowl; five of them played defense.

After playing for the Packer's coach in a couple Pro Bowls, Cogdill viewed Green Bay with unbridled admiration. Gail said, "I played for Lombardi twice in the Pro Bowl and the guy had so much class. He would tell us, 'You know what your job is; you know what you have to do, let's get it done.' That was the first year.

"The second time I played under him, he used this reverse psychology. He said, 'Boy, you guys look terrible. My grandmother could outrun you.' This guy could pick up the time, the tone and the atmosphere when he walked in the room with the ball players and completely change it to the way it was supposed to be."

Bingo. It was precisely his ability to manage and motivate people that allowed Lombardi to use all players, including black players, in Green Bay without incident.

Players like Cogdill were at an immediate disadvantage when they played Lombardi's teams because they knew the best coach in the business was on the other sideline.

Gail said, "The left side of Green Bay's defense, we called the tough side, Devil's End. I always told the quarterback, 'These guys are the best. Don't wait for me to make my break. The only way we will have any success to that side is to throw the ball before I break. When I make my break, I want the ball right at my shoulder.' If we had any success at all, it's because we threw the ball quick. If I made my break and had to make three steps and go for the ball, those guys would react. They could do anything they wanted."

Detroit tight end Jim Gibbons said, "That left side didn't make a mistake; that's what we knew about them first and foremost. You didn't bank on them making a mistake. If you were going to run a pass pattern against them you had to run it, you had to do your best job or you were not going to get open. Lombardi had them tooled to play the game. I think Lombardi brushed every player in the league with his greatness and anybody who cared about the game wanted to play for him. Every player who played in the league at that time, *every player*, would say, 'Boy, this is a coach I would love to play for.'"

And Gibbons gives the impression he would have liked to play in Titletown. "We used to go to mass in Green Bay. The priests would always pray for the players' safety and for a Packers' win. We would laugh and the people would laugh. It was always special to play in Green Bay."

NFL Films President Steve Sabol admired the left side and the special talent of the cornerback. "You can see in our films that Adderley was an instinctive player who played his man loose. He concentrated more on the ball, yet he was rarely beaten. He became a specialist at making the big play. He would bait quarterbacks into thinking the receiver was open and then he would close real fast and many times make the interception."

Green Bay's backup quarterback Zeke Bratkowski faced Adderley in practice every week and said, "His reaction was absolutely tremendous, and he intercepted so many passes for touchdowns during his career it was unbelievable. There is a term, 'He broke on the ball real good.' Herb had an ability to react to the ball and shut down receivers."

Going into a Packers game, Cogdill said he would think, "I hope I get through this. It was not so much they were going to hurt you; they were so good and quick on that side. They didn't kill you or run over you; they just finessed your jock strap off. If I went to run a pattern or ran downfield to throw a block on Herb or anybody, I better stay on my feet because they were going to be past me to make the tackle or make the coverage. It was the 'awesome side' as far as I was concerned. Of all the other teams we ever played, I never ran across those types of people in those positions who could do their jobs as well as they did. It was great teamwork."

Game four of the '62 season may still be reverberating in Motown. Going into the contest, both teams were undefeated and the winner was going to be in the early season driver's seat. With less than two minutes in the game Detroit held a 7–6 lead and possession of the ball. The Lions kept moving and the clock kept ticking to under a minute. Green Bay was in trouble. Detroit quarterback Milt Plum was faced with a third down on a soggy field and he went after the new guy on the left side. A first down would give the NFL's second best team a win over the best.

Adderley said, "I always played the receivers a couple of steps deeper than usual because of a sloppy field." Always was in the future, this was just his fourth game as a starter.

Bad things happen to offenses that mess with the great ones, things like interceptions, fumbles and big hits. It is safer and smarter to try to do business to the other side of the field.

All-Pro Terry Barr went one-on-one toward Adderley; Barr cut inside, Plum made the toss and Barr made a move to the corner. Adderley said, "A good example of slipping on a wet, sloppy field was in '62 when Terry Barr did just that. I stepped over him, picked the ball off and ran it down to field goal position. One slip cost the Lions the game and they still haven't recovered from that major slip!"

The Lions won three world championships in the 1950s and have not been back to a title game in a half-century. Fatalists and Adderley fans say his interception was the ruination of the Lions.

Adderley's name needs to be mentioned in any discussion of the greatest Green Bay Packers of all time. He never made a mistake at a crucial time in a big game to cost his team a chance to advance or win. Isolated at left corner-back, he didn't handle the ball frequently like a quarterback, running back or receiver. But when he did …

Detroit's fine team reportedly split between offense and defense after the game as defensive tackle Alex Karras fired his helmet at Plum in the visitors'

Adderley (26) scored a first quarter touchdown on this 103-yard kickoff return against the Colts on November 18, 1962. An unidentified Packer threw a key block on Baltimore kicker Dick Bielski (31). Packers Forrest Gregg (75) and Norm Masters (78) are shown with Baltimore's Bill Saul (50), Alex Hawkins (25) and Dan Sullivan (71). Tom Moore scored on a 23-yard fourth quarter run to secure a 17–13 Packer win as Lombardi's best team finished the year 13–1.

locker room. Associated Press and *Detroit News* writer Jerry Green quoted Karras as saying, "I missed him by this much." The All-Pro tackle held his fingers six inches apart.

Green Bay kept mowing down opponents and entered game 10 against the Colts with an unblemished record. Players and fans would touch a spectrum of emotions in a gut-wrenching game played November 18, 1962.

Baltimore hit a first quarter field goal to take a 3–0 lead and then drilled the ensuing kickoff. "I knew I was in the end zone when I caught the ball, but I didn't know how deep," Adderley said. "I had my mind made up to run it out because the guys coming down on the coverage team have a tendency to slow up when they see the ball going in the end zone. When I caught it, I yelled, 'Go!' which alerted Tom Moore and the guys in the wedge that I was running it out. I headed straight up the field and saw an opening to my right. I slowed up enough to let Tom cross in front of me to set up the key block on the Colts safety man Lenny Lyles."

Adderley staked the Packers to a 7–3 lead with a 103-yard touchdown return and the Green Bay crowd was delirious. Adderley and Willie Davis were joined by second-year linebacker Nelson Toburen from Wichita State.

"I worked with Nellie more in practice than in any games and I remember him being a very intelligent, quick, strong, athletic football player with the potential to be an all-star in the NFL," Adderley said. "He didn't make many mistakes during practice and none during the games. To top it off, he was a friend and a real nice guy."

Late in the fourth quarter of a close, hard-fought game between the Packers and Colts, Johnny Unitas dropped back to pass. Nelson's assignment was to go to the left flat, which he did. Green Bay's defense covered all Baltimore receivers, forcing Johnny "U" to run. A bright man, Toburen knew the Colts were closing in on field goal range and separating the ball from Unitas was the objective. Nelson explained, "He took off running and my idea was to make him fumble, and I did. Just as I threw myself at him, he twisted his hip to try to get away from me and the top of my head hit him in the solid part of his hip. I was going full speed and he was too; it just broke my neck."

"He fumbled and Nitschke recovered. It was toward the end of the ball game, late in the fourth quarter." With the win secured, Green Bay's record remained perfect; Nelson Toburen's life did not.

Adderley said, "I was about fifteen yards from the spot on the field where Nellie closed in on Unitas. After the play Nelson laid motionless on the field with no signs of movement and that's when I knew that it was a very serious injury. It took a lot out of me when they carted him off on a stretcher and headed for the hospital." The Green Bay crowd was numb.

"I felt like crying, but I had to hold back the tears because the game continued and I had to focus on shutting down the Colts great wide receiver Lenny Moore," Adderley said.

Nelson Toburen is not famous in Packers history; however, of all the players Lombardi ever coached, none have literally picked themselves up from a fall in a nobler and more conquering fashion. A promising career was snapped in one play, but a life of triumph followed.

Judge Nelson Toburen and his wife, Helen, are retired and living in Pittsburg, Kansas.

"The only good thing about the game was that we won, but we lost a potential great linebacker and outstanding person, which stopped us from celebrating big win after the game," said Adderley. If Toburen had stayed healthy, who knows what Dave Robinson's career would have been in Green Bay?

Late in the fourth quarter, the man who threw the key block on Adderley's kickoff return, Tom Moore, scored on a 23-yard run to seal Green Bay's win.

Reeling from the Toburen injury, coming off a difficult win, having one practice day and facing a team bent on revenge, Green Bay's undefeated season went by the wayside on Thanksgiving Day 1962. Detroit's pass rush pinned their ears back and sacked Bart Starr 11 times, including once for a safety. The game ended with a 26–14 Detroit win, and the game was not that close. The following week, Lombardi informed the league office he had enjoyed all of the Thanksgiving Day games he could stand and insisted his team end the tradition.

"Nellie's injury was not an excuse because Detroit just kicked us around," Adderley said. "A lot of guys worried about him, and you can't just get something like that off your mind overnight. That was on everybody's mind, especially Lombardi's. He was really shook up bad about that. He knew the potential of Nellie."

The powerful Packers gathered themselves and smashed everything in sight on the way to a rematch of the '61 championship game. Lombardi was back in his native New York against his former team and Adderley was nervous in pre-game warm-ups walking the hallowed ground in the House that Ruth Built: Yankee Stadium. The wind was cold and swirling, the Giants were seething a year after the 37–0 whitewash in Green Bay and a nation was watching the team from the prairie play in the Big Apple.

Always thinking, Adderley's mind ran through the list:

1. Shut down Frank Gifford.
2. Watch the slippery footing.
3. Some spots will be frozen.
4. Babe Ruth played here.
5. The first plays set the tone.
6. Miserable weather.
7. They're pissed about 37–0.
8. We are 13–1.

Veteran New York quarterback Y. A. Tittle came out throwing in the wind and didn't stop. He launched it 41 times with 18 completions. The great Gifford was held to 34 yards on four catches and the game was a classic defensive stand off.

"The game turned out the way I expected," Adderley said. "It was a hard-fought defensive game and the offenses were also shut down by the weather. For the second straight championship game we kept the Giants out of the end zone. We shut them out for eight quarters." New York's seven points came off a blocked punt and the Pack got a Jimmy Taylor rushing touchdown and three field goals.

Adderley said, "A lot of credit has to be given to Jerry Kramer because he played an excellent game and, more importantly, he kicked three field goals to seal the victory for us. It would have been a tough assignment on a warm clear day in Yankee Stadium, but the difficulty of the assignment was increased ten times or more because of the weather. He came through for us in a big way, in a big game."

Football is a team sport and getting Adderley on the field made the entire defense better. The year of the move, 1962, marked World Championship number two for the young Dynasty, with a final score of 16–7.

Jesse Whittenton was an outstanding corner in his own right. In his book *Run to Daylight*, Lombardi said Jesse was, "As close to being a perfect defensive back as anyone in the league." Not coincidently, when Adderley became a starter, Jesse received his first postseason honors validating Lombardi's praise. Whittenton closed out his Green Bay career with three trips to the Pro Bowl in 1962, '63 and '64.

NFL Films, in their "Greatest" series, selected Green Bay's tandem of Adderley and Bob Jeter as the fourth-best set of cornerbacks in NFL history. Steve Sabol offered an observation about a category that was *not* part of the series. He said, "I think Herb Adderley and Willie Wood ended up as the greatest cornerback/safety combination in the history of the game."

The '62 club was Lombardi's best. Like a band of coordinated criminals, the secondary victimized rival quarterbacks with interceptions: Willie Wood picked 9; Adderley, 7; Gremminger, 5; and Whittenton, 3. Thefts were on the rise in Green Bay as the team lost just one game all year and beat New York in the championship game to claim their second straight crown.

As good as Adderley was in 1962, he did not play left corner in his first Pro Bowl; he was moved to the right side. NFL royalty was on the left: Dick "Night Train" Lane.

Dave Robinson (l) and the man considered to be the greatest cornerback of all-time, Dick "Night Train" Lane.

Stalking Three Crowns

A bitter year in Packers' history was 1963.

The club was poised to accomplish a coveted Lombardi goal by winning three consecutive championships in the playoff era. "That '63 team was really good," said wide receiver Boyd Dowler. "We lost only two games, but we lost both to the same team."

The pre-season opened with Lombardi's most embarrassing defeat, running back and place kicker Paul Hornung was forced to sit out the entire season while serving a one-year suspension for betting on games, and for the first time Lombardi named a rookie to start the opening game. Additionally, a very strong Green Bay team played in "The Losers Bowl" at season's end. The '63 championship is the one that got away.

The fourth year of the decade also provided an opportunity for Lombardi to deliver a resounding blow against bigotry with one of the strongest racial statements in NFL history in the pre-season's final game. Regrettably, the accomplishment received little coverage in the press.

On Friday, August 2, 1963, Lombardi suffered his most humiliating loss as head coach of the Packers. In front of a national television audience, his defending World Champions were beaten by the College All-Stars, 20–17, at Chicago's Soldier Field. Packers' first-round draft choice, Dave Robinson, was a member of the college squad and had University of Wisconsin great Pat Richter for a roommate.

"It was the first time I roomed with an African-American, although I was very close to Merritt Norvell, who was a teammate on the football and baseball teams," Richter said. "I know one thing, we got along very well and since I can't recall any crazy, out-of-the-ordinary stories, we were probably a bit boring. Maybe Robby's being such a conversationalist had me mesmerized, or put me to sleep!" Robinson always had a fall-back career because if football wouldn't have worked, he could have been an auctioneer.

Going into a game against the pro team he was going to join, Robinson found himself in a no-lose situation, or so he thought. He said, "If we won, I'd party with the All-Stars; if we lost, I'd join the Packers for a victory party."

The hard fought game was knotted at the half 10–10 and Green Bay's locker room got lit up like never before. Adderley was getting to be an old hand at College All-Star games because he played for the collegians in '61 and for the Packers in '62 and '63. With the game deadlock at intermission, Herb saw his coach blow up. "Lombardi was yelling at us during the half time break because he felt the potential of an embarrassing defeat if we didn't play better in the second half," Adderley said. "His yelling, cursing and screaming was my first time seeing him and hearing him go off like that, so I was nervous and scared just like the other guys."

The game featured a distinct touch of University of Wisconsin football. Badger quarterback, Ron Vanderkelen, born in Green Bay, hooked up with UW teammate and Madison native Pat Richter for a 74-yard scoring strike. Green Bay's reliable right cornerback Jesse Whittenton slipped on the play, allowing for the decisive score.

Richter said, "A funny thing did happen about 15 years later when I was in Las Vegas for a Badger golf event. A fellow with a wide brimmed hat came down the fairway towards us and said, 'Well there's the S.O.B. who almost cost me my job.' I looked at the guy and then recognized it was Jesse Whittenton."

Let the record show Whittenton made a complete recovery from the traumatic event and became a golf course owner, member of the PGA senior golf circuit and put a young golfer by the name of Lee Trevino on the regular tour.

"We didn't play any better in the second half and time ran out with the All-Stars leading 20–17," Adderley said. "Lombardi yelled and screamed like we had just lost the NFL Championship game, and he cursed a few guys out for their performances. He said more than once that we would get back to the College All-Star Game and win."

For the next few hours and days, the distasteful defeat was clearly etched on the coach. "After the All-Star game, we had this little team get-together to eat salad and stuff. Mostly it was to have a beer," Dowler said. "The game was played at nine o'clock at night, so by the time we played, showered and got dressed, it was well after midnight before we went to this eating thing. When Lombardi came in the banquet room, his color was gone. He looked like he was ready for a casket."

Dowler believes the loss was the most demeaning one suffered during the Lombardi era. "First of all, there weren't that many to choose from, but yes, you could say that game was the most embarrassing. It was worse than losing the 1960 Championship game to the Eagles, because he knew we would be back to win it all."

Lombardi almost never attended defensive film meetings, but the loss infuriated him to the point that he made an exception. After a bunch of fuzzy-faced college kids rolled up 323 total yards in offense, the Old Man made an appearance when the defense broke up into their gathering.

It was not a social call. Adderley said, "The film session was worse than his rampage in Chi-Town because he came in the room with the defense to view the films with us. It was like, 'get ready,' because he was still very upset about losing to the college kids."

Robinson's first practice day with the Packers was Monday, August 5, 1963, and the questions, events and information whirled in his mind at warp speed.

"I didn't know how good I was," Robinson said. "I knew the Green Bay Packers were the greatest team in football; these guys were better than anybody I ever played against. I didn't know how good I was and it's a hell of a thing, you don't know."

A real attention-getter for the rookie was the racket created by two of Green Bay's all-time greats. "The loudest pad noise I ever heard in my life occurred that first day. Forrest Gregg and Willie Davis faced each other in practice and it sounded like gunshots going off." Welcome to the bigs.

Ron Kramer and Robinson also went head-to-head in the first practice during Lombardi's famous nutcracker drill. After Lombardi's pointing out during the film session how Robinson defeated Kramer in a block, Kramer was more than ready to face Robby in practice. "Everybody was telling me after the old man got on Kramer during the film session that Ron was gonna light me up," Robinson said. "Lombardi lined us up so Nitschke went first and I went second so I got Kramer. I did OK against him."

Dowler said, "Ron Kramer told me right away Robby was going to be really good. He told me that several times in training camp."

Gregg took note of the new guy and said, "We ran a play and I thought, 'I'll clean this rookie up right quick.' It was like I hit a tree."

It was also on day one when Lombardi put Robinson's role in context and explained why Robinson was used at three different positions in various college bowl and all-star games.

Robinson said, "When I came to the National Football League in 1963, there were no starting linebackers in the NFL who were black, none. The rumor at the time was that blacks couldn't play linebacker. Now, the AFL had linebackers in it — the AFL was way ahead of the NFL with the racial relationships."

Lombardi told his Penn State rookie, "Phil (Bengtson) wanted you to play linebacker all along. I'm the one who had you moved around and I'm very happy. I think you can be a great linebacker. This year we're trying to win our third consecutive World Championship, the first team ever to do that, and we don't need any distractions; we don't want anything that's going to disrupt the flow of the team. Winning three consecutive championships is the most important thing around here."

Green Bay's head coach had peered into the future and had seen a potential problem. He told Robinson, "The reason I didn't want you to play linebacker at first was you'll be the first black linebacker in the National Football League and I don't want a bunch of reporters going around writing stories about that and not about us winning the championship. So, if anybody comes to you and asks you about being the first black linebacker, you just refer 'em to me."

Robinson said, "Every time somebody asked, I just referred 'em to Vince. There never was an article that I knew of anyway."

Much like as had been the case with Adderley, Robinson oozed with athletic talent but his NFL playing position was not certain. "All of us read about Dave when he was announced as the Packers' No. 1 choice and we read that he was an honor student majoring in engineering, so we knew he was intelligent," Herb said. "We read that he played both ways at the end position and was an All-American, but it didn't mention anything at all about him being a linebacker."

Where Robinson would play was made easier with the development of two rookies in Green Bay's training camp. While Robinson was with the All-Stars in Chicago, Lionel Aldridge made huge strides to nail down the right defensive end job and Marv Fleming earned a spot behind Ron Kramer at tight end. Aldridge became the first rookie starter for Lombardi in Green Bay.

Robinson's acclimation to the position of linebacker in Green Bay unfolded in storybook fashion. He was not going to start as a rookie because Lombardi was the coach, but a fellow 'backer took Robinson under his wing and poured 10 years of experience into his brain. Veteran Bill "Bubba" Forester wanted to hang it up, and the kid wearing number 89 was the key to Forester's exit.

Robinson said, "The very first day in practice Bill Forester told me, 'You're my ticket out of here. I'm retiring after this season is over.' Bill had wanted to retire after the '62 season, but after Nelson Toburen's injury Vince wouldn't let him. Bill and I worked together after practice every day. I practiced at all the linebacker positions."

The teaching sessions continued at the team's training camp facilities because Robinson was intent on learning and Forester was set on retiring. After the nine o'clock evening meeting, most of the guys went downtown and that gave the veteran and rookie time to talk, but it had to be done on the sly.

"In Sensenbrenner Hall, the rookies were on the second floor and the veterans on the first floor," Robinson said. "I used to sneak down the back steps to his room because rookies weren't supposed to be on the first floor. If a veteran found a rookie on the first floor he'd rip him a new one. Bubba and I would talk for a half hour or hour about playing outside linebacker, how to read keys, what tips to look for and things like that. I took my playbook down and we went over everything. Ninety-nine percent of what we did was verbal, not on the chalkboard or watching film. The big thing was that I learned all 11 defensive positions. When I would ask Bubba a question, he would tell me what I was supposed to do, but he could also tell me what any of the other ten guys were going to do. Forester was much more thorough with me than Phil Bengtson. Phil would tell me about the 'Xs' and 'Os', but Bubba Forester would tell me why the X is here and the O is here."

With all the satisfaction of a successful 5-year-old cookie burglar, Robinson said, "The point is, we worked together a number times and the veterans didn't know I was coming down to their floor. We did our work and then I would sneak back upstairs."

If the rookie had been caught on the wrong floor, it would have been a big deal. Under Lombardi's system, it would have been no issue at all that a white man was helping a black man. Adderley said, "Bill Forester was a very good linebacker and he was a white guy from Texas. He didn't judge a man by the color of his skin and he wanted Dave to be successful as a linebacker."

Adderley spent the last three years of his Hall of Fame career on a Cowboys team riddled with racial division. Adderley said, "If Dave had been in Dallas, the white linebackers wouldn't have helped him with anything. But Bill Forester did it for the good of the team, and he thought it was the right thing to do."

As if Robinson didn't have enough to worry about, he had to keep one eye on his draft board and the other on a set of x-rays. Uncle Sam was closing in and wanted Robinson in fatigues. Robinson was able to delay induction because he had a potential pair of aces. Mrs. David (Elaine) Robinson, a petite woman, was getting bigger than a house, and her physician suspected she was carrying more than one fetus, but there was no proof.

"We had to wait until the seventh month to take x-rays, so we needed a little more time," Robinson explained. "When they finally took them, the doctor said, 'It looks like at least two because I saw two backbones.' He wasn't sure if there was another one or two hidden." The Robinsons, and the draft board, were forced to wait to see if Elaine would have one, two or a litter.

Lombardi used the final '63 pre-season game to settle a score with Redskins owner George Preston Marshall. The previous year, Marshall laughed at Lombardi because the Green Bay coach was mistaken for being black and denied a table at a restaurant in North Carolina. Green Bay's head man was insulted by the events and supposedly asked to terminate the long-standing agreement between the two teams. Washington's owner reportedly refused; therefore, Lombardi found another way to put the screws to Marshall.

The Packers were World Champions and had become the darlings of the NFL. Any team would have loved to have Green Bay on the pre-season schedule because they could sell out huge stadiums and generate lots of revenue. In those days, players were only paid $50 for each pre-season game, and the teams were basically printing money.

Robinson explained how his head coach solved the problem. "It was the smallest crowd I ever played in front of as a pro. We ended up playing the Redskins in 1963 in Cedar Rapids, Iowa, at a high school football stadium. Frank Budd, a black track star and (at the time) world's fastest human being, was trying to make the team with the Washington Redskins. There were something like a hundred press credential requests, and the press box could accommodate about twenty. The lights were so low that all the punts and half of the kickoffs went above and out of the lights. It was terrible. The locker rooms couldn't handle it, the crowd was small and both teams lost their shirt."

Green Bay won the game 28–17; the score between Lombardi and Marshall was more lopsided.

Conditions of the contract called for the Packers and Redskins to take turns selecting the location of the game in alternating years. Following the Cedar Rapids contest, Lombardi reportedly found George Preston Marshall and told him the teams would play at the same high school stadium every other year, at which time Marshall asked Lombardi if he would like to break the contract. Apparently, Lombardi didn't have to tell Marshall it was as clear as black and white he wanted out of the deal.

Lombardi repeatedly stood for racial advancement while others around the league resisted progress.

Adderley said, "We played the Redskins on a high school field, but we all stayed at the same hotel. It blows my mind thinking about how Lombardi hated racism and discrimination in the '60s and all of the shit I had to deal with ten years later with the Cowboys."

Three "new breed" black players made the team in 1963. Robinson, Lionel Aldridge and Marv Fleming were not willing to do business as usual and wanted a nice place to live. Aldridge had a unique talent: he could speak "white" and was put to work.

"It was not illegal to refuse to rent based on racial concerns in 1963," Robinson said. "There were no laws on the books. We would have Lionel call and use his 'white' voice to find out if landlords had apartments for rent."

"Oh, sure, we have plenty left."

Robinson said, "We would go look at places and once the landlords saw us, we'd be told everything was rented. There was nothing we could do; it was not against the law."

When Ruth Pitts, wife of running back Elijah Pitts, took a substitute teaching job in Little Rock, Arkansas, Robinson had a place to live, moving in with Elijah.

The Mt. Airy Badgers of 1955 included Herb
Adderley and Bill Cosby. Top row, left to right:
Herb Adderley (12), Ronald Byrd (6) Coach
Charles "Chicken" Jones, Alonzo Ellis
(9) unknown (5). Front row: Bill Cosby (10)
Leonard "Bunky" Rhodes (4) and Mel Sharp (11).

Herb Adderley's high school basketball coach,
Albert "Ike" Woolly

Herb Adderley, freshman year at
North East High School, 1954

The Northeast Varsity Baseball Team posted a record of 12–3 during the 1956 season. Herb Adderely is third from right, top row.

High School Football Team, 1957. Herb Adderley, (23), far right, third row.

At the end of his high school career, Herb was voted the best athlete in Philadelphia. He said, "That award was big because there were some great athletes in all major sports. The great Wilt Chamberlain won the same award the previous year and that made it even more special, adding my name next to his as 'best athlete' in the city."

Herb with MSU standouts Fred Arbanas (84) and Fred Boylen (55), 1960

Adderley played in more College All-Star games than any man in history. Shown here as a member of the '61 team, Herb played in the game five times after the Packers won world titles under Lombardi and was a member of the Cowboys club in the '72 game. Seven times he played in the charity game at Soldier Field.

Herb Adderley, High School Senior, 1957

*High School Head Football Coach
Mr. Charles Martin*

Dave Robinson, Moorestown High School, 1959

*Elaine Burns and Dave Robinson hung out at
Coney Island in the late 1950s. The two dated
for six years and were married for 44 years.*

*Wedding day March 22, 1963, Dave and
Elaine Robinson*

After a 1965 practice, wearing number 83, Dave poses with his twin boys:
David standing and Richard on dad's leg.

The Robinsons at Happy Valley on the campus of Penn State University in the mid-'70s.
Robert has a Nittany Lion by the ears, followed by Richard and David, plus Elaine and Dave.

Vince Lombardi and Herb Adderley: Greatness admires greatness.

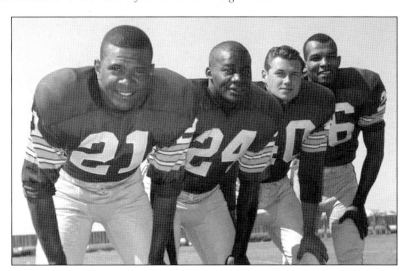

The only defensive backfield to win three consecutive world championships in the modern era: Bob Jeter (21), Willie Wood (24), Tom Brown (40) and Herb Adderley (26).
Photo courtesy of *Green Bay Press-Gazette*

Packers' linebacker Dave Robinson (89) made one of the greatest plays in team history during the 1966 Championship game against Dallas. On fourth-and-goal, Robby got to Cowboys' quarterback Don Meredith, forcing him to lob a wobbling pass to the end zone. Green Bay safety Tom Brown intercepted with 28 seconds left in the contest to secure a trip to Super Bowl I. The magnitude of the Ice Bowl, played a year later by the same two teams, overshadowed the '66 game and Robby's great play.

Dave Robinson became the NFL's first black starting linebacker in the modern era. Boyd Dowler said, "Robby was just as good a player as Nitschke, there isn't any doubt in my mind. If Robby had been with us two years earlier and been on all five of the World Championship teams, he would have been a slam-dunk for the Hall of Fame." Former defensive tackle and long-time defensive coordinator, Dave "Hawg" Hanner said, "He was the best linebacker we had."

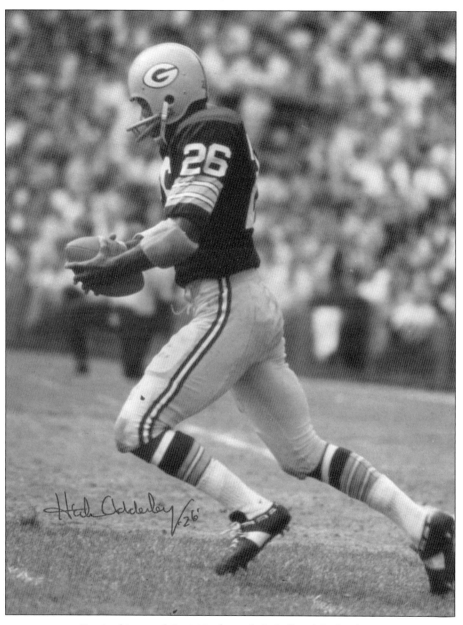

Trusting his great skills, Adderely caught kickoffs with his hands, not his arms, allowing him to get a fast start.

Paul Hornung and Herb Adderley are shown at the annual black tie affair for players and their wives or girlfriends in Appleton, Wisconsin. Herb said, "In Paul's last year, 1966, near the end of the season we had a couple days off in California where Number 5 and I had a night to remember in Sausalito. Paul was a great teammate both on and off the field, and race was never an issue."

1964 Packers linebackers: Dave Robinson (89), Lee Roy Caffey (60) Ray Nitschke (66) and Dan Currie (58)

Herb Adderley Green Bay Packers 1961–69.

Adderley is crawling to recover a Don Meredith fumble forced by Henry Jordan in the Ice Bowl. Bob Jeter (21) and Ray Nitschke (66) are part of the gathering crowd.

A defining moment in a great career occurred in Super Bowl II. Adderley said, "I had an easy day covering Fred Biletnikoff (25) and I was in the right place at the right time in the fourth quarter. Quarterback Daryle Lamonica tried to hit Fred with a deep turn-in and I picked off the pass for an interception."

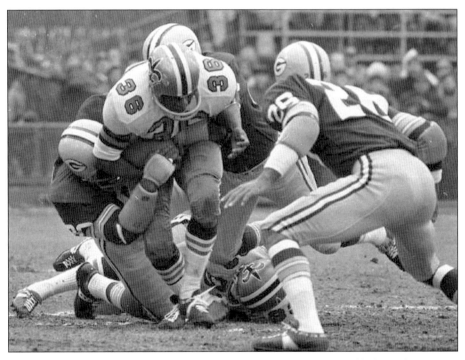

Robinson and Adderley were as adept at stopping the run as covering a pass. Adderley said, "We corraled running backs and Robby and I never ran into each other. Seen here against the Saints, Robinson and Adderley conbine to bring down Don McCall.

Photo courtesy of *Green Bay Press-Gazette*

President Lyndon Johnson asked to meet Adderley and the two men shook hands in the Dallas locker room. During his three years with the Cowboys, Herb shook hands with the President of the United States and Dallas head coach Tom Landry the same number of times. Once.

Adderley's close friend Gregory Eaton and President Obama. Eaton was a star running back at Sexton High School in Lansing, Michigan, when Adderley was at MSU. Herb hitchhiked to Sexton games to watch Eaton play and the two have been friends ever since.

During induction ceremonies on August 2, 1980, Herb Adderley sat beside his Pro Football Hall of Fame bust. He became the fifth member of the Lombardi Dynasty to be inducted at Canton, Ohio. Boyd Dowler said, "The only guy that Herb had trouble with was Gary Collins." Adderley and Collins are depicted in the picture on the table.

Reva Adderley and her son Herb are at the Pro Football Hall of Fame in 1980. During his induction speech Adderley said, "Mom, I appreciate you taking care of me and leading me on the right road with your guidance." In the Hall of Fame of life, Reva is a first ballot, unanimous selection.

Herb Adderly's classmates at Michigan State University, Ernie Green and Carolyn Rush. Mr. Green was a member of the Little Rock Nine, and Carolyn was the sister Adderley never had.

Dave's sister Retta said, "You might as well say Dave and Elaine grew up together. They went together in high school, through Dave's college years and were married for 44 years. They were meant to be together; it was preordained."

An indication of the racial harmony in Green Bay is displayed in this 2010 photo of Dave Robinson and Packers great tight end Ron Kramer. Both players refer to the picture as "Chocolate and Vanilla." Robinson said, "Ron was the best tight end I ever played against and one of the best friends I ever had." The likeable Kramer passed on September 11, 2011.

Photo courtesy of John Smits

143

Toni Adderley, DDS, stands between her children, Joshua Satchel and Justice Page. Dr. Toni said, "My dad lives for his grandchildren and the Green Bay Packers, but my son is a humongous Cowboys fan and they go at it during the season." Toni is a tremendous source of pride for father.

Dave Robinson, his sister Retta, Lombardi's former correspondence secretary Lori Keck and Royce Boyles attending the Broadway play "Lombardi," in which Dave was one of six characters in the production.

On the field, Lombardi was an excellent judge of talent and a very thorough man with a large ego. Because of Hornung's long suspension, guard Jerry Kramer was pressed into duty as a kicker. Jerry proved serviceable for extra points and field goals, but kickoffs were a problem.

Late in pre-season, Robinson, who had kicked off at Penn State, was watching Kramer struggle getting depth on his boots in practice. Robinson said, "He'd kick the ball down to about the 10 and the return team would consistently get the ball to the 30 or 35 yard line. I was complaining like everybody else. I was laughing and told Willie Wood it was no big deal to get the ball to the goal line. He asked if I could do that."

"Oh, yeah."

Wood apparently told Lombardi about Robinson's kickoff abilities and the Old Man pounced on it.

Robinson said, "The next day in practice Vince told me, 'I checked the scouting report and saw you kicked off in college.'"

"Yes, Sir."

"Son, your best way to make this team is as a kicker."

Robinson said, "I was a number-one draft choice and had to make the team as a kicker." Lombardi loved the idea of having a 245 pound kicker on young legs with a running start who could break the wedge. Robinson was not as enthused as he assumed his new duties.

Robinson said, "When training camp was over I was pretty much ready to play linebacker and wouldn't have made a lot of rookie mistakes partly because Bubba Forester was very helpful to me; he was the man. But Vince had his veteran starters with Forester, Nitschke and Currie, and I was the swing guy."

Green Bay lost only two games all year, both to the hated Chicago Bears. In two losses, Packers quarterbacks threw nine interceptions. Bart Starr was picked off four times in the opening game of the season and Chicago still only managed to score 10 points on Green Bay's excellent defense. The Pack mustered just a field goal.

Green and gold muscles were flexed the next eight weeks as Packer opponents fell in rapid succession. In week 10, Chicago drubbed Green Bay 26–7 to beat the Pack for the second time during the season and take a one-game lead with four to play. San Francisco and its 2–9 record was up next and the Packers had a chance to get to feeling better about themselves.

During the eight-game winning streak, on October 1, 1963, Elaine Robinson delivered healthy baby boys, Richard and David. Pappa Dave kept wearing Packer green instead of the Army issue.

The turbulent 1960s delivered America its cruelest blow two days before the 49ers game. On Friday, November 22, the chaotic decade claimed a

With acrobatic grace, Herb blocked a Fred Cox field goal attempt and teammate Hank Gremminger returned it 80 yards for a late fourth quarter touchdown. Adderley was stunned when the ball slapped him on the side of the face, and he needed time to realize the play resulted in a 37–28 Packers' win over the Vikings at Metropolitan Stadium in October, 1963. Following the play, Minnesota head coach Norm Van Brocklin vehemently told the officials Adderley was off sides. After watching the play on film the next day, the "Dutchman" apologized to Herb and called the play "a super-human effort."
Photo courtesy of Vernon J. Biever

President's life in Dallas, Texas. "We came off the practice field and heard about the shooting when we got to the locker room," Robinson said. "We were listening on the radio and reports were sketchy at first, so we really didn't know what was going on. Vince came in at one point and looked very somber. He really liked Kennedy. When we heard that the President had died, it was like someone poured cold water on the whole team. I was devastated."

John Kennedy had been a friend to Lombardi, and the young President was the best hope black America had felt since Abraham Lincoln. "My first thoughts were that JFK was the first president in a very long time who gave black folks any hope of equal rights and the chance to advance civil rights," Adderley said. "I thought that it was a huge setback for the struggles that had been going on for equal rights."

Herb said, "Lombardi was terribly upset; very upset. He called Rozelle and told him the games should be called off. None of the guys wanted to play."

The National Football League decided to proceed with its games while the four-year-old AFL cancelled its entire schedule. By his own admission, NFL Commissioner Rozelle made the wrong choice and took severe condemnation for playing while the nation mourned.

No one could reach AFL Commissioner Joe Foss for a decision because he was pulling weekend duty in the Air Force reserve. Assistant Commissioner Milt Woodward was left with a lonely decision and made the right call.

In a September 24, 2001, *Sports Illustrated* article entitled "Football's Forgotten Choice," *SI* reported, "Sportswriter Red Smith was relentless in his criticism of Rozelle's decision. When Smith saw Rozelle in the press box during that week's Eagles-Redskins game, Smith said, 'Now which one is the big league?'"

The renowned Smith was a Green Bay native.

Adderely was a durable competitor who failed to answer the NFL bell just once. "I missed one game in Green Bay because of a badly pulled hamstring muscle. Doug Hart replaced me and did a great job against the 49ers in Milwaukee. It was two days after President Kennedy was killed and no one felt up to playing that Sunday, including me, so I was happy to sit that one out."

Coverage of the games was nearly pushed off the air and completely out of the newspapers. On live television at 11:21 a.m. CST, about 45 minutes before kickoff, Jack Ruby murdered JFK's accused assassin, Lee Harvey Oswald, at Dallas Police Headquarters.

Later that Sunday afternoon, a stunned nation sat numbly before its televisions and watched a horse-drawn caisson transfer a flag-draped casket from the White House to the Capitol. Hundreds of thousands gathered to pay final respects to the slain president as the games played on.

If only Rozelle had taken Lombardi's advice.

A miserable week only got worse for Green Bay's coach, his country and his team. The President, who had given Lombardi his private phone number, was laid to rest on Monday, November 25. Three days later, the Packers suffered a 13–13 Thanksgiving Day tie in Detroit as Jerry Kramer missed an extra point and middle linebacker Ray Nitschke broke his arm.

"Bad break for you, good break for me," Robinson told Nitschke. Bubba Forester took over at middle linebacker and Robinson became the starter on the right side. Aldridge had opened the year as the first rookie to start for Lombardi and Robinson became the first black staring linebacker in the modern era when Nitschke broke his arm. Stereotypes were melting like icicles.

"The bad thing was that it put two rookies, Lionel Aldridge and I, on the same side," Robinson said. "Teams came at us with everything but the kitchen sink." The tandem held up to the onslaught as their team chased an elusive third consecutive world championship.

Green Bay took its 9-2-1 record on the road for the customary regular season ending trip to the West Coast, looking for two wins and hoping somebody could knock off Chicago. The Packers played a Saturday game against the Rams in Los Angeles on December 7, where a little animosity was brewing on Adderley's side of the field.

It was another one of those West Coast games against an inferior team that saw Green Bay struggle. Los Angeles took a 14–10 halftime lead and by the third quarter, Rams wide receiver Jim "Red" Phillips had gotten on Adderley's nerves. "He was always giving me an elbow or something," Adderley said. "We'd been feuding for three years so I knew something would happen sooner or later."

Rams quarterback Roman Gabriel threw a pass toward Phillips that never found its target. An Associate Press story said, "Adderley intercepted a pass intended for Phillips and the Auburn redhead literally rode the Packer down the sideline near the Packer bench."

Herb didn't mind giving Phillips a ride; it was the other stuff that got his cork. "He was choking me, and when the play ended, he kicked me in the shin and called me the n-word," Adderley said. "So I aimed a right—I didn't want to miss—and hit him on the jaw. I stepped in front of him and hit him under his face bar square on his chin and the punch knocked him out."

Robinson said, "Herb impressed the hell out of me. One punch and the guy was laid out."

"That is the only game I was ejected from during my twelve year career," Adderley said. "Lombardi paid my fine and told me not to let it happen again, and it didn't."

The incident ignited a second-half fire under the green and gold that resulted in Jimmy Taylor ripping off a 40-yard rushing touchdown and Bart Starr hitting Max McGee with two scoring passes as the Pack rolled to a 31–14 win. Green Bay also won the following Sunday at San Francisco, 21–17.

Adderley and Robinson are left to wonder, "what if." What if the Lions had beaten the Bears in the last regular season game?

In the end, the death of a great female singer may have taken Green Bay's last, best hope. Detroit was forced to play Chicago in the season finale without "Night Train" Lane on the Lions' left corner. Lane's wife, blues, R&B and jazz singer Dinah Washington, passed in her sleep a day before the game. Bears wide receiver Johnny Morris and tight end Mike Ditka caught scoring passes on the side "Night Train" vacated. Chicago won the game 24–12 and closed the door on Green Bay's hopes for three in a row.

Despite winning both West Coast games and finishing the regular season with a sparkling 11-2-1 record, the '63 Packers were relegated to the "Runner-up Bowl." Officially, the NFL named it the Bert Bell Benefit Bowl in honor of the man who served as league commissioner from 1946 to 1959. For the record, Green Bay beat Cleveland, 43–20. Also for the record, nobody gave a rip. The game proved to be so insignificant the league eventually categorized it as an exhibition.

A bitter taste lingers these many years later for players who barely missed winning three in a row. Boyd Dowler said, "We repeated once in '61 and '62 and *should have* won it in '63 and *didn't*. It was a disappointment."

"If we had just gotten to the championship game," Robinson said.

The Last Hiccup

If 1963 is the year Packer players would like to forget, '64 may be the one they did.

Boyd Dowler said, "That year is a fog to me. I really can't remember too much about it."

The most nondescript and forgettable season of the Glory Years was 1964, when the Packers went 8-5-1. Two losses were suffered by a single point, another by three. Three losses by five points made the record look worse than it should have been, and '64 would be the final year Lombardi's Packers did not win a World Championship.

Paul Hornung returned from a one-year suspension for betting on games and had a miserable year kicking as he made just 12 of 38 field goal attempts and missed two extra points. The offensive line was thrown into a scramble when Jerry Kramer went out with an injury. Rookie center Ken Bowman became a starter, Forrest Gregg shifted from tackle to guard, Bob Skoronski and Norm Masters manned the tackles and Fuzzy Thurston played his normal left guard position.

Stability was also a concern on the other side of the ball at linebacker. Bubba Forester retired and second-year man Robinson had the inside track on the right side job, but it was not going to be handed to him. "For the first time, I came into training camp knowing where I was going to play," Robinson said. "I got myself in really good shape during the off-season because I knew we picked up Lee Roy Caffey in a trade. I had played in the College All-Star Game with Lee Roy and I knew he was a good player and that I would have to struggle for my job."

Robinson started the first couple of pre-season games and things fell into place quickly, partly because his new roommate was Lionel Aldridge, the right defensive end. "We played side-by-side and were roommates, so he and I talked a lot. In the hotel before the game we went through the program and over the game plan together, which helped a lot." Robinson won the starting job.

"The linebackers in Green Bay always got along well as a group," Robinson said. "That year it was Nitschke, Dan Currie, Lee Roy, Tommy Joe Crutcher and myself, and it probably meant more to our wives who was a starter. But we were like the Musketeers: all for one and one for all."

The defense had problems in '64 with injuries and field position; 26 missed field goals helped put the defense in a bind, repeatedly giving the other teams great field position. Only in Lombardi's first year as coach did his defense give up more points. Green Bay's '59 squad surrendered 246 points; the '64 group allowed one fewer. Green Bay's opponents scored an unacceptable 39 more points in '64 than '63. It was a season to forget. Pat Cochran, widow of backfield coach Red Cochran, said, "We won second place twice: 1963 and '64, and boy, it wasn't going to happen again. There was a playoff bowl in Florida and Lombardi said this was the end of that, he wasn't gonna be in any more of them damn playoff games. He was ornery. He was not a happy camper down in Florida."

Some real good came about as a result of the poor season. In order to improve his team, General Manager Lombardi made several in-season and post-season changes that allowed his team to win an unprecedented three consecutive world championships.

In '64, Green Bay's defenders gave up an unheard-of 20 or more points in eight of 14 games. Part of the problem was at left linebacker where Dan Currie struggled on a bad knee, and the unit was depleted when Robinson got hurt during a kickoff.

The Packers played five lackluster, but close, games to open the '64 schedule and wobbled to a 3–2 record. Game six at Baltimore put Robinson's career in jeopardy.

Robinson was still handling the kick-off chores and Lombardi liked the idea of having a 245-pounder as his wedge buster. "Vince told me I should be the first guy down because I had a running start, so I tried to do that," Robinson said. "As a matter of fact, there were times Elijah Pitts would challenge me to see who could get down there first and I figured out pretty fast he was happy to finish second."

In game six at Baltimore, the first kickoff of the game went textbook perfect. "Tommy Joe Crutcher went down and threw himself into the wedge and broke it all apart; it just scattered," Robinson said. "We went in and made the tackle because the wedge disintegrated. Baltimore wasn't stupid, so the next time we kicked off they sent two guys after Tommy Joe and they spun him around twice so he couldn't get into the wedge and he was late getting there. I beat him down field and was locked up with the point man in the wedge and Tommy Joe threw himself in there crossways to break it up like a bowling ball. He hit me in the back of the leg and tore the cartilage. I knew right away because when you tear one it makes a terrible sound; you can feel it, too."

As Robinson agonized with the injury on the team bench, trainer Dominic Gentile checked on the linebacker/kicker's condition and determined significant cartilage damage had, in fact, occurred. Gentile went down the sideline and delivered the bad news to Lombardi that number 89 was done for the day. Dominic and the head coach discussed the situation; Gentile went back to Robinson and said, "Coach wants you to stay loose in case somebody gets hurt and you have to go back in there." Robby told Gentile, "Tell that S.O.B. somebody *is* hurt; it's me."

Robinson stayed on the active roster all year but was involved in just one more play. He ran straight downfield on a kickoff against the Rams, but his season ended in Baltimore.

With Robinson out and a sputtering offense, Green Bay lost to the Colts 24–21 and followed it up with a West Coast loss to the Los Angeles Rams. The unimaginable had happened: Vince Lombardi's team sank to one game under .500 at mid-season, and there was trouble in Packerland.

Green Bay's head coach, one of Fordham's Seven Blocks of Granite, decided to overhaul his offensive line. Before the '64 season Lombardi had traded All-Pro center Jim Ringo to Philadelphia for Caffey and a huge void was created when Number 51 left town. Ringo was extremely quick and his replacement in Green Bay, converted left tackle Bob Skoronski, had excellent skills but not quickness. The offense perked up when a rookie was plugged in at center, and it didn't hurt that 'Ski' went back to his old position as the line found stability.

Robinson was able to observe from the sidelines while his damaged knee put him on the shelf. He said, "When Vince put Ken Bowman at center the offense started to jell." It sure did, to the tune of 186 yards rushing and a 42–13 waxing of the Vikings. With a revitalized running game, Bart Starr had time to toss four touchdown passes, and a glimmer of hope flickered when the team climbed to 4–4.

Bowman restored the quickness needed for fundamental Lombardi plays and had immediate success in his first start. "We had some trouble at the beginning of the year. Bob Skoronski, was a big, strong man with straight-ahead power," Bowman said. "Lombardi always said you had to make the onside 'cut-off block' to make his plays work and one of those was the sweep." In his first start against Minnesota, Bow had a big game. "The Vikings had a big fella by the name of Gary Larson playing tackle. If you got into his legs, he went down." Bowman said modestly, "I just remember a pretty good day chopping people down." He became a rookie starter for a coach who tried to avoid such things.

Not only did Ken Bowman restore the needed quickness to the center position, he was a rugged gamer who played with injuries for a good portion of his career. It's hard to imagine anyone from the Dynasty with a bigger heart.

After Bow became a starter, Green Bay went 5–1–1 to finish the season and put an offensive line in place that would see better years.

Now serving as a judge in Arizona, where he resides with his wife, Rosann, Bowman was a cerebral rookie whose learning curve was a trajectory.

The strong finish assured Green Bay a second straight appearance in the "Runner-up Bowl" at the Orange Bowl in Miami, and the team needed some changes. Lombardi's success as a coach has hidden his accomplishments as a General Manager and the dismal '64 season exposed problems with the ball club he addressed in a series of bold maneuvers that returned his team to championship form.

The last game of the year, like the season itself, was forgettable. St. Louis beat the Packers, 24–17. As proof positive, Robinson's knee required surgery; it locked up during the week leading up to the "Losers Bowl." He said, "I was on the practice field when it tore and it sounded like a gun shot. Vince sent me back to Green Bay and surgery was performed January 2, 1965."

Lombardi and the fellas wanted to be playing for large rings, larger trophies and championship money. The insertion of Bow in the offensive line was the first of several personnel moves made by the general manager.

Lombardi made two major acquisitions when he shipped Dan Currie to the Rams for speedy receiver Carroll Dale and a third-round draft choice went to the Giants for kicker Don Chandler. The vertical passing game and long-suffering kicking ailments got well in a hurry.

During training camp in '65, "Lombardi's Left Side" was assembled when Robinson was shifted over to join Adderley and Willie Davis. Lee Roy Caffey moved into the starting role at Robinson's vacated spot on the right side, and the major adjustments put the team in position to make history.

Without winning the championship, Lombardi was also unable to play in the prestigious College All-Star game and showcase his title winners at the start of the following football season.

Adderley was convinced 1965 was a pivotal year for the players on the roster. "We had just about all of the same guys who appeared in both of The Losers Bowls," he said. "I read in-between the lines; if we didn't win the title in '65, some of the guys would not be Packers in '66."

Adderley added, "I made a commitment to get in the best physical condition possible for a tough 1965 training camp. I wanted to be a Packer and play for Lombardi, so I made another commitment to shut out every receiver that I had to cover in '65. I wasn't able to *shut out* all of the guys I covered; however, in trying to shut the receivers out, I was able to keep them from catching a TD pass."

Robinson was a third-year man in '65 with a solid working knowledge of the linebacker unit. As a rookie in '63, he was pressed into duty as a right side 'backer when Ray Nitschke broke his arm in the Thanksgiving Day game at Detroit. Veteran Bill Forester was moved to the middle and Robinson took over the vacated spot on the right. Robinson played well enough to earn the starting job for the 1964 season; however, in game six at Baltimore he tore up a knee and played just one more down the rest of the year.

Lombardi's players were expected to know the game of football and know where each of the other 10 guys was supposed to be on a given play. Because he made them responsible to think during the games, his teams were able to adapt on their own. "We had the freedom to talk and make adjustments on the field during the games," Adderley said. "Our recognition of formations, along with using our keys to react, gave us a big advantage against both the run and pass. We gave up less points in the second half of many games because the teams didn't have a plan 'B' to use against us and because of that, they had to run the same plays they did in the first half."

The Old Man had a well-earned reputation as a control freak, but on game day he let his players play, and his game management allowed his outstanding individuals to function as a unit.

Bill Wade played quarterback for 13 years in the NFL, seven with the Rams and six with Green Bay's bitter rival, the Chicago Bears. Wade said, "The Green Bay Packer team was one thing; the individual players were another thing. They were good both as individuals and working as a group. Adderley was as good as anyone against both the run and the pass."

Week two set the tone for the '65 season when Green Bay and the Colts played for the first of what would be three games in the same year. Quarterback Johnny Unitas led a powerful Baltimore club into Milwaukee's County Stadium for an early season showdown that saw Adderley step up big.

"I was named Defensive Player of the Week after that game against the Colts and the great Johnny Unitas," Adderley said. "I picked off two passes and recovered a fumble to stop a potential go-ahead TD." A trend also developed that saw Green Bay's defense give up noticeably fewer points in the second halves of games.

Adderley's second quarter 44-yard interception return for a touchdown helped the Pack squeak out a 20–17 win. Adderley said, "Unitas threw only one interception the entire season the year before, so picking off two of his passes in the same game was a very difficult thing to do."

Even a great signal caller like Johnny "U" had to pick his poison when facing Green Bay's great defenses. Highly-regarded former quarterback coach, offensive coordinator and head coach Ted Marchibroda said of Lombardi's

Left Side, "You couldn't stay away from everybody, but with those guys on that side, you looked to go away from them. You went after Bob Jeter on the other side because Adderley was so good and Robinson was the first of the really big athletic linebackers."

For Lombardi's players, the ultimate goal was always apparent. "Winning the game was the most important thing," Adderley said. "However, knowing that I contributed to the victory was very satisfying."

The *really* powerful Packer teams of the Glory Years were 1961, '62 and '63. After winning two World Titles, the '63 club lost just two messy games. Unfortunately, both defeats were suffered at the hands of the Bears, who captured the championship that year. During the three-peat years of '65, '66 and '67, there were several close championship or playoff games won by Lombardi's disciplined teams. The defense was solid for a decade, and the nature of the offense changed to some extent throughout the years.

Legendary *Green Bay Press Gazette* sports editor Art Daly said, "The early Lombardi teams had a great running game; the later ones relied more on passing. The defenses were always strong during those years."

One major personnel change was made in the secondary in '65: Tom Brown replaced veteran strong safety Hank Gremminger. With a new left side linebacker in the person of Robinson, and with Brown as the strong safety, Adderley was the veteran glue expected to make the new parts work together.

Brown joined an elite secondary of Adderley, Bob Jeter and Willie Wood on a team that was *supposed* to return to championship form. His addition gave the Packers a bit of a youthful look as Robinson was in his second full year as a starter, Tom was in his first and Adderley was a seasoned fifth-year veteran. Youth and inexperience usually mean mistakes, but Lombardi's cerebral players kept blunders to a minimum and did not beat themselves. Mental mistakes fell in the zero-tolerance category during the Dynasty.

"In my opinion, there was no outside linebacker in either the NFL or AFL who was smarter or better than Dave Robinson," said Adderley. "He made very few mistakes and would never make the same mistake twice in a game. He held up the tight ends from coming off of the line better than any linebacker in the league and that made it easier for Tom Brown to cover them."

While not playing the left side per se, Brown found himself on that side a majority of the time in order to cover tight ends. "Tom Brown was a good tackler and he supported the run well," Robinson said. "We used to call him the garbage man because he was always hanging around the action to get interceptions."

Adderley said, "Tom Brown was equal to Grimminger at the safety position. He was smart, consistent and didn't make any coverage mistakes. He did a good job when he had to force the run to our side. Tom determined who would force the end run by the split of the end from the tight end, or tackle if the formation was weak our way. After working together with Robby and Tom during the pre-season, I got to know what to expect from both of them."

Brown was a second-year man and first-year starter who knew the stakes were high. "Absolutely there was a lot of pressure," he said. "Herb was looking out for me, he was a great support. He would tell me what to look for. It wasn't like he was a mother hen, but he would say, 'You're part of the eleven players out here and we're only as good as the weakest link. We expect you to pick it up just the way Gremminger did.' Everybody was expected to know their job and do it."

The chemistry between Robinson and Brown clicked immediately. "If Dave Robinson was supposed to be in a certain place, I knew he was going to be there and that was the most important thing," Brown said. "I could count on it; Robby was such an intelligent player. There are a lot of teams that lose because players do not do their jobs; they're freelancing out there. That's why the Packers were so good; we did our jobs first. Lombardi didn't like to play rookies because it takes more than a year to know where your help is. That's why that left side was really, really good. You could count on those guys doing their jobs."

In '65 the undefeated Packers went searching for win number five at Tiger Stadium in Detroit against a familiar nemesis: the Lions. Robinson's ability to keep guards away from Adderley paid huge dividends in the first half. "I was tied up with the guards and running back Joe Don Looney jumped outside and Herb hit him," Robinson said. "The rest of the day Joe Don Looney didn't really run; he ran like a baby."

Adderley said, "I got a good shot on him."

One of Detroit's offensive tackles was upset with the Looney lick and said to Adderley, "What the hell are you doing?"

Adderley shot back, "Look, you carry the ball and I'll hit you like that."

Green Bay's defense turned in a second half shutout on the way to a 31–21 win.

Lombardi's resurgent '65 Packers reeled off six straight wins to open the season and put the world back on its correct axis. A mid-season stumble saw them go 3–3 in a six-game stretch, and they entered a must-win game against the Colts in Baltimore during week thirteen. Robinson said, "It was a big, big game and Vince took us out to Washington D.C. for the entire week before the game. We had to win that game or we would have been eliminated from the Western Division race."

With the nation's capital just 45 minutes away, all kinds of distractions were within easy driving distance for those who wanted to stray off the reservation. According to Robinson, "Everybody said Washington was a 'sin city' and the guys would be drinking and partying if we spent the week out there. Vince scheduled a meeting, film session, lunch, dinner or something with no more than an hour and a half in between." Lombardi created a quasi-training camp compound. "No beer was sold in the place we stayed; the bar was closed. On Wednesday night Vince brought in two beers per person for dinner and that was it."

As he often did, Robinson came up big in the crucial game against the Colts. "My mom brought a bus load of people down from Jersey for the game, so most of my family was there," Robinson said. His two brothers, Byron and Les, were sitting in the stands with some Baltimore fans who were feeling pretty good about their team's chances late in the second quarter. Fog had settled into Memorial Stadium, and Colts signal caller Gary Cuozzo had his team deep in Green Bay territory. When Byron Robinson said his brother Dave would come up with a play, a Colts fan sitting next to him wanted $50 of that action.

On the very next play, Cuozzo threw a pass in Robinson's direction. Adderley said, "Robby made a great interception, leaping very high in the air in front of me. Cuozzo was trying to hit my man, Jimmy Orr, for a crucial first down."

Robinson carried the pick 87 yards for the longest return of an interception against the Colts at Memorial Stadium. "Unfortunately, I was 97 yards from the goal line when I intercepted it," Robinson said.

According to Adderley, "That was a play that helped us win the game."

Green Bay took over at the 10-yard line where Lenny Moore had tackled Robinson, and Bart Starr promptly hit Boyd Dowler with a touchdown pass. The Packers never relinquished a 21–13 halftime lead and Byron Robinson pocketed a quick 50 bucks.

Adderley said, "I had an easy game because the passing games were shut down by the foggy conditions. My jersey didn't have to be washed after the game even though it was a muddy, wet and sloppy Memorial Stadium field."

Paul Hornung scored a team-record five touchdowns as the Pack rolled to a 42–27 win.

Green Bay took a 10–3 record into the season's final game against a mediocre San Francisco team in California. A win and Green Bay would clinch the division to secure a championship game date against Cleveland. The 49ers game should have been meaningless, but three weeks earlier the Packers couldn't get a win against the Rams. Green Bay was beaten 21–10 at the L.A. Coliseum by a Rams club that was 2–9 going into the contest.

West Coast trips were always a struggle for Lombardi's clubs. From '61 to '66, Green Bay finished the regular season with a road game at either Los Angeles or San Francisco. The Packers were clearly superior to either of the two teams, yet, the average margin of victory for the six games was a mere three points per game. Two contests ended in ties.

The 49ers should have been ripe for the pickin' because they had nothing to play for and had been soundly drubbed the previous week by Gale Sayers and the Bears. Chicago's great running back scored six touchdowns and accounted for 336 combined yards in a muddy 61–20 rout at Kezar Stadium while Green Bay was beating Baltimore in the fog.

In the '65 season finale at San Francisco, an obscure play added to the Packers' West Coast scuffles.

Renowned NFL referee Art McNally described the weird events. "John Brodie made a pitch-out to running back John David Crow and the ball wound up on the ground," McNally said. "Willie Wood picked it up and ran it in for a touchdown. While Green Bay was huddling up for the extra point, rookie line judge Chuck Heberling told me the play was a 'grounded lateral.' In those days, a 'grounded lateral' could be recovered, but not advanced. In today's game it's called a 'muff.' I asked Chuck, 'Are you sure?'"

"Yes."

"Positive?"

"Yes."

McNally said, "I went over to the Green Bay huddle and said to Bart Starr, 'Captain, you do not have a touchdown. Willie Wood could not advance the ball.' Bart then told me, 'Art, go tell The Man.' So, I had to tell Lombardi."

When McNally informed Lombardi, the Green Bay coach said, "Art, Art, what are you doing to me?" Art said, "I told him it was his ball. He never said a word. No one hollered or screamed."

Twenty-five years later, in 1990, John David Crow told former NFL official Red Cashan of the play, "It was the right call."

On that December 19, 1965, day, Green Bay came out of the visitors' locker room at Kezar Stadium with a tenuous 7–3 halftime lead. They needed a big play and Adderley was poised to make it. Lombardi's Left Side, Adderley, Davis and Robinson, were fine physical athletes, but their mental capacity and ability to make "in game" changes made them great. Lombardi knew he had intelligent human beings playing for him, not programmable robots.

With an assassin's diligence, Adderley prepared and waited for his moment. "The field at Kezar was always either dirt or mud depending on whether it rained or not. High schools and colleges played on the field also, so there was no grass left at the end of the NFL season.

"John Brodie was the quarterback and I was shutting down an excellent wide receiver by the name of Bernie Casey. I was lining up a little deeper than usual because of the field conditions. Brodie and Casey noticed my alignment, so John started throwing hitch passes. A hitch pass is when the receiver comes off his side of the field, stops after three or four strides, turns towards the QB and the ball is there for a few yards gain. When Brodie saw my deep alignment, he would call an automatic for Casey to run the hitch. After a few of those plays, I picked up on Brodie's language that alerted Casey to run the hitch. I let them run it a few more times to make sure I figured out the language calling for the hitch."

There is a difference between a calculated risk by an intelligent player and the reckless gamble of a chump. Adderley explained how he hedged his bet, "During a time out, I told free safety Willie Wood what was happening and that I was going for the next hitch pass. I asked him to cover me deep if it was a hitch n' go route. Willie didn't have to cover me deep because I picked the next hitch and jogged into the end zone for a 13-yard touchdown. I was 'right on' about picking up the language calling for the hitch pass. The Left Side became one of the greatest units of all time because we were alert to everything that happened on the field."

The calculated precision described by Adderley illustrates how Lombardi's disciplined teams adjusted on their own and did not beat themselves. Herb was so exceptional throughout his career that "no receiver was ever awarded a game ball for an outstanding game against me."

While patrolling the left corner, Adderley was awarded 12 game balls; nine while playing for Green Bay and three with the Cowboys. He also has a lucky number 13 game ball that was presented for his historic interception return for a touchdown in Super Bowl II against the Raiders.

In back-to-back games against Baltimore and San Francisco, Robinson and Adderley intercepted passes in crucial situations that allowed Lombardi's team to pursue the first of three straight championships.

The 1965 season ended in spectacular, quirky fashion, requiring a playoff game between Baltimore and Green Bay to decide the Western Division Champion.

The Packers could only manage a 24–24 tie against the 49ers and ended the season in a deadlock for the division championship with Baltimore. Lambeau Field played host to the historic playoff game against the Colts, and it was a stomach-turner that went into sudden death overtime.

"No mental mistakes" was a cardinal rule for a Lombardi team. In many close, critical games, the lack of blunders by Green Bay meant the difference between winning and losing, between a dynasty and a good run, between a storied franchise and a good story, between World Championships and anything else. Lombardi's teams did not beat themselves and, in the process, won several critical games by razor-thin margins.

Robinson said, "All week long before the game the sports writers and sports announcers were all saying it was going to be tough for us to beat the same team for the third time in the same year. Lombardi told us, 'You can beat the same team ten times a year if you have a better team. And we are better.' He was right."

The Packers had a clear advantage entering the playoff game against the Colts because Baltimore had lost starting quarterback Johnny Unitas and his backup Gary Cuozzo. Running back Tom Matte made a noble attempt serving as the emergency third-string signal caller.

Adderley sized up the situation and said, "We knew it would be easier defending against Matte's passing game because of his lack of experience and, more importantly, his accuracy. He also had the game plan taped to his wrist, so that indicated he couldn't remember the plays. Our game plan was to force him into passing situations by shutting down the run, and we did that."

Green Bay's best-laid plans literally took a hit because quarterback Bart Starr's day lasted one play. He opened the game with a 10-yard pass to tight end Bill Anderson who was hit by Colts cornerback Lenny Lyles and fumbled. Baltimore linebacker Don Shinnick recovered the ball and ran 25 yards for a touchdown. Starr missed the rest of the game due to bruised ribs suffered on the play when he tried to make a tackle on Shinnick.

Tom Brown said, "They weren't going to win by throwing passes against us with Tom Matte at quarterback. Lombardi told us, 'Listen, the only way they are going to beat us is if they get a touchdown from the offense on an interception. Because we are not going to let them march down the field.' Sure enough, Baltimore's defense scored on the first play."

Lombardi's off-season acquisition of Don Chandler delivered a clutch win as the gentleman kicker drilled a controversial 27-yard field goal in regulation and then hit a 25-yard game winner in overtime. There was lots of pressure on the first-year Packer. "You put a guy out there under those circumstances and you're not supposed to miss those," Chandler said. "If it would have been back 50 yards, why then, if you'd have missed it, people would have accepted it."

Another source of pressure came from the guy on the Packers' sideline in the hat. "Absolutely there's a lot of pressure in that," Don said. "You bet, you didn't want him giving you that look."

Of the Lombardi championships, the '65 title game against Cleveland is the one buried deepest in the recollection of most Packer fans. The title games against New York in '61 and '62 and the two wins over Dallas for trips to Super Bowl I and II are memorable for many reasons.

Because the Cleveland Browns and Green Bay Packers faced off in the slop at Lambeau Field on January 2, 1966, it is only fitting the game has been mired in memory mud similar to the playing conditions. The game should be remembered if for no other reason than it marked the end of Jim Brown's record shattering career.

Entering his first NFL Championship Game, Robinson's personal pride was on the line. "It wasn't so much I was afraid of screwing up or anything, it was just pressure," Robinson said. "I knew that everybody in the country would be watching. It was like the Super Bowl is now—all my friends, neighbors, people I went to high school and elementary school with and family, they would all be watching on national television. And at some point I would be going one-on-one with Jim Brown."

Cleveland's great running back was of equal concern to Adderley. "Every time we played the Browns I was more nervous than usual because of having to meet the great Jim Brown head-on before the game was over," Adderley said. "I saw him on film running over defensive lineman, line backers, and once he got into the secondary he would look for d-backs to run over or outrun them to the goal line. I don't remember tackling him alone because we knew we had to gang tackle the greatest running back to ever play in the NFL with more than one guy. We always held him under 100 yards rushing and that was a very difficult assignment. He was known for breaking a long gainer sometime during the game, but he never did it against us because of our game plan to gang tackle him."

Adderley also faced two other slick obstacles: a flanker and the field.

Boyd Dowler said, "The only guy that Herb had trouble with was Gary Collins. I know Gary was just giving Herb fits and we used to talk about it. Herb used to say, 'How come I can't cover him? It must be a mental block because he's a lot like you but not as good.'"

Adderley's riddle with Collins was never really solved. "Gary Collins was the guy who I had problems with for two reasons," Adderley said. "Number one: his height and weight; and number two: having to force the end run when Jim Brown ran wide to the left. The Cleveland Browns never beat us, so it wasn't like Collins was taking me to school even though he caught a few TD passes. I had more trouble with Gary Collins than any receiver that I had to cover one-on-one. He caught a scoring pass on me in the '65 title game on a 17-yard post-corner move in the end zone and gave the Browns' fans something to cheer about when he caught a few passes in front of me."

Adderley was a thinking man's cornerback and adjusted to the quagmire Lambeau Field had become during the championship game. "I always played the receivers a couple of steps deeper than usual because of a sloppy field," he said. "I felt I had the advantage because the receivers had to slow up to make moves during their routes and that gave me more time to react, so I never had a problem playing on a wet, sloppy, or frozen field. I knew that one slip by me could allow my man to catch a TD pass and cost us a game."

Quarterback Bart Starr effectively sent a steady diet of running backs Paul Hornung and Jim Taylor at the Browns in the muddy conditions. Green Bays' Hall of Fame backs were called on 45 times resulting in Hornung gaining 105 yards and Taylor, 96. With Green Bay chewing up the clock, Jim Brown spent a lot of time on the sidelines, and when he played, middle linebacker Ray Nitschke's laser focus on the great fullback restricted Brown to 50 rushing yards.

The hard-fought game was not decided until late in the fourth quarter when Adderley got the best of Gary Collins. Adderley said, "With less than two minutes remaining in the game, Collins tried to run past me on a fly route and I was on him closer than his shadow. I picked it and Collins tackled me after I ran into Tom Brown on or about our 20 or 25 yard line. The play ended all of the hopes the Browns had to win the game because time ran out after our offense ran a couple of plays." Championship number three had been secured by a Lombardi-coached Packers team.

Robinson said, "For the guys who had been there in '61 and '62 it was a return to normalcy and, of course, that's how Vince looked at it. But for me, it was the greatest experience I had ever had; better than winning bowl games or anything else. This was the World Championship and we didn't think about money or anything else because we were World Champions. Best in the world."

In true Lombardi fashion, Adderley put his phenomenal year in perspective. "The '65 season was my best as a Packers' player, but it wouldn't have meant anything if we wouldn't have won the title. Because we won the title in 1965 and I had my best year up until that time in my career, I felt as though I lived up to my personal commitments for the season. I removed any doubt in Lombardi's mind about me wanting to be a Packer."

For the third time in his career, Adderley was voted to the Pro Bowl as a first team All-Pro following the '65 season.

The five personnel moves made by Lombardi going into the season not only put Green Bay football back on course, it launched a three-year orbit.

A Full-blown Trend

As the Packers stood on the eve of the 1966 season, Wisconsin sports fans had reason to cherish their team more than ever.

The Milwaukee Braves, who had been loved and supported by baseball fans who packed Milwaukee County Stadium in record-shattering numbers, had absconded to Atlanta, Georgia, after the '65 season. In the process of becoming big business, sports proved it could break hearts from Ashland to Racine.

The structure of professional football in America was changed in the summer of '66, and it put Lombardi's team in a position of increased importance. In June, the National and American Football Leagues announced a merger agreement. Terms of the deal included a championship game to be played between the two leagues for four years, until all teams would form a revamped NFL with American and National Conferences. Some NFL team was going to have to uphold the honor and prestige of the established league in an unprecedented face-to-face showdown with the junior circuit. The game would become known as the Super Bowl.

Adderley said, "Lombardi reminded us during the first day of training camp that we would not embarrass him, the Packers and the NFL by losing to the All-Stars again. He was just as serious about winning the game as he was about beating the Browns for the Title in '65. It was a tough camp because he wanted us in the best of shape as soon as possible because of the limited amount of time to prepare for the game."

The team was back in a familiar position as defending champions of the National Football League, but Lombardi pointed his club to the future, not the past. "When we returned to training camp, there was hardly any conversation about being the champions," Adderley said. "We were more concerned about the two-a-day practice sessions, the hated grass drills, winning pre-season games and repeating as NFL champions. Lombardi made sure that we didn't get complacent by reading our clippings, so it was back to business as usual: God, family and the Green Bay Packers. Not necessarily in that order."

Robinson agreed, "It was the hardest training camp I have ever been through and I was never worked so hard. Vince was not going to lose to the All-Stars again." The 1966 camp became famous for grass drills. "Ken Bowman would count 'em and when we set a record, Bow would yell, 'New record,' and Vince would stop. We told Bow to either quit counting or start lying,"

Robinson said. "By the time we went to the All-Star Game, I was down to 231 pounds and one of their coaches asked me if I was sick."

Back on the national stage as defending world champions, there was a bit of unfinished business. Lombardi bristled at the thought of the '63 loss to Robinson and the College All-Stars. There was a pool of Green Bay Packer youthful talent in the collegiate camp with first-round draft choices Donny Anderson, Jim Grabowski and Gale Gillingham ticketed to join the World Champions after the exhibition game.

Gilly broke his hand during practice in Chicago while holding a blocking dummy when teammate Larry Gagner's helmet hit the back of Gale's hand. "It was the best thing that ever happened to me, by the way," according to Gilly. Green Bay's coach wanted his injured guard out of Chicago and in camp at Green Bay. Gillingham said, "Lombardi made no bones about it; he told them, 'He's my property, get him up here.' Away I went."

The injury got Gilly out of the collegiate sessions and he missed only about five days of Packer practices. Phil VanderSea said, "He came in from the All-Star camp with this big cast on and Lombardi put him right into the scrimmages so he could play *against* the All-Star team."

Gilly said, "I had my right hand in a cast and Lombardi just told me to do what the hell I could do to get ready." Immediately upon joining the Packers, Gillingham knew the All-Stars were going to get drubbed. He said, "I told Grabowski the night before the game, 'For God's sake, you and Donny need to get hurt warming up because you are going to get massacred.' I had seen both camps and I thought there was a little different approach in Green Bay."

With a light-weight, somewhat removable cast, Gilly played nearly three quarters of the predicted annihilation. The Packers mauled the kids 38–0. Robinson said, "The game wasn't that close, Vince called off the dogs."

According to Adderley, "We had a bitter taste to get out of our mouths from the '63 All-Star Game and if we would have lost that game, half of the team would have been placed on waivers the following week."

Adderley and his teammates asserted themselves early and often in a domination of the youngsters. "I picked one and ran it back 34 yards for a touchdown in the first half," Adderley said. "Lombardi came over to me at halftime with a big smile on his face and patted me on the shoulder pad. He didn't have to say anything because we knew what it meant whenever he did that. He didn't do it that often to any of us, so it was always a special feeling."

In 1966, a young public relations man by the name of Chuck Lane was hired by Lombardi. Lane knew immediately what he believes to this day, "I was truly blessed to be associated with and represent such classy athletes and men of character. I never had an issue with anyone on that team as long as

Vince Lombardi was there, as he would never have allowed anyone to conduct themselves in any manner unbecoming to the image that he felt the Green Bay Packers must embody."

––––––––––––

The Dynasty was well in place when Lane joined the team, and both the local and national press constantly clamored for player interviews. Chuck could proudly trot out anyone on the roster for the press, but especially the two from The Left Side. Lane said, "When writers interviewed these men, they learned something from them. Those interviewed talked to, not down to, reporters and thus earned the respect of the media."

Lombardi's Left Side was earning respect around the league as the unit worked better and better with experience. "We were really starting to click," Robinson said. "After working together in '65, we knew what we were doing. I knew Herb, Herb knew me. I knew Willie Davis, and he knew me. We had meshed as a veteran squad."

Game two of the '66 regular season was a rematch of the previous year's NFL championship game, but with a different venue. Green Bay made the trip to Cleveland's "Mistake by the Lake," cavernous Municipal Stadium. A massive overflow crowd of 83,943 saw the home team surge to a two-touchdown lead as Adderely's personal antagonist, Gary Collins, did it to him again. Twice.

"Collins caught two scoring passes against me in the first half and they were ahead 17–7 at the break," Adderley said. "I had to cover him all over the field with *no* help from Willie Wood in the middle of the field and Collins caught a post route, and a post corner route for touchdowns."

No receiver had ever caught two touchdown passes in the *same* game against Adderley, not to mention two in one half. The Packers were a bit stunned.

Willie Wood was not making mistakes; he was working with right corner Bob Jeter in double coverage on the great Paul Warfield.

A significant measure of a good football team can be determined by its adjustments at halftime, and the Cleveland game was a prime example. Adderley said, "In the locker room Lombardi told us we could win the game if I could shut Collins down in the second half. I told him I could do it if Willie would be in the middle of the field to help me with the post pattern."

It's easy to miss an important element of the Lombardi genius: he trusted his players and relied on their judgment. "When you look at our football team and you look at our lineup, both on offense and defense, there aren't any dumb guys in there," said Boyd Dowler. "I mean, guys were football smart and they were basically intelligent people. Lombardi just wasn't going to have it any other way."

What good are smart players if you don't listen to them?

According to Adderley, "Lombardi told Phil Bengtson to make the changes I suggested and have Willie Wood help me on the post pattern. Because of a major adjustment that was suggested by a player, we were able to shut Collins out of the end zone in the second half."

Adderley could not resist making a comparison between Lombardi's trust in his players and the rigidity he experienced in his later years with Tom Landry and the Dallas Cowboys. "Landry wouldn't have made the adjustment because he depended on the defense he called to stop plays and not the players," Adderley said. "That way, he took credit and not the players. When the defense called did not stop the plays, the players were blamed."

With Green Bay's defense in sync during the second half of the Cleveland game, the Browns could manage only a Lou Groza field goal. Veteran quarterback Bart Starr directed Green Bay's offense for two touchdowns and the last one was a thriller.

Starr was brilliant in '66 on his way to being named the league's Most Valuable Player. In no small measure, his work in the final minutes at Cleveland helped secure the award. Starting at his own 20-yard line, Starr calmly moved his squad to the Browns' nine, where he faced a do-or-die fourth-and-goal.

Starr's first two choices on the play were wide-out Carroll Dale and flanker Boyd Dowler; both were covered. Bart dumped a pass off to his third option.

Refusing to give in to the biological clock, 31-year-old full back Jim Taylor turned in one of the best plays of his Hall of Fame career.

"He made one the greatest runs to get the ball into the end zone," Adderley said.

Robinson agreed, "It was a hellaveu play by Jim."

Three very good Cleveland Browns took aim at the great Number 31 as time ran down. Adderley said, "Bill Glass was more than an average defensive end and Jim ran out of his grasp. Jim Houston, an excellent linebacker, was there to clean up the play and Jim ran over him. The last guy to have a clean shot was a great cornerback who in my opinion should be in the Hall of Fame, Erich Barnes. Jim put a couple of shake-and-bake moves on Barnes that we had never seen before and Barnes was left with two arms full of air."

The Herculean effort was not a big deal to the man who made the play. "You only had six or eight yards to get," Taylor said. "It was instinctive, spontaneous reaction combined with some desire and whatever. I thought I would juke one way and went the other."

No one was more thankful than Adderley to see Taylor cross into the end zone. "I was so happy that Jim scored the winning touchdown," Adderley said.

"I met him coming off of the field with a bear hug and thanked him for bailing me out of an embarrassing situation."

Lombardi's club breezed through the regular season and took a 10–2 record to the East Coast for a contest with the Colts.

Two late season games, one against Baltimore and other in the Cotton Bowl against Dallas in a playoff tilt, were cliffhangers with huge contributions from Lombardi's Left Side. Robinson came up big in both games. Against the Colts, Willie Davis caused a late game fumble that Robinson managed to recover in a standing mass of humanity. In a gesture no father of twins would welcome, somebody grabbed Robinson's testicles in an effort to distract him from the task at hand.

"I was struggling, struggling, struggling and John Mackey or somebody did that and I went right to the ground," Robinson said. "I asked Mackey if it was him. He said, 'I wouldn't touch those things.' He swears it wasn't him."

Robinson escaped with both the football and his manhood as Green Bay earned a 14–10 win and locked down another division championship. Robinson's fumble recovery stopped a drive that, in all likelihood, would have given the Colts a three-point lead and a win.

Green Bay players were nationally known, so imagine how many distractions awaited them the following week when they went to Los Angeles to close out the regular season. Lombardi did not like the West Coast trip. "He thought his players were getting too familiar with the starlets and celebrities there," *Milwaukee Sentinel* sports writer Bud Lea said. "He would take the team to California early for the good weather, but not to L.A., so he took them to Palo Alto." Green Bay went West with an 11–2 record and tried to focus on the game.

Adderley said, "We were playing against the Rams in the L.A. Coliseum and a security guard came over to me during the game and said a guy in the front row was attempting to get my attention. I said, 'Hey man, I don't have time to be involved with the fans.' The next time I came to the sideline between plays, the guard walked over to me and said the fan was Bill Cosby. When I looked in his direction, it was Cos. I asked the guard to let him come on the field, but he told me that he couldn't do it unless he had a sideline pass."

What happened next defied logic. "I walked up to Lombardi during the game while he was coaching from the sideline," Adderley said. "I told him that my friend Bill Cosby wanted to join us on the sideline but he had to have a pass. Lombardi looked at me like I had just landed from a UFO, and walked away. The next time I came off the field in-between plays, Lombardi came up to me and said, 'What did you say to me about a sideline pass?' I repeated what

I said and shortly after that he ripped off his pass and gave it to me. I gave it to the guard and he walked over to the stands and escorted Cos to our sideline. We shook hands, he said 'thanks,' and he viewed the game from the sideline"

Adderley said, "When I introduced him to Lombardi after the game, Coach said, 'Why didn't you tell me that you knew Bill Cosby, *I Spy* is my favorite program.' I invited Cos in the locker room after the game, introduced him to all of the guys, and yes, he started cracking jokes while telling them about our friendship while growing up in Philly. The guys also asked me why I never mentioned that Cos and I were friends. No one ever asked me!"

In a recent conversation, Cosby asked, "Do you know how angry I am that I didn't have the sense enough to save it? Do you know how much money I could make with that pass?"

Especially if Lombardi had signed it.

"No, he wouldn't have to sign it," Cosby said. "All I have to say is, 'That's it.' I was not going up to him. Herb is lucky, that man had a reputation, boy oh boy. With that cap."

The great comedian could not resist thinking about asking Lombardi for an autograph during the game.

"Can you sign this?"

"What ta hell is going on out there?"

The Packers managed a 27–23 win over the Rams and moved on to a remarkable showdown in Dallas.

We are left to wonder: If not for the Ice Bowl, what if?

If not for the Ice Bowl, Robinson may have the most memorable play in Packers history. If not for the Ice Bowl, the 1966 NFL Championship Game may be remembered for its historic significance.

In an article entitled, "Before the Ice Bowl" on the website Cold Hard Football Facts.com, the game was put into context:

"The Cowboys, for their part, were an important cultural phenomenon in the rise of the South from a cultural backwater and as a second-class citizen of sports into a power player on the wider American stage.

"The Cowboys, most notably, were the first pro sports franchise in the Deep South (along with the AFL's Houston Oilers). The 1966 NFL championship game, meanwhile, was the biggest and most important pro sporting event in the history of the South to that time.

"It was played on their home turf, at the Cotton Bowl, making it the first postseason NFL game ever played in the South—and it came against no less a power than the mighty Packers, the most northerly team in the NFL, a team that represented everything that the staid old-boy Midwestern league had stood for since its foundation in 1920.

"The 1966 NFL championship game, in other words, was the day that the South finally joined the wider world of American professional sports—a full 101 years after the end of the Civil War."

There was another little twist to the game. Whichever team won would represent the National Football League in Super Bowl I.

In some regards, Tom Landry was the ideal opponent for Lombardi. The stoic Dallas head coach was a bright man who threw complicated assignments at his players. Some argue Landry made the game so complex and robotic he beat himself, and the contrast between Lombardi and Landry became clearer in the '66 title game.

The contest opened in a furious way when Green Bay scored two quick first-quarter touchdowns and Dallas came back with two of their own. After 28 first-quarter points, it was a defensive struggle.

"The Cowboys picked up momentum from somewhere during the half-time break and came out the second half with a new attitude," Adderley said. "They were able to move the ball on the ground with Don Perkins running at his best on quick-hitting plays between the tackles. Nothing came out to The Left Side, and they really ran the ball with the plan to control the clock."

It all came down to the final seconds, but few remember because of the Ice Bowl.

"Once they got into the red zone, the Cowboys made three killer mistakes," Adderely said. "Number one, a tackle was flagged for moving before a snap count. Number two, running back Dan Reeves dropped a pass in the right flat. Number three, Bob Hayes lined up in an unfamiliar position on the goal line."

Dallas was poised for a tying touchdown in the game's final moments as Green Bay's defense was pressed against its own goal line. Sitting on the two-yard line, offensive tackle Jim Boeke jumped off side. The refrain of Boyd Dowler explaining Lombardi, "…you better not go making mental mistakes," was a story line that would be played out in two consecutive championship games. After Dallas worked its way back to the Packers' one-yard line, Green Bay found a way to win and Landry found a way to lose.

Apparently, Landry was the only one allowed to deliberate during a Dallas game.

Facing a fourth-and-goal from the two-yard line, Landry, inexplicably, had 185-pound wide receiver Bob Hayes lined up against Green Bay linebacker Dave Robinson.

What was he thinking?

Robinson said, "Hayes couldn't have blocked me if he'd had a twin with him."

From his position on the corner, Adderley heard the chatter of a rattled Dallas team. "Hayes came out wide to my side and people from the Cowboys bench were yelling to him to get in closer to the offensive tackle, which he did," Adderley said. "Because of that alignment, I told Tom Brown that he and I would cover Hayes in and out. Robby then lined up in front of Bob and forced him to make an inside release. Robby recognized the rollout quicker than a New York second and forced quarterback Don Meredith into hurrying his throw towards the end zone on our side."

After getting rid of Hayes, Robinson draped himself over Meredith. On his way to the ground, Dandy Don looped a pass to Packers safety Tom Brown, who intercepted the ball and secured a trip to Super Bowl I. The pick came with 28 ticks on the clock, making Robinson's play one of the greatest in Packers history.

"How about that," Adderley asked. "Two guys, Dave and Tom Brown, making their biggest plays on the same historic play."

According to former Cowboys tight end and noted author Pete Gent, Hayes had not played in a similar goal line situation all year. Of Landry, Gent said, "He was such a loser. When we got behind, he acted like he's still a loser, playing guys who hadn't played at all, like it's still exhibition season instead of a championship game."

Adderley agrees with Gent on the inconceivable game plan. "Hayes jogged into the end zone and stopped between Tom and me looking towards Meredith because he didn't know what to do," Adderley said. "Hayes became a spectator and watched Brown catch the ball and made no attempt to catch the ball or prevent Tom from catching it."

Brown said, "Dave Robinson was the guy who made the play. Obviously you have to be at the right place, and we had a certain defense called with Herb Adderley and myself, but Dave made the play. He was the one who forced Don Meredith to throw the ball up in the air—it was fourth down."

The play still stands as the biggest, most under-publicized one in Packer history, and it was turned in by Robinson and safety Tom Brown in the '66 championship game against the Cowboys. It is buried in history because of the Ice Bowl.

"If there's any man who should be in the Hall of Fame, it's got to be Dave Robinson," Brown said. "It's a crime that he is not in the Hall of Fame. He was the smartest linebacker, outside linebacker. I can't imagine anybody smarter than he was. He knew his responsibility, he knew the responsibility of the guys behind him and he knew the guys in the back counted on him to be in a certain spot and that's what made the Packer defense so good."

Robinson's intelligence and ability to adjust during the game was a huge factor in the Tom Brown interception. When Lombardi evaluated the play, he gave Robby a minus-two because he was supposed to make Meredith commit to a run or pass. Robinson said, "A couple plays earlier, the one where Boeke jumped, they ran a rollout and tight end Pettis Norman dropped a pass in the end zone. It hit him right in the chest. I wasn't going to take a chance on someone dropping another one."

Pete Gent put the blame on Tom Landry, "On the sidelines, I don't know where he got this reputation of being Mr. Calm and Collected. He did nothing but screw up on the sideline. He started to play guys who hadn't played all year. He lost the first two games against Green Bay in the championship games."

Bart Starr also had a hand in things when he turned in one of the best playoff performances in history during that game. He completed 19 of 28 passes for 304 yards, four touchdowns and no interceptions. His passer rating was 143.5.

By season's end, Green Bay's legendary ground game was gone, ranking 14th out of 15 teams. The defense held Bob Hayes to one reception for a single yard in the title game and hardly anyone remembers because of the Ice Bowl.

One of the most fascinating aspects of Super Bowl I is the influence of Vainisi. Lombardi, who was originally recruited to Green Bay by Jack Vainisi, led nine future Hall of Fame players—all scouted by Vainisi—onto the floor of the Los Angeles Memorial Coliseum: Starr, Taylor, Hornung, Gregg, Davis, Jordan, Adderley, Nitschke and Wood.

No human being, including Lombardi, could have envisioned how big the Super Bowl would become, but he was aware the prestige of the NFL was squarely on his shoulders. He took his team to beautiful Santa Barbara, California, to prepare for the game and packed the daily schedule like it was training camp.

It was breakfast from 7–8 a.m., buses to practice at 9 a.m., practice from 10–11:30 a.m., lunch 12–1 p.m., meetings 3–4:30 p.m., dinner 6–7 p.m. and another meeting from 8–9 p.m. Curfew was 11 p.m.. Only the serial street runners like McGee and Hornung could beat the system.

"We knew Lombardi was feeling the pressure because he talked about reputations of the NFL, the Packers and us as individuals being on the line," Adderley said. "He mentioned those things many times leading up to the game and we understood clearly what he was saying."

A plain-old simple win was not what Lombardi was looking for. "He told us we needed to win by at least three touchdowns," Robinson said. "Vince wanted to stop all speculation about which league was superior."

Leading up to the game, Green Bay's coach told his guys they had played teams all year that were better than the Kansas City Chiefs. He was talking about the Colts, Bears, Rams, Lions, Vikings and Cowboys." Adderley said, "We all believed it, too,,and that gave us even more confidence that we would win."

However, the Chiefs had at least one player who was as good as any Adderley had seen in the NFL. "My assignment was to shut down the great flanker Otis Taylor. Yes indeed, he had size, speed, quickness, intelligence, hands and he ran good patterns." The two would match up on game day.

During pre-game warm-ups, Adderley noticed, "The Chiefs had as many as, or more, black players than we did." Once the game started, it was a familiar site at the Los Angeles Memorial Coliseum: the place was about a third empty. The massive stadium held 93,607 and the announced attendance was 61,946 for the only Super Bowl not to sell out. Perhaps pricey tickets kept the crowd away because end zone seats were ten bucks and it cost twelve for the expensive ones on the sides. Adderley said, "Seeing the empty seats was no big deal or factor because that's the type of crowds we drew when we played the Rams."

Like a heavyweight boxing match, the teams felt each other out in the beginning. "Their plan was to establish their running game with Mike Garrett and use the play-action pass to get their passing game going," Adderley said. "It worked for them in the first half when Chiefs quarterback Len Dawson caught right cornerback Bob Jeter peeping in the backfield and threw a seven-yard scoring pass to Curtis McClinton." Kansas City also hit a field goal and Green Bay held only a 14–10 lead at the half. Not exactly what Lombardi had in mind.

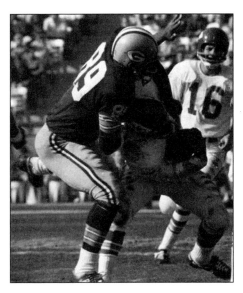

The game turned on the third play of the second half. "The Chiefs were putting five men in the pass pattern in the first half and we did not blitz once. At the half we decided to change that," Robinson said. "We knew there would be no one in their backfield to block, so

Shown here stopping Kansas City's fine running back Mike Garrett in Super Bowl I, Dave Robinson was a sure tackler. The Chief's starting backfield of Garrett and Curtis McClinton were held to 33 rushing yards in the game.

Photo courtesy of *Green Bay Press-Gazette*

on their first third down, we brought the house. All three linebackers, Lee Roy, Ray and I, went in on Len Dawson and he had that deer-in-the-headlights look." Dawson's pass was intercepted by Willie Wood, who returned it all the way to the 10-yard line and Green Bay scored to put the game away early in the second half. Adderley said, "Willie's interception was the biggest play of the game because it changed the momentum."

Robinson said, "We blitzed on every passing down in the third quarter. Either Lee Roy or Ray would go and I stayed with the tight end on the strong side." Years after the game, Lenny Dawson told Robinson the Chiefs' game plan was disrupted because of the blitz. Once again it was a defensive adjustment that allowed the Packers to throw a second-half shutout and win a game. The final score was 35–10 and Lombardi had his three-touchdown margin with four points to spare.

According to Adderley, "The Left Side shut down the Chiefs from doing hardly anything to our side."

Destiny Fulfilled

According to Robinson, Lombardi was on a mission in 1967.

"From the first day of training camp, Lombardi's goal was to win the third-straight championship." It was the first year Green Bay's running game would be without Jim Taylor and Paul Hornung, who both ended up in New Orleans. Taylor signed a 20-year contract with the Louisiana franchise and Paul was claimed in the expansion draft.

Massive changes had been made to both the team and city of Green Bay by Lombardi's ninth year at the helm.

The splendor of a rainbow is best viewed from a distance. If observed too closely, it is impossible to see where the colors separate. So it is with life. We can be so close to a situation we miss the reality of our good fortune.

As twilight was descending on a *Chosen* few who conquered a league and propelled a city forward, a newcomer assessed Titletown.

Detroit native John Rowser, an African American, was a rookie defensive back in '67 and had an uncommon adjustment to the little city by the bay. "I was more prejudiced than the people of Green Bay," Rowser said. "I came out of Detroit and we stayed a little separate. You just kind of stayed your ground. I got to Green Bay and all these white people invited me over to their houses, they were hugging me and all this stuff. They would invite me and I would have an excuse not to go."

It took a full year for Rowser to trust what he was experiencing in Wisconsin. "The next year Claudius James was my roommate and we would go visit and do all those things," he said. "It was a real nice time, it was real smooth. I said to Claudius, 'You know what, I must be the one who is prejudiced when all these people are open to me and I keep making excuses why I'm not going.' I was so used to separation. At first I couldn't accept they were genuine. I loved it up there."

By 1967 many of the young men Lombardi had collected on the way to greatness were seasoned-veteran leaders solidly entrenched as lifelong Green Bay Packers.

Rowser said, "They were good human beings so I learned a lot from them. They didn't talk a whole bunch to you until you made the team because the veterans don't like to really invest a lot of time and information into rookies because they might get cut."

On and off the field, Lombardi's teachings molded a group of confident men. "They weren't threatened very much because most of them were All-Pros and wanted the best players on the team, so they willingly helped you so you could eventually take over and play," Rowser said. "I learned a lot from Herb and Dave. Green Bay was a great place and the vets helped the rookies out. I was the only cornerback backup, so once I made the team, Herb, Bob Jeter and Willie Wood each helped me out; each one would give me their perspective."

Young linebackers would come into camp and be surprised how willing Robinson was to share his knowledge of the position. One rookie asked Robinson if he was afraid he might lose his job by sharing his wisdom. Robinson said, "The guy who is going to take my job is in third grade."

Veteran players were guarded with their information early in training camp, but once a rookie made the final cut, the spigot opened all the way. "I didn't want somebody to get released and end up with the Bears or Vikings and tell them my tricks," Robinson said. "Once a guy became a Packer, I would tell him everything I knew."

Old, injured and probably a little weary, a 1967 green and gold patchwork was dedicated to making football history by winning a third straight World Title and a second consecutive Super Bowl. Black, white, offense, defense and regardless of college or region of the country, in the fall of '67, a familiar group of players congregated at St. Norbert's college determined to get the Old Man one final jewel for the crown.

Robinson said, "I liked that team a lot; it won every game it had to win."

Any hope for a three-peat was nearly knocked off the rails in game five at Milwaukee County Stadium. Adderley tore his right bicep while tackling Minnesota's blocky fullback Bill Brown, and the injury was gruesome. It wasn't until being interviewed for this book that Adderley's family physician, Dr. Kevin Fleming, first learned of the grisly injury.

"It was in the first quarter when I tackled Brown and my right bicep hit his thigh pad," Adderley said. "It didn't hurt at the time of the initial blow, but as the game went on I could feel the pain."

Robinson said, "The bicep was hanging down; it was ripped off the bone. It was ugly. I've seen compound fractures; as a matter of fact, I've had them, and Herb's injury looked worse. When I looked at it I felt queasy. It was the ugliest thing I'd ever seen."

Dr. Fleming said, "That injury hurts like hell. That's the muscle that flexes the arm, and obviously you have to extend and flex the arm to make a tackle, so every time he would make a tackle it would have hurt. Today if that happened, it would be a season-ending injury. That is unbelievable."

By the fourth quarter, Adderley was in severe pain and shared his misery with Minnesota. Quarterback Joe Kapp threw a post route to Red Phillips that failed to find its mark. "Phillips never looked for the ball," Adderley said. "He knew I was waiting to put a legal shot on him so I stepped in front of him and picked it." Phillips is the same guy Adderley coldcocked two years earlier in the Los Angeles Coliseum for using the n-word.

Adderley's back-up, John Rowser, thought he would get some playing time with significant arm damage to the star cornerback. "My only problem in Green Bay was that the guys were extremely durable and they played hurt," Rowser said. "Herb lacerated his bicep muscle and told Vince the doctor may have to operate. Vince told Herb they didn't have time to operate because they were going for the championship. Later on that year Herb had half a bicep; the lower part of the muscle atrophied because it didn't get sewed up."

Rowser's description was verified by Dr. Fleming, who said, "Yes, that's exactly what would've happened."

All of the grass drills, the gassers, the nutcrackers and everything else Lombardi had thrown at his players were designed to develop mental toughness. With a mangled arm muscle hidden in his jersey and a third straight world championship in his sights, Adderley' gutted out the season. Adderley said, "I never took pain killers or got shots to ease the pain. I was in a lot of pain before, during, and after games the remainder of the '67 season."

Adderley's mental toughness was put in perspective by Dr. Fleming, "Today they would do surgery, reattach the muscle and let it heal for about six weeks and then start rehab very gingerly to make sure it didn't come off the bone again. So, yes, that would probably be a season-ending injury today. He played through it not only that year but obviously years after and for the rest of his career."

The game in which Adderley got injured, Minnesota won 10–7. Green Bay then took to the road the following weekend with their wounded All-Pro corner.

The Packers entered a huge game six with heightened emotion at Yankee Stadium against the Giants. It was a return trip to Lombardi's native New York where the lights were always a little brighter. Fullback Jim Grabowski said, "We knew it was a big, big game because Vince was going back to New York. You could tell by his actions that week during practice, he didn't have to say anything because he was pretty intense."

Adderley, fresh off the injury, had to face the man who may have been the league's top receiver at the time. Robinson said, "In 1967, Homer Jones was like Calvin Johnson in today's game, and Herb made tackles, covered him, everything. Unless you knew about Herb's injury, you could never tell. He had an above average game by Herb Adderley standards; it would have been a great game for anybody else."

Adderley said, "I was hurting a lot against the Giants before the game started. Having to hit and bring down Jones was a very difficult assignment that day with a bad arm."

New York held a 14–10 halftime lead, but Green Bay blew it open in the second half to rack up a convincing 48–21 win. As he frequently did, Robinson came up big in a big game by intercepting Fran Tarkenton twice and recovering a fumble. For his efforts the left linebacker was selected Associated Press Defensive Player of the Week.

Robinson was quick to credit both Lombardi and Adderley for the defensive success against New York. "The Old Man knew they would not mess with Herb. If Vince would have put someone else in, the Giants would have picked on him all day and worn him down." Robinson said. "That's the big thing about The Left Side; people didn't pick on our left side. They came over there every now and then to keep a balance, but they tried to get away from us."

By 1967 Adderley, Davis and Robinson were an experienced trio with the "it" factor. "We really watched out for each other. I never felt so good in my life as I did coming of the field in New York with the win. Vince was excited because he went back to New York, but I was happy for Herb. He made it through the game with the worst looking arm I had ever seen in my life. I question if I could have played with that injury."

Adderley was in agony after the game and said, "It was pain that I had never felt before." Adderley's friend, Andy Pinckney, went in the Packers' locker room to give the ailing star a hand. "His arm was separated, and I had never seen anything like it," Pinckney said. "It was a mess. It was like a loaf of bread that someone had pulled a couple slices out of the middle. I helped him get the jersey off and helped him button his shirt and tie his neck tie."

Adderley reached deep within himself and into the past to fight through the pain. "I thought about Bernie Dobbins and the pain he endured for all those years," Adderley said. "Bernie was my inspiration all year long."

Including the Ice Bowl and Super Bowl II, Adderley played 13 games with the damaged arm. Robinson said, "Herb deserved to be Defensive Player of the Year for playing with that injury."

Robinson added, "Vince coached the last part of the year like a maestro; he knew when to bring in the strings, horns and percussion."

Not to mention running backs and kick returners.

Green Bay's record of 4-1-1 looked a lot better than Adderley's arm when the nation heard a "beep, beep" from a Road Runner. On Monday, October 30, in St. Louis, the Cards kicked a fourth-quarter field goal to take a surprising 23–17 lead over the Pack.

Lombardi then inserted rookie Travis "Road Runner" Williams on the ensuing kickoff and put an electric charge into Packerland. In training camp Travis had earned a reputation for unreliable hands, but that concern vanished when he touched the ball. Williams had never returned a kickoff, not in college, not in the pros. The plan was to have the other returner, Adderley with his bad arm, field the boot and give Green Bay good field position.

"Before the kickoff, I told Travis that I would take kickoff," Adderley said. "But, if it came to him, I would get the first man and he should run to daylight. That is what he did for a 93-yard return for a touchdown."

Robinson said, "He ran out the end zone. We asked him why he ran out of the end zone and he said, 'Herb told me to run 'til they tackled me.' Very good."

Raw speed was a new dimension that made a real difference for the fundamental Packers. "With Herb, our field position after kickoffs was good; with Travis it was great," Robinson said.

Boyd Dowler added, "When you watched Travis on film, it was like somebody cut out some of the frames."

With a lethal return game and Phil Bengtson's defense, the Packers headed for a third straight title.

"Our defenses in those days were pretty doggone good," said Director of Public Relations Chuck Lane. With pure intentions of giving the defense a little publicity, the young PR man bumped into Lombardi's ego.

"I used to write the game programs and the news releases," Lane said. "The program had a story on the upcoming opponent; the news releases gave the guys in the media some tidbits they could build upon for the promotion of that upcoming game. I happened to make the mistake of writing in there that Phil Bentson's defense was ranked number-one in various categories. Of course, I had to clear the news release every week with Coach Lombardi. Well, he got down to the part where it was 'Coach Bengtson's defense.' He corrected me that in no uncertain terms, that wasn't Coach Bengtson's defense."

"That is my defense."

With a lethal return game and Lombardi's defense …

Until the New York Giants of 2011, only one team had made it to a Super Bowl without winning at least 10 regular season games: the '67 Packers. They lost a couple of games late in the year but won when it counted, including the Ice Bowl.

Akin to swearing in church, let it be said that winning the last three games of the regular season may not have been "the only thing" for Lombardi. If true, it was a radical departure from the way he viewed the value of winning every game, including pre-season match-ups. He had an option on a special place in football history and his boys needed to be healthy at season's end to enter the unoccupied room reserved for three-time champions.

At the end of the 1967 season, Green Bay's offense relied on the wily skills of veteran quarterback Bart Starr, who was saddled with a makeshift running game that had been decimated by injuries. The offense ranked ninth in a sixteen team league.

But the '67 team won championship number five under Lombardi and the third in a row with the Ice Bowl win over Dallas and a convincing drubbing of Oakland in Super Bowl II.

For the first 45 years of the Super Bowl, only the '67 Packers won the crown with single-digit regular season wins. Ironically, no Lombardi team ever locked up a division championship earlier; they sealed it with three regular season games remaining. Green Bay lost two of the last three, including the season-ender to a lowly Pittsburgh Steelers club. More than one Packer player was upset that an all-out effort was not made to beat a Steelers club that took a 3-9-1 record into Milwaukee County Stadium. It was standard practice for Lombardi to put a "10-game clause" in contracts: 10 wins was worth a $2,000 bonus per player. Lombardi had a bigger goal.

The Packers' head man was acutely aware of press coverage of his team, and reporters got in trouble by crossing a line, real or imagined, into his world of coaching. Respected sports anchor Bob Schulze of WFRV-TV in Green Bay recalled one such incident. "The Packers lost a late-season game to the Rams on the west coast. (They) had already clinched the divisional title, so the outcome didn't really matter all that much. Still, I felt compelled to go on the air with the comment, 'whoever was wearing green and gold at the Los Angeles Coliseum had to be imposters. They certainly were not the Green Bay Packers.' He heard about it.

"When I stepped from my car the next day at the Packers administration building on Highland Avenue (later to be renamed Lombardi Avenue), he got out of his car at the same moment."

Lombardi said, "Good morning, you goddamned super expert!"

Green Bay won the division and faced the Cowboys for the honor of playing in Super Bowl II

Oh yes, the Ice Bowl, perhaps the most scrutinized football game in history. Not!

The game had the most analyzed *final drive* in history, and therein lies the problem.

Adderley was stunned like everybody else the morning of the game, December 31, 1967. The temperature had plunged about thirty degrees overnight. "I opened my front door and found out the weatherman on TV was right, it was ten degrees below zero. My first thought was, 'I hope my 1967 Lincoln starts.' It didn't. I wasn't too worried because some of the other guys lived in the same area."

Absolutely. Thank God for dependable teammates.

Adderley said, "Travis Williams was driving past and I waved to him trying to let him know I needed a ride to the stadium; Travis waved back and kept on driving in the new Plymouth he had gotten from a local car dealer. It was a Road Runner with a woodpecker or something on the side." Another rookie mistake.

"Willie Davis lived a half block away and picked me up," Adderley said. "We didn't say too much on the way to the stadium because we were in a semi state of shock. We took turns saying, 'This is unbelievable.'"

Inevitably the locker room talk was about the temperature. "Lombardi put a stop to that," Adderley said. "He told us, 'We cannot let the weather distract us from our game plans and focus.' He also said both teams would have to make adjustments because of the weather."

Lombardi was right, of course, but so was Boyd Dowler's father, Walter, when he told his son, "Don't worry about a thing. This will bother Bob Hayes more than you." Living in Wyoming teaches such lessons.

Green Bay's coach told his players that anyone who would handle the ball, running backs, receivers, linebackers and defensive backs, could not wear gloves. There was one sneak in the bunch.

Robinson knew Lombardi was physically color blind and asked trainer Dominic Gentile for a pair of brown jersey gloves that were popular at the time. "I wore them during running plays and stuck 'em in my pants on obvious passing downs," Robinson said. "Vince never knew."

Adderley, Robinson and their teammates stayed in the locker room to stretch and loosen up rather than face the bitter cold in something that was supposed to be a "warm up."

In addition to great players and a great head coach, the '67 Packers had a secret weapon and ritual that involved Adderley's unborn daughter Toni. Olive Jordan Frey said, "When Barbara was pregnant with Toni I happened to rub her stomach before a game early in the year and I asked, 'Barbara how does that baby feel?' We won. Being the superstitious bunch we were back then, I rubbed it before the next game and we won again. From then on, for the rest of the season, I had to rub her tummy."

Brutal weather the day of the Ice Bowl meant fans wore layer upon layer of clothes to stay warm. They were bundled beyond recognition and Olive and Barbara had trouble finding each other. "Barbara and I knew we had to find each other so I could rub her stomach so we would win," Olive said. "We stumbled around and found each other and I patted her tummy. What we didn't realize, Herb and Henry were standing on the floor of the stadium peering through the crowd and praying we would find one and other so I could rub her stomach."

Adderley was also checking out the footing and said, "In between the hash marks the turf was soft, but I knew it would be frozen eventually. I always felt the wet, muddy and frozen field gave me an advantage because the receivers had to slow up and be very careful when making their cuts. That is exactly what happened."

The Ice Bowl has it faults in Packer history. The game has taken on such magnitude that Robinson's great play a year before in the same game has not received proper recognition. The same thing happened in the Ice Bowl. The final drive has obliterated a great performance by Dowler, who caught touchdown passes of eight and 46 yards to prove his dad was right. Bob Hayes spent the day trying to stay warm by putting his hands in his pants on plays he was not designed to get the ball. Adderley picked up on that and held the speedster to three catches for 16 yards.

Green Bay's great Number 26 is not remembered for intercepting a pass and recovering a fumble in the game because the final drive has stolen the thunder.

Just as Adderley figured might happen, Hayes slipped on one of his routes. "The ball hung up there and I made the play on the ball. As cold as it was, that ball was as heavy as a brick. I was also able to jump on a fumble

Green Bay Packers cornerback Herb Adderley (26) intercepts a Don Meredith pass in the second quarter of the Packers' 21–17 victory over the Dallas Cowboys in the NFL championship game at Lambeau Field on Dec. 31, 1967. Linebacker Dave Robinson (89) is at left.

Photo courtesy of *Green Bay Press-Gazette*

caused by Henry Jordan when he hit Meredith." Both of Adderley's big plays stopped potential scoring drives. With all due respect to Chuck Mercein, the running back has received more publicity for his role in the final drive than either Boyd or Adderley has for their outstanding plays. They all came up big, including Mercein.

Herb Adderley intercepted a pass and recovered a fumble in the Ice Bowl. His great game has been lost to history because of the final drive that sealed the win. Cowboys running back Dan Reeves (30) gets an arm full of the frozen tundra, and Adderley gets away with an interception.

Center Ken Bowman and the entire offensive line was mistake-free on the final drive. But it was a bare-handed Bowman who handled every snap without an error.

In the final analysis, the Ice Bowl will be remembered for the drive. Everything Lombardi taught for 10 years was wrapped up in 68 yards with four minutes and fifty seconds remaining. No mistakes and lots of mental toughness.

"The real difference was Vince Lombardi and the Green Bay Packers' will to win," Robinson said. A somewhat gimmicky fifty-yard option pass from Dan Reeves to Lance Rentzel gave Dallas a 17–14 lead late in the fourth quarter. Robinson added, "We felt really bad when we gave up that touchdown and when we went to the sideline, I thought we had lost the game. We didn't fault the offense for not scoring enough points; we thought it was our fault for giving up the points."

Adderley said, "In my opinion, the final drive and the quarterback sneak was the greatest drive ever in the history of the NFL, especially considering the conditions. Bart was the master of a flawless drive on a frozen field and Ken Bowman had as much to do with the play being successful as Jerry Kramer."

At game's end, Adderley put his foot speed into high gear. "When I heard the crowd yelling and screaming, I sprinted to the locker room and was the first one to enter," he said. "Willie Davis said he wasn't far behind."

These many years later we now know why the Ice Bowl was such a nail-biter. "When the game was over, we told the guys the reason it took so long to win was because the baby had a hard time feeling the pat through all those clothes," Olive Jordan said.

Lombardi's Left Side looked really good in Super Bowl II and was even better than it appeared. The Green Bay defense sent an early message to Raiders' running back Hewritt Dixon to open the game. "He ran the first play and tried to go wide and Ray jacked him with a solid shot," Robinson said. The play provided a signature moment in a Hall of Fame career for Nitschke when he literally upended Oakland's running back. Robinson said, "Dixon hit the ground, got up, and in a real high voice said, 'they're hittin' they're hittin', they're really hittin' *hard* today.' I told him, 'You damn right we are, and if you come here again, we'll hit you some more.' Sometimes teams just don't hit, but we did."

Adderley said, "My assignment was to shut down Fred Biletnikoff, and after watching him on film I knew he wouldn't present the type of big play potential Otis Taylor did in Super Bowl I. Biletnikoff was not blessed with the size, speed and quickness of Taylor. I was concerned about having to tackle those tough running backs."

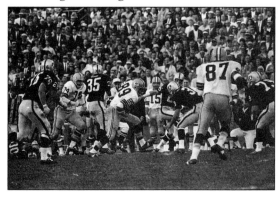

Lombardi's Left Side created a big turn over against Oakland in Super Bowl II. Adderley said, "When I hit Pete Banaszak, I yelled, 'Give it up,' and he fumbled just in front of our bench." Dave Robinson (89) picked up the fumble.

Two members of the left side combined for a big play when Adderley hit Oakland's Pete Banaszak to jar the ball loose. Robinson recovered and returned it six yards.

The first two Super Bowls bore a strong resemblance because they were close at the half and blowouts after intermission. Green Bay brought a 16–7 lead out of the locker room for the third quarter and took a 33–14 win back in at game's end.

Adderley said, "I had an easy day covering Biletnikoff, and I was in the right place at the right time in the fourth quarter. Quarterback Daryle Lamonica tried to hit Fred with a deep turn-in and I picked off the pass for an interception." The kid from P-Town made Super Bowl history on the return. "All I had to do was get by Lamonica and I did that with a slowdown move and a head slap. I saw my teammate Ron Kostelnik hustling downfield to throw a block for me, so I slowed up again so 'Kos' could knock Gene Upshaw on his butt and I jogged into the end zone."

Robinson said, "Herb went into the end zone and held the ball up, and he was one of the first guys to score and put the ball in the air." When Adderley crossed the goal line he became the first man in Super Bowl history to score a defensive touchdown, an accomplishment that stood by itself for ten years.

Following the contest, Oakland's classy quarterback paid high tribute to Lombardi's Left Side. Robinson said, "Daryle Lamonica and I talked for a long time after that game and he said, 'We couldn't get outside of your linebackers.' He was talking about Lee Roy and me, and then he said when they did try to pass, out drops were fifteen to twenty yards. He hadn't seen that in the AFL."

Lamonica saved the best for last, according to Robinson, "Daryle told me the coaches told him before the game not to throw to his right side, which is our left side. By the fourth quarter he hadn't thrown over there all day and thought, 'I'll try one.' Herb picked it."

Talent against talent, there has been speculation how the Packers stacked up against their Super Bowl opponents, Kansas City and Oakland. What if Lombardi would have had a year or two coaching either of the AFL teams? Some think the results may have been different.

To this day, no team has duplicated the great feat of winning three consecutive World Championships as the Packers did from 1965-67. Seven times since 1967 teams have won two consecutive titles, but no one has yet matched the accomplishment of the Dynasty.

Following the season, on February 11, 1968, in Philadelphia, the Ice Bowl good luck charm, Toni Adderley, was born.

Drifting Toward Obscurity

From the summit of greatness, Green Bay's Dynasty began to crumble February 28, 1968.

Lombardi resigned as head coach, named Phil Bengtson as his replacement and remained as general manager; the transition produced no winners. In Packers' history, it was "The Day the Music Died." The fabric of a great franchise began to tear from top to bottom and continued to do so for 21 years.

Although the term had not yet become part of standard football vocabulary, Phil Bengtson served as defensive coordinator for the great Lombardi teams. Some guys are great assistants but just can't cut it as head coaches. Bengtson was one of those. On some level the new coach must have immediately known he was not up to the task.

Packers Director of Public Relations Chuck Lane described Bengtson's expression at the introductory press conference saying, "Phil looked like he swallowed a porcupine backwards."

At the event Lombardi said, "Fortunately, I've had a very capable and loyal assistant. He has been with me from the beginning in Green Bay. I am positive that under his leadership and under his direction, Green Bay football will continue to be excellent, Green Bay football will continue to grow and Green Bay football will be everything you want it to be."

For one of the very few times, Packer employees did not believe Vince Lombardi. Lori Keck, correspondence secretary for the Great Coach, said, "From day one, I think we all knew Phil was in over his head, but we didn't talk about it much. Bengtson had no backbone at all."

Adderley said, "Bengtson was a top defensive coordinator in the NFL, but he couldn't handle the head coaching job. He didn't know too much about coaching the offense and he lost touch with the defensive guys as individuals."

According to Robinson, "Phil Bengtson was the best defensive coordinator I ever played for; I would walk through fire for Phil. I think it was the Peter Principle with him. He was great as a coordinator and should have stopped there, but was promoted one place beyond his capabilities."

Longtime *Milwaukee Sentinel* beat writer Bud Lea said of Lombardi's selection, "Phil Bengtson was a hell of a defensive coach; he was not a head coach and, hell, the players took full advantage of the situation."

Logically, Bengtson needed to be Lombardi's successor as head coach. Green Bay's defenses were consistently great throughout the Dynasty and

Bengtson was the man at the wheel. But he had a weak personality. Player Personnel Director Pat Peppler said, "Phil was second in command. We'd been successful and the defensive players really had confidence in him, so Vince was locked into that."

Bud Lea asked, "Do you think Lombardi really wanted a strong guy to follow him?"

Receivers coach Bob Schnelker spent two years as an assistant under Lombardi and three as offensive coordinator for Bengtson. Schnelker spoke volumes of Coach Phil's personality and coaching style when he said, "I don't really remember much about what Phil did on the practice field when he was head coach. His disposition was not meant for that job because he was so quiet and in the background all the time."

Lori Keck said, "We all knew Lombardi regretted his decision to give up coaching and he was miserable the entire year. He was miserable not only because he wasn't coaching, but because he saw the team being mishandled by Phil. He would not let himself undermine Phil's authority."

Using his Jesuit discipline, Lombardi did not interject himself in either coaching or player personnel decisions, even though he was general manager.

The robust, dynamic, confident Vince Lombardi was not in the Packers offices in 1968. Another Lombardi had taken his place. Keck said, "He was dejected. Resigned, literally and figuratively, is probably more accurate. He was visually different in '68. He would walk around the office with his shoulders slumped, his head down. Within the organization, he was aimless and meandering trying not to interfere with Bengtson. I prefer to remember Lombardi in any year except 1968."

Peppler agreed, "That year, Vince was aimless."

Lane said, "Lombardi scheduled golf games whenever possible to get away from watching what was happening with 'his team' in 1968. He would come out to the practice field and observe, but you could just see the 'steam' rising from the back of his neck. He never said anything to me, but he didn't have to."

Jack Koeppler, Lombardi's best friend, saw the former coach languish in his role as general manager only. "Oh, no question about," Koeppler said. "He didn't know what to do with himself. They went into training and we were on the golf course one day and he says, 'Man, what a blunder.' I said, 'Well, why don't you tell Phil you're going to take it back?' He said, 'I can't do that to him. I absolutely can't do that to him.'"

Koeppler said, "But, some of us who knew him could have given him some advice."

If Koeppler was correct and if Lombardi's friends would have convinced the coach to take his time to make his retirement announcement, he may not have left Green Bay. "All we had to do is say to him, 'Coach, you don't have to make an announcement now. Hell, wait to make the announcement. Make it in May or June.' None of us were bright enough to figure that out at that time and had we gotten him to delay making that decision, he'd have never retired. Because by the time they went to camp, he wanted to go."

From a player personnel standpoint, Lombardi did not want to obstruct Bengtson. Peppler said, "He bent over backwards not to interfere. Too far, I thought, which I told him one time."

If winning cures everything, losing exposes problems. Past success, intense pride and team camaraderie could not prevent major cracks from developing in the team's performance. A major contributor to the '65, '66 and '67 championship teams, place kicker Don Chandler decided to retire when Lombardi stepped down as head coach. Chandler's replacements scored 42 fewer points in '68 than Don had in '67. Under first year head coach Phil Bengtson, the offense scored 51 fewer points, the defense allowed 18 more and the team lost three more games than the previous year. It was over.

Green Bay's great offensive guard Gale Gillingham believed the Packers had one more championship in them if only Lombardi would have stayed on as coach for the 1968 season. "I think we would have walked through the whole frickin' thing; there ain't no doubt in my mind," said Gilly. "For one thing, we would have had a field goal kicker."

Robinson said, "Don Chandler would have stayed if Vince would have stayed. And if Don would have wanted to retire, Vince wouldn't have let him. Lombardi was something; he wouldn't even let guys retire if he wanted them to play."

For nine years, Lombardi had controlled the team and everyone knew it was his. It wasn't the team of his assistant coaches, of quarterback Bart Starr or defensive captain Willie Davis. It was the Old Man's. Truth be told, it was his organization. Bengtson was in a tough spot.

The once precise practices became flawed, mistakes were not corrected by the coaching staff and the players knew it. There was good news for Bengtson because he inherited a veteran team. There was equally bad news because shrewd veterans like Adderley, Robinson, Wood, Jordan, Skoronski, Dowler, Gregg, Starr and others instantly knew a decade of pursuing perfection had departed. The players knew it, Phil knew the players knew it and everybody knew Lombardi knew everything.

Schnelker said, "Phil was very quiet. He was a defensive guy and really didn't know that much about the offensive part of it. I was really the offensive coordinator under Phil, and we used to go round and round because he didn't understand things. We couldn't seem to match up when it came to game planning."

Except for occasionally yelling, "Grab, grab, grab. What the hell's going on out there," Lombardi didn't interact much with the defense and concentrated on the offense. When Bengtson became head coach he strayed away from the defense, his area of expertise. "Phil spent time with the offense," Robinson said. "Put it this way, he spent more time with the offense than Vince had with the defense."

There was an elephant in the room and occasionally on the practice field. Robinson said, "The players and Phil were leery Vince would step in, but to his credit, Vince never, never, never said a word; never got involved. We could see there were times Vince wanted to say something, but it was Phil's team and Vince let Phil run the team. Phil was nervous and guarded how he said things. I think he kept wondering if Vince was going to say something, and the ball players kept wondering if Vince would have done things the way Phil did. It was a very unnerving situation."

Bengtson became a different person when he got the head job in 1968.

The pressure of trying to succeed Lombardi would have been immense under any circumstances, but the burden became even more complicated in '69 when Bengtson added the responsibilities of general manager. According to Robinson, "Phil really went through a metamorphosis when he got both jobs after Vince left. Phil found out what it meant to be coach and general manager and I think that was just too much for him."

Lane said, "Yes, Phil changed, and I think it was the pressure that got to him. Phil Bengtson was a great human being, who was like your favorite uncle. 'Hail fellow, well met' and a father figure to many of the defensive players, but once put in the lead role, he had to be a disciplinarian, and he did not excel there and knew it. Phil started drinking a good bit, and the players 'tested' him whenever they could. He tried to gain the authority and respect that Lombardi earned, and it just never was to be."

The same can be said of Bengtson's relationship with the coaching staff. Packers' assistant coaches noticed an annoying dimension to his behavior; a personality change which was supposedly caused by the drinking. Phil was a considerably more difficult man to deal with during evening sessions following a break for supper.

According to Peppler, Bengtson's trouble with alcohol was an ongoing problem, "Lombardi semi-cured him of alcoholism. He told Phil, 'I know you have a drinking problem. If you can handle it you've got a job; if not …' Phil bitterly resented that; he really despised Lombardi because Vince treated him like he had to, like a little kid." In Lombardi's one-man outpatient alcoholism treatment program, Phil got better for a while and Ray Nitschke made a complete recovery.

As he was leaving Green Bay, Lombardi told the Packer Executive Board not to allow one person to hold both the head coach and general manager positions. They did not follow his advice and much to the detriment of the franchise, Bengtson was given the GM job, too.

In 1969, Lombardi was in Washington and the power void in Green Bay was beginning to swallow Green Bay's once dominant franchise. Bengtson's mousey leadership style inflicted mortal wounds and ended Adderley's career as a Packer.

It was Bengtson's role of disciplinarian that produced a major fracture in his relationship with his players, and it is possible to identify the day and event that caused him to lose his team. It was after dinner Friday, October 24, 1969, when Bengtson basically raided a Green Bay nightclub because he heard that players were hanging out there.

Adderley said, "Myself, Chuck Mercein and Phil VanderSea were in My Brother's Place. The bartender said, 'Phil just came in.' I thought he was talking about Phil VanderSea. When I looked up, Bengtson staggered in. He was bombed. He staggered in, so I saw him and dropped to my knees. I was near the back door, so I just crawled out. I stayed on my knees and crawled about twenty-five yards to get out of the place."

VanderSea said, "Coach Bengtson arrived with a police escort."

Adderley was easy to pick out of a crowd with his mutton chop side burns and spiffy wardrobe. Bengtson was reportedly so drunk his wife needed to tell him whom she saw, and she noticed the nattily-clad Adderley.

John Rowser said, "I was there that night but had just gotten out of the place. Phil's wife said that was 'the entertainer' she saw." She was referring to Adderley.

Adderley added, "When I got out in the parking lot to get to my car, two police officers were there waiting for any of the guys who came out the back door. He had already planned for that. One of the police officers was a good friend of mine and said, 'Herb, get the hell out of here. Bengtson's trying to get you guys and he's gonna lower the boom on you. Get the hell out of here as quick as you can.' So that's what I did, I bypassed and hauled ass."

Robinson said, "The seeds were sown for Phil Bengtson losing the team when he raided that bar. That started a downhill slide and it never stopped. After that, he lost the team, he lost everybody. After that, everybody thought, 'that rotten S.O.B.' After that, everybody criticized everything he did."

Lombardi had rules about players being in bars, but he didn't go hunting for his guys at Speeds Bar, the Tropics, Piccadilly or other popular places.

"Vince would never have gone down to My Brother's Place looking for ball players," Robinson said. "He knew players hung out there. After that raid, nobody would defend Phil. In fact, if you wanted to be kicked out of the locker room, all you had to do was defend Phil Bengtson."

The incident had no adverse effect on Adderley's play two days later in a game against the Atlanta Falcons. He picked off a pass and returned it 80 yards for a score. Packers' public address announcer Gary Knafelc informed the Lambeau Field crowd of 50,861 that Adderley had set an NFL record with his seventh return of an interception for a touchdown.

"I received a tremendous standing ovation the next time I went on the field," Adderley said. "I acknowledged the fans with a fist salute held high in the air."

Herb set an NFL record with his seventh return of an interception for a touchdown on this 80-yard sprint against Atlanta. Doug Hart (43) and fallen teammates Bob Brown (78) and Jim Weatherwax (73) cleared the way on October 26, 1969, at Lambeau Field.

Bengtson managed to parlay the episode at My Brother's Place into a succession of self-inflicted body blows as he continued to alienate the team. Adderley said, "We played Pittsburgh, in Pittsburgh, a week later and Bengtson let Mercein get dressed, go out on the field for pre-game warm ups and everything. When we came back in the locker room, Phil Bengtson came over to Mercein and said, 'We just cut you. Take your suit off, you gotta go.'"

VanderSea was miffed by Bengtson's double-jeopardy treatment of Mercien. "Chuck and I were found guilty by a player committee and fined $750 each," VanderSea said. "Chuck was then cut after warm-ups at the game in Pittsburgh. It was an unnecessary and heartless decision, especially because we were on the road, as well."

Adderley said, "When Bengtson did that, I said, 'Oh, my goodness.' A lot of guys said, 'I wonder what would have happened if he would have caught you? Would he have cut you like that?' Bengtson knew I was in My Brother's Place, but didn't have enough proof. It stuck in his brain; he started criticizing me, nit-pickin' in films, this and that. Finally it all broke after the '69 season."

The Steelers wobbled into the game with a 1-6 record and for the second consecutive week, Adderley was electric. He intercepted three passes, but one was not allowed because of an off-side penalty. The Packers needed everything Number 26 contributed, and Green Bay squeaked out a 38–34 win to improve their record to 6–2. Four of the next five games were losses and a once promising '69 season was lost.

Adderley said, "Bengtson set the Packers back years because of his inability to be a head coach and the trades he made. He sent me to Dallas, John Rowser, my backup, to Pittsburgh, Bob Long to Atlanta, Elijah Pitts, Lee Roy Caffey and Bob Hyland to Chicago, Marv Fleming to Miami and a few more I can't think of." Safety Tom Brown went to Lombardi's Washington team and Ron Kostelnik, a solid defensive tackle, was sent to Baltimore for a fourth-round draft choice. The pick was used to select placekicker Skip Butler, who never scored a point for the Packers.

"Phil was a strategic person as far as telling you how to play, but he wasn't used to running the whole organization," John Rowser said. "He may have been a good coach if they hadn't made him general manager and all that other stuff."

The loss of two veterans, Adderley and his backup, Rowser, weakened an aging secondary. Adderley had told Bengtson he would not play for him again, so Bengtson should have known he would be able to take the All-Pro's salary off the books and keep Rowser.

"I hadn't had a raise in three years with those All-Pro guys in front of me," Rowser said. "I wanted to play, and I asked for a little increase. I was only making $20,000 and I wanted $25,000. Bengtson didn't even talk to me about it. I said, 'I'm really serious. I need to get some kind of increase.' I guess they punished me by trading me to Pittsburgh. I went to the Steelers and they gave me $45,000. So, Green Bay wasted those three years of training me."

Trading away talent was only half of the problem. Bengtson was draft-challenged. Peppler said, "I'm inclined to think Phil was just a rotten judge of talent."

To verify Pepper's point, Bengtson had four No. 1 draft choices in three years and used them to select Rich Moore, Bill Lueck, Mike McCoy and

Rich McGeorge. Not one of them has made it to the Packers Hall of Fame.

Adderley said, "I asked Bengtson to trade me to a team near Philly, my hometown. That included the Eagles, Giants and Redskins. He knew the last team I wanted to play for was the Cowboys because of the racism and history of the Cowboys not paying guys equal to what other teams paid."

Bengtson sealed his fate in Green Bay when he sent Adderley to Dallas. Robinson said, "The problems for Phil built into a crescendo, and Herb Adderley's trade was the last straw."

The trade accelerated Green Bay's downward spiral and changed the fortunes of a Dallas franchise that had never won the "big one." Phil Bengtson deserves credit for ending the gag-a-thon in Big D.

"Yes, Bengtson supplied the missing piece of the puzzle; he didn't know that I would be the missing piece of the puzzle to get the Cowboys over the hump," Adderley said. "I helped them both on and off the field to get to two Super Bowls and the Cowboys beat the Packers for the first time in the regular season in '70, my first year in Dallas."

Peppler found Bengtson's treatment of the battle-tested Adderley particularly disrespectful. Peppler said, "Phil turned on Adderley, and Herb had played with a bad arm. Adderley had a torn bicep or something and Phil treated him like he was a piece of trash." Complications from that 1969 right bicep injury bothered Adderley the rest of his life.

"Frankly, I was delighted he got to go with Dallas," Peppler said. "I would have hated it if he would have gone to a team that was not a winning team. He didn't deserve that."

Rather than shipping Adderley out of town during the off-season or early in training camp, Bengtson waited. "He made it as difficult for me as possible by waiting until the week before the final exhibition game to trade me to the Cowboys," Adderley said. "I played the second half of the final preseason game against Joe Namath and the Jets. We opened the season against the Eagles in Philly and I was awarded the game ball for shutting down outstanding receivers Harold Jackson and Ben Hawkins."

As poorly as Bengtson functioned as head coach and general manager of the Packers, he nearly made it worse. He could have etched his name in Green Bay Packers' infamy with a move he contemplated making with legendary quarterback Bart Starr. Peppler said, "Bengtson wanted to get rid of Bart. In those last years, Bart was injured a lot and Phil had no respect for Starr at all."

The team took a great tumble during three years under Bengtson before he was relieved of his duties following the 1970 season. For Robinson and other holdovers from the Glory Years, accelerated deterioration would hit the franchise when a quirky, bizarre college coach was hired to succeed Bengtson. The new coach and general manager may have been responsible for one of the more accurate slogans in sports history: Devine happens.

Following a decade of unprecedented greatness with Vince Lombardi and his renowned players, it was agonizing to watch and smell the Green Bay Packers decompose.

Forward to The Past

As much as they could, Adderley and Robinson appreciated what they had in Green Bay.

The championships, individual honors, celebrity status and money transformed their lives from meager beginnings. They played for the best coach, during the best dynasty, for the best fans and the best organization.

At the same time, Birmingham was bombing, Watts was burning, racist cowards were belittling themselves while attempting to suppress others, Vietnam was raging and the Cold War moved the world to the brink of nuclear war.

There was a problem with Vince Lombardi's groundbreaking and championship use of black players. During his reign beginning in 1959, his historic racial advancement worked so well in Green Bay it received virtually no publicity. At times, life should imitate sports teams, at least the great ones.

Adderley said, "I have always felt that Lombardi used his position as head coach of the Packers to show the country and the world that black and white men could get along as human beings, teammates and become World Champions in an all-white city and remain friends 50 years later. It happened when the racial unrest was at its worst.

"He used his position to integrate housing in an all-white city. Because of him, the black players could live where they chose to live without any problems from the neighbors."

Adderley said, "Those things happened because of Lombardi's zero-tolerance for racism and discrimination. The man understood that he ended up in Green Bay not only to coach the team, but to bring change to the NFL and city of Green Bay."

For a championship athlete with a social conscience, winning is *not* the only thing. Winning without dignity is sitting in the back of the bus, drinking out of a separate water fountain or being told separate is equal. Winning without dignity is insulting.

———————

Herb Adderley was traded to the Cowboys, a team plagued with cliques and racism. Adderley said, "It was a culture-shocking change for me after being a part of what Lombardi did in Green Bay. I had to implement my discipline to keep from expressing my feelings. It was a situation where I had to use tact to ease the racial tension between the white and black players off the field and in the locker room. It was bad when I got there and just as bad when I left three years later."

Adderley was on an airplane flying to his new team in Dallas on September 3, 1970, the day Lombardi died and three days after the weekly issue of *Sports Illustrated* hit newsstands.

In an August 31, 1970, *SI* article entitled "Big Ifs in Big D," legendary sports writer Tex Maule offered the following comments about the Cowboys: "Most of the black players on the club are less than enchanted with Dallas and the attitude of its citizenry toward blacks. Don Perkins, who was a fine running back, retired while still in his prime and gave as one of the reasons his difficulty in finding suitable housing in Dallas. Another black player said, 'Sure, they cheer us when we're on field, but they can't see us off it. They make you feel like an animal act.' Moreover, a few of the white players have no love for the blacks and don't bother to conceal it ..."

Adderley had been traded into *that*.

More so than white players, the African-Americans in the NFL during the '60s and '70s talked to each other about various franchises and living conditions in different NFL cities. Dallas had a reputation. "I hated like hell to report to the Cowboys because of the terrible racial rumors that all of the black players in the league were aware of," Adderley said. "I had two strikes against me before I reported to the team because, one, I was a Packer who helped kick the Cowboys' asses and, two, the color of my skin."

Former Cowboys defensive end and author Pat Toomay said, "This is Dallas, Texas. This is 1970. It was an intolerant place, no doubt about it."

In 1965, NFL Commissioner Pete Rozelle interjected himself into a private racial matter in Green Bay. However, he was not willing to address racial problems in the Dallas locker room five years later. As first reported in *The Lombardi Legacy*, and later on HBO's documentary, "Lombardi," Rozelle wanted Vince Lombardi to stop a mixed race marriage between Packer's black defensive end Lionel Aldridge and his white fiancée, Vicky Wankier. Rozelle also took a pass on confronting the Cowboys' problems even though a national article published in *SI* under Tex Maule's respected name exposed the turmoil.

"Lombardi did in Green Bay what Rozelle should have done with the known racism in the NFL," Adderley said. "Tex Schramm and Rozelle worked together for the Rams before Schramm took over the Cowboys in 1960. Schramm was a powerful general manager because he ran the Cowboys, not the owner."

Adderley believes Commissioner Rozelle was aware of the racial problems in Dallas and chose not to act because of his history and friendship with the Cowboys GM. "Schramm pushed for Rozelle to be the Commissioner after Bert Bell passed and that is the reason Rozelle ignored the racism six years after meddling in the personal lives of Lionel and Vicky. Rozelle's response to the racism going on within the NFL, the unwritten quota system of five or less black players, meant he went along with the shit and never did a damn thing about it."

Historically, the Cowboys, Washington Redskins and St. Louis Cardinals were the most undesirable teams for African American players. The Redskins made an abrupt about-face when Lombardi took over in 1969.

Just as he coached, direct and fundamental, Lombardi addressed and prevented racial or ethnic issues in Green Bay. Cowboys head coach Tom Landry, cerebral and complex, used an approach that can be described as selective apathy and had persistent racial problems on his teams. In sharp contrast to Green Bay, notable black Cowboy players encountered racial difficulties both on the team and in the greater Dallas Metroplex. The franchise eventually known as "America's Team" chose not to deal with America's problem.

Mel Renfro joined the Cowboys in 1964 and said, "In the early years it was very tense. There were some (white) players on our team who were from Alabama; that's just the way they were. We realized that and we just dealt with it."

It never got tense in Green Bay because Lombardi dealt with *it*.

No racial problems were caused by Southern whites on the 1959 Packers team. The list included Bart Starr from Alabama, Louisiana's Jimmy Taylor, Paul Hornung from Kentucky and Arkansas' Dave "Hawg" Hanner. No fewer than eight players on Lombardi's first roster had Texas ties: Jesse Whittenton, Bobby Dillon, John Symank, Hank Gremminger, Bill Forester, Don McIlhenny, Forrest Gregg and Ken Beck.

Dallas defensive back Cornell Green, another black player, said of the racial tension, "I always thought there was some of that on the team. Blacks lived on one side of town and the white kids lived on the other side of town. We had to go twice as far to practice as they did."

Unlike the Green Bay Packers with Lombardi in charge, the Cowboys did little or nothing to improve living conditions for the black players.

Renfro took matters into his own hands and confronted the issue directly. He said, "When I first came to Dallas, Coach Landry directed me to a part of town to live where all the black players were living, in the black part of town. I had some problems with housing and what not. A big developer refused to rent to me and it got pretty nasty in court. I filed a civil rights lawsuit and won."

Coach Tom lived in a nice house in a nice neighborhood that was not located on "the other side of town."

Former Cowboys tight end and *North Dallas Forty* author Pete Gent said, "We trained in California because there was no place in Texas where black and white guys could stay in the same room."

Dallas defensive back Mark Washington said, "In the early '70s when I got to Dallas, it's not like we hung out with each other. To me there was an apparent chasm between some of the white players and the black players. We didn't go over to each others' houses for dinner; we didn't socialize after the games and all that sort of stuff. It wasn't there. We just came together and played football is what it amounted to."

Adderley's Dallas teammate Toomay said, "Herb's soothing presence in the locker room defused racial tensions that had plagued the team for years." Toomay is white.

Calvin Hill, the exceptional Cowboys running back from Yale, said, "If there was a racial divide, Herb as much as anybody helped that become less of a factor."

In addition to racial problems, the Dallas Cowboys were lacking the heart of a champion.

The 'Boys lost four consecutive league championship games, including two bitter defeats at the hands of Green Bay in 1966 and '67. Dallas also lost Super Bowl V to Baltimore, before finally claiming the title in 1971. Three of Green Bay's proven champions, Adderley, Forrest Gregg and Lee Roy Caffey, just happened to be a part of the club when Dallas won it all.

According to Hill, "We were always 'next year's champions' and had lost some crucial games against the Packers and back-to-back games against Cleveland. We were at a crossroads. We were a great team and just couldn't get over the hump. All of a sudden Herb comes and we get over the hump."

More to the point, Toomay said, "In an attempt to incorporate the Lombardi mystique, since it was impossible to defeat it, Cowboy General Manager Tex Schramm acquired three of the Packers' aging veterans. Uncharacteristically, Schramm, in making this move, overrode the strong objections of his coach, who reportedly wanted nothing to do with former Packers. One thing was certain, if Herb was a product of Lombardi, then Lombardi the man couldn't be as bleak as I'd imagined."

Here is a simple fact: the Cowboys were unable to win a world championship until players from the Green Bay Dynasty were added to the Dallas team, and Landry didn't want them.

In Adderley's first year, 1970, the Cowboys went to their first Super Bowl and won it in his second.

How much Landry resented Schramm's insistence on using former Packers, we do not know. It may have been substantial. Perhaps Landry was coaching against himself as much as against Lombardi. We know how many times Vince beat Tom, but unknown is the number of times Landry beat Landry.

Green Bay's great head coach had the Cowboys' number and Mel Renfro knew it. Nicknamed "Brother 'Fro" by Adderley, Mel was Herb's roommate in Dallas. Renfro said, "The Packers would always beat us and we were a better football team, but there was something about them. Coach Landry coached with Vince. He knew Vince and knew Vince knew how to win."

Lombardi's Packers attained mythic status in the '60s. Hill recounted a surreal experience from his rookie year of 1969. "We used to play the Packers in a pre-season game every year in the Cotton Bowl. I remember walking out of the locker room and walking down the concourse to the field. I saw Bart Starr, Herb and Willie Wood in their uniforms; they looked like gods. It almost looked like there was an aura around their helmets; that's who they were."

America's Team was obsessed with the club from Titletown.

Adderley said, "The first thing I noticed when I walked into the locker room in Dallas was a bulletin board with a message stating, 'The Packers owe us blood, flesh and money.' 'Blood' was written with red finger nail polish. It didn't take me too long to realize the Cowboys and Landry hated the Packers. Landry proved it to me my final year because of the way he treated me for personal reasons and his hate for the Packers and me."

Green Bay's ability to win close championship games was the hallmark of Lombardi's greatness. In big, tight games the Cowboys played just well enough to lose; they were in need of a heart transplant.

Hill is an Ivy Leaguer, usually the smartest guy in the room and not easily impressed. "The first day Herb was in our meeting, Tom Landry introduced him and Herb stood up," Hill said. "He was like a movie star; he was wearing a Super Bowl ring. I was saying, 'Wow, I'm on the same team as *Herb Adderley.*' That was the first time I'd seen a Super Bowl ring and that was kind of cool. He was the first World Champion I knew."

Apparently, Coach Tom Landry was not nearly as impressed with the five-time World Champion and didn't think he could learn anything from Adderley's experience in Green Bay. Adderley said, "I was never asked about the defenses or anything else about the Packers. Landry never asked my opinion about anything."

The Dallas coach knew everything and had second place trophies to prove it.

The highly-respected Hill said, "Herb came the year we went to our first Super Bowl, the year we got over the hump. In addition to his play, he brought an attitude. He was a very charismatic and positive guy who *had won.* I don't think any team has dominated a decade like the Packers did in the Sixties.

Herb was a Hall of Fame part of that. When he came to us, he brought that winning persona. He was a great team guy."

Adderley's impact on Dallas' black players was profound, immediate and palpable. One of Adderley's biggest admirers, defensive back Mark Washington, said, "I say this from a black player's standpoint: When Herb came to the Cowboys, he brought mutton chop side burns. Guys didn't have those things."

Adderley stretched the parameters for black players on a Texas team plagued with a few influential rednecks. In the Dallas Cowboys' culture, Adderley tried to make it OK for blacks to be black, on the same level as whites who were being white. It was cowboy boots, "just a pinch between the cheek and gum," pickup trucks and "Cotton Eyed Joe" for some; mutton chops, Afros, beards and Fu Manchus for others. The times were a changin'.

One morning during Adderley's first training camp, Mel Renfro was given a glimpse of Adderley's mindset. Renfro said, "On our way to the practice field, we saw some hawks flying up near the mountains. Herb said something I never forgot, 'Brother 'Fro look, those hawks flying around up there are looking for something to kill.' He was just that kind of a guy; he was an attack guy. He was a go-after-it guy, a win guy and a team guy."

The entire Cowboys team felt the championship sting of Adderley on November 16, 1970. In front of a national audience on Monday Night Football, the Dallas Cowboys stunk. With the team's former quarterback, Dandy Don Meredith, calling the game on ABC television, the Cotton Bowl crowd began chanting for him to come out of the booth and lead the team. The St. Louis Cardinals thrashed Dallas, 38–0. Most disturbing to Adderley was the ability of his new team to quit, and the club's record fell to a mediocre 5–4.

After the game, a team leader emerged when all hell broke loose from inside a Number 26 jersey.

According to Renfro, "Our guys were sitting around with their heads down and Herb just exploded. He said, 'What in the hell is wrong with you guys? You act like a miserable bunch of losers.' The whole locker room got a wakeup call. Nobody had ever taken that approach before because Landry was so laid back as far as his emotions were concerned. Herb just tore into us and it got our attention. He brought that Lombardi ambiance of 'no crap,' 'let's get it done.' He was very tough-minded."

A new heart had been transplanted from Green Bay to Dallas and the Cowboys were being taught how to win.

During the blowout loss Adderley tried to rally the troops, but his teammates spit the bit. "For the first time, I started talking to the guys on the field," Adderley said. "I was saying things like 'let's not give up, we have to keep hustling every play. Let's go, we have to stop the run!' I kept repeating the same things the entire second half. The guys heard me but they didn't respond. On some of the plays I was the only one in the secondary chasing Cardinals running back MacArthur Lane."

The great cornerback had never been associated with quitters in Green Bay and couldn't stomach the experience in Dallas. The locker room rant raised the dead. "I yelled out, 'Get your heads up you bunch of losers!' I also told them that *was not* the type of effort they gave when they played against the Packers," Adderley said. "I told them our defense was as good as or better than any in the NFL and we needed to prove it in the final five games."

Adderley's detonation worked and the team reeled off five straight wins to finish 10-4, earned a place in the playoffs and found their emotional leader following the Monday night fiasco.

"I continued giving pep talks during the week at practice, saying over and over again that we had the best defense in the NFL," Adderley said. "I did this every week right up to and after losing Super Bowl V."

Adderley supplied what Tom Landry was innately incapable of providing: genuine emotion.

"Herb was a catalyst on a team that needed a catalyst," said Toomay. "His presence in the locker room and everywhere else was tremendous and it pushed the team over."

Running back Duane Thomas said, "Herb was the spirit of the team."

According to Adderley, "Landry, the other coaches and all of the guys noticed that I was speaking out and backing it up with my performance on the field. It helped the team to win the final five games including beating the Packers for the first time in the regular season. My response to the defense not giving 100 percent in the 38–0 game resulted in the real Doomsday Defense showing up and shutting down the final five teams."

Super Bowl V was the continuation of Cowboy teams losing winnable big games, and an old symptom returned. Early in the second quarter, Colts quarterback Johnny Unitas tossed a poorly thrown ball to wide receiver Eddie Hinton that bounced off Hinton's hands, was then tipped by Renfro and ended in the hands of Baltimore tight end John Mackey. "After Mackey caught the ball, the other three d-backs started jumping up and down and made no attempt to chase Mackey," Adderely said. "They were hoping to get a flag thrown to nullify the play because the ball was tipped. They quit on the play and that is what most of the team did in the 38–0 ass-kicking Monday night game." Mackey scored on a 75-yard play as Baltimore won 16–13 when kicker Jim O'Brien hit a 32-yard field goal with five seconds left in the game.

Dallas made it to the Super Bowl in each of Adderley's first two years with the team, '70 and '71. "The Cowboys never went to the Super Bowl until Herb got there," Hill said. "We went to the Super Bowl, then went again the next year and won it. To me, it doesn't happen without Herb Adderley."

Wide receiver Margene Adkins spent the 1970 and '71 seasons in Dallas and said, "One thing about Tom Landry, he could never talk to his guys. At lunch break we'd be in the locker room laying on the floor and he would come walking through and you could tell he wanted to stop and kind of hold a conversation with us, but he never would do it."

Tom Landry may have become the first coach to go undefeated if the game had been played by robots.

Relegated to working with humans, he tried to get them to obey.

The Packers' outstanding flanker Boyd Dowler won five championships with Lombardi. He played in every game the Old Man coached in Green Bay and spent over 40 years in the NFL as a player, assistant coach and scout. Dowler compared his coach with anybody else he encountered. "Lombardi was there to motivate; before the game, and he'd make his half-time talk. Vince was best at it because Vince motivated better than anybody. That's the difference: the motivational skill."

Adderley said, "I never did any talking during the week or before games to motivate my Green Bay teammates. Between Lombardi and some of the guys who did talk, sometimes we had too much motivation."

Lombardi and Landry's view of inspiration were completely opposite according to Adderley. "Landry said many times that it wasn't his job to motivate players because real pros motivate themselves. Yeah, that's true, but it sure as hell has been proven that motivation from your coach helps teams to win," Adderley said. "Landry, in my opinion, didn't know what to say to motivate the team; if he did, he didn't do it during my three years there."

America's greatest coaches and managers held a view about motivation that was contrary to Landry's. To varying degrees, Lombardi, Knute Rockne, Red Auerbach, Phil Jackson, John Wooden, Bob Knight, Casey Stengel, Earl Weaver and others had dynamic personalities capable of generating enthusiasm.

The leadership void in Dallas was filled when Adderley showed up. "I saw and felt they needed a guy who was an example on the field—a winner," Adderley said. "They needed someone to take the lead and speak up during the week at practice, in the meetings and before the games. I did this on my own my first year there and Landry never said that it was a good thing or bad thing; however, he did appoint me one of the captains for a reason."

Adderley's emotional leadership could have complemented Landry's icy, stoic, standoffish personality and sustained a prolonged domination by Dallas. Apparently, Coach Tom was not ready to win championships if it meant sharing part of the leadership stage with anyone, least of all a Lombardi man.

Forrest Gregg, who joined the Cowboys in 1971, believes the former

Packers made a difference for a Dallas franchise that couldn't win the big one. "I'd like to think so. I know one thing, Herb was the starting cornerback and attitude about winning was a factor. Cowboys players tell me, 'Having you guys on that team made a difference. Because we decided we wanted to win now instead of wait 'til next year.' The play of Bob Lilly, Mel Renfro, Roger Staubach and Duane Thomas was good, but we made a difference, I think."

The differences between Lombardi and Landry are many and could not be clearer than in the area of race relations. In his first significant personnel move at Green Bay, Lombardi traded for Emlen Tunnell. The addition of Tunnell to Green Bay's 1959 roster was one of many messages the Packers' coach sent to anyone who bothered to notice. Tunnell was a winner, a leader and black. He was coveted by Lombardi.

Over a decade later, Tom Landry was handed a 1970's version of Tunnell in the person of Adderley and mangled the opportunity. Adderley was a winner, a leader and black. He was loathed by Landry.

As if in a time warp to the past, Adderley saw the black and white issues for what they were when he joined his new team in Dallas. "Racism was a part of some of the white players' agenda," he said. "They didn't want to be associated with the black players, nor did they want black players as teammates."

Calvin Hill, who is among the classiest, most intelligent and honorable men to wear a Cowboys uniform, spent half of his 12-year career as a running back in Dallas. Each week the statistical leaders in the NFL were posted on a bulletin board in the team's locker room. On one occasion, someone on the Cowboys' squad took it upon himself to write the word "nigger" on top of the page listing the rushing leaders. There was an arrow from the n-word to the name of the person who held down the top spot on the list as the league leader, Hill.

"I remember that," Hill said. "There was a bulletin board as you walked in the practice facility. I didn't see it and then Billy Parks or someone brought my attention to it; I saw it. I was offended by it. It hurt."

Ever the consummate gentleman, Hill said, "You feel sorry for the person who wrote it."

Adderley said, "Whoever did it used a red Sharpie pen and used all caps, including the arrow pointed at Calvin's name. It offended and hurt all of the black guys and all of us didn't feel sorry for the racist who insulted us. Calvin was a divinity major and accepted it differently than others of us."

The incident was apparently no big deal to the Dallas head coach. Adderley said, "Landry told us in the meeting after he read the insult, 'someone from outside came in and wrote the insult.' We knew that it was an attempted cover up, but didn't comment on his lie. Believing that would be like believing the leadership in Pakistan didn't know that bin Laden was hiding out there."

It is beyond comprehension that such a thing would have occurred in Lombardi's Green Bay. The Great Coach, his assistants and players prevented, eliminated and dealt with such problems.

"With the Green Bay team and Coach Lombardi, from what I understand, if there were somebody who would write 'nigger' on anything, Lombardi would figure out who it was and get rid of them," said Hill.

That is fact, not theory.

"I can think of one guy who had a problem, a real serious problem, and Vince traded him out of Green Bay," Robinson said. "I don't want to mention the player's name, but Vince got something for him and got him off the team."

In a pointed accusation, Adderley said, "Tom Landry and Tex Schramm knew what was going on in Dallas and were a part of it for not stopping it. The two of them made the decisions to keep a less talented white player and cut the more talented black player. That racial tactic told me Landry didn't put his best players on the field because of the color of their skin. This stuff was the exact opposite of Lombardi's policy of putting the best players on the field and not judging anyone by the color of their skin."

The February 26, 2012, fatal shooting of Trayvon Martin in Sanford, Florida, raised echoes from the past. In the aftermath of the killing, investigations revealed the possible use of a racial slur that had been a favorite of a certain Dallas running back.

Adderley said, "The funky word 'coon' has surfaced with the mess about the killing in Florida. Allegedly, the shooter referred to the 17-year-old slain kid as a 'f***in' coon.' That word alerted my memory back to a white player referring to Bob Hayes as a 'coon' in front of the entire team before one of those long Landry film sessions. The guy waited until all of the other guys were in the room before he entered and stood in front of all of us who were seated at the time, reached into his shirt pocket and pulled out a bone that looked like a chicken wishbone. He then called Hayes' name out and asked Bob if he knew what 'this' is, referring to the bone." The apparent meaning was it was a 'coon bone.'

"Hayes stared the guy down and did not respond," Adderley said. "There was complete silence until Landry entered the room. The assistant coaches were in the room at the time and none of them said a word."

Despite the bigotry, Adderley became the fourth black starting player on Landry's defense, joining Jethroe Pugh, Mel Renfro and Cornell Green. Three years earlier in Green Bay, six black defensive starters, Davis, Aldridge, Robinson, Adderley, Jeter and Wood, contributed greatly to Lombardi's fifth and final World Championship.

Toomay said, "Herb, from the beginning, was someone special to me. He was disarmingly open and friendly — unusual for a veteran of his stature, who normally wouldn't pass the time of day with an obscure rookie. On more than one occasion, Herb joined me for a meal and, until he arranged for his own transportation, often rode with me to practice."

Toomay added, "Everybody was enthusiastic about him. A consummate professional, sporting a glittering Packer Super Bowl ring, Herb, who is black, was a magnetic figure in the locker room, for both black and white alike. 'Peace, love and happiness' was how he concluded nearly every exchange. 'Brother A' was what he came to be called."

When Bengtson traded Adderley, the Cowboys' Doomsday Defense was handed the missing piece. Right cornerback Mel Renfro said, "Before Herb got there, that left cornerback position was a problem for us. I would hardly ever get any passes thrown at me because they were attacking the other side effectively. When Herb got there, that stopped." In 1970, Adderley's initial year in Dallas, the Cowboys beat Green Bay for the first time in regular season play. In the game, Bart Starr completed nine of 21 attempts for 83 yards, no touchdowns and one interception against a revamped Dallas secondary. That was Green Bay's total aerial game as the franchises were moving in opposite directions.

Deja vu. Remember when Adderley took over the left corner in Green Bay and Hank Gremminger was moved to safety? It made a championship team even stronger.

Adderley's addition in Dallas had a similar effect. Left cornerback Cornell Green moved to strong safety and made the Cowboys' deep defenders among the league's best. Green said of Adderley's contribution, "We were a struggling team, a good team, but we never got the big one until Herb came. Herb knew what it was all about. We took his lead. He made a big impact."

Toomay's praise for Adderley is boundless. "On the field, Herb was equally impressive. Even at the age of 31, the future Hall of Famer moved with the grace of a gazelle. He could hang

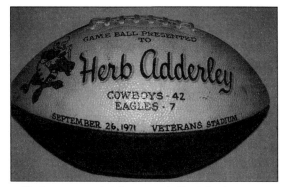

Adderley was awarded three game balls while playing for the Cowboys, and head coach Tom Landry did not congratulate him on any of the three.

in the air like Dr. J. His instincts were impeccable. Predictably, however, his technique was in conflict with the technique required of a cornerback to play Landry's Flex defense."

Toomay described Adderley's contributions as a first year Cowboy as "mighty." Dallas made it to Super Bowl V, losing 16–13 to Baltimore when Colts rookie kicker Jim O'Brien hit a 32-yard field goal with five seconds on the clock.

Unlike Lombardi's Green Bay, significant racial splits, rifts and sniping remained in Big D. Black running back Duane Thomas and white linebacker Steve Kiner of Tennessee became roommates in 1970 and drew the ire of a select few players. Thomas said, "We had an apartment together." According to Thomas, one of the prominent white, starting linebackers asked Kiner, "What are you doing rooming with this nigger?" To which Thomas asked, "Who is he talking about?"

The demeaning slur better described the person asking the question than the African-American running back at whom it was aimed.

Midway into the '71 season, Dallas signed an aged and seasoned former Packer, Forrest Gregg, as insurance for the offensive line. On a Cowboys team divided along racial lines, a message of championship unity was delivered by Adderley and Gregg. Calvin Hill said, "The first time Forrest came in the locker room and Herb saw him, they hugged one another. It was the kind of hug that indicated these guys had something besides being on the same team. That was very eye opening for me. Forrest was a Southern white guy from Dallas …"

Not everyone got the message.

It is a God-given right to remain ignorant, and at least one member of the Cowboys exercised that right during the run up to Super Bowl VI. Symptomatic of a divided team, a significant racial incident occurred when a white Dallas running back threw a drink on black backup wide receiver Margene Adkins. The episode took place while members of the team were experiencing Bourbon Street in New Orleans. Nothing confrontational happened immediately following the episode, but trouble was festering. In the locker room later in the week, Adkins and the other player got into a fist fight. Margene won a unanimous decision but paid dearly for his momentary win.

Without an audience with Landry, no meeting at all, Adkins was cut from the team and sent home. The young receiver did not get a Super Bowl VI ring or paycheck.

"That type of Landry justice was nothing new," Duane Thomas said.

With former Packer Herb Adderley serving as co-captain, the Cowboys overcame the off-field squabble and won Super Bowl VI in convincing fashion. Doomsday came of age and smothered Miami in a 24–3 yawner.

"If Herb hadn't come to us when he did, we don't go to any Super Bowls, period. It's that simple," said defensive back Mark Washington. "That's the kind of effect he had on our team; there was nobody on the team who was more positive."

Duane Thomas agreed, "Absolutely. Herb was the spiritual component that you have to have on the field."

Defensive back Cornell Green said it was Adderley who pushed Dallas over the top, not the other two former Packers, Lee Roy Caffey or Forrest Gregg. Green said, "Lee Roy and the other one were not as big a part of the team as Herb was."

Whereas Lombardi's Green Bay teams built championship upon championship, it was one and done for Dallas.

Toomay said, "The following season, as younger players began to develop enough to step in, things changed. Abruptly, for Herb, it got ugly."

Intellectual Ruins

Sitting atop the football world, optimism was running high when Dallas reported to Thousand Oaks, California, for training camp in 1972.

One of Adderley's greatest heroes was conducting a basketball camp at the same college that housed the reigning NFL champions. Adderley said, "I walked over to the great John Wooden one afternoon and said, 'I just want to say hello, and you are a winner!'"

The Wizard of Westwood said, "Herb, you are a winner, too, and it's also a pleasure meeting you."

It didn't take Coach Wooden forty seconds to compliment Adderley on being a winner. Tex Schramm and Tom Landry didn't get around to it in three years.

Like the truly great coaches, Wooden put a jolt into his players. "He is right up there, in my opinion, with Lombardi and Red Auerbach as the greatest coaches ever," Adderley said. "John Wooden was one of the best motivators in the history of sports."

It should have been the best of times in Cowboys training camp. Instead, Landry refused to let the optimism penetrate his controlling nature. He wore a whistle around his neck and a shirt with an inscription that said "Head Coach." Some contend it should have read "Head Case."

Perhaps a March, 15, 2011, article by Dr. Peter Milhado regarding obsessive personality sheds light on Landry's behavior: "The need to control is easily recognized by others. A refusal to delegate, suspiciousness, evasiveness, hoarding, moral superiority, emotional isolation, and mistrusting warmth and love, can all be personality characteristics. No matter how bright, the obsessive is slow to recognize feelings—they think rather than feel."

One has to wonder if Landry would have rather lost Super Bowl VI without Adderley than win it with him. If Pat Toomey is correct in his belief that Landry felt the Lombardi guys were forced on him by Schramm, Coach Tom may have spent the off-season fixating on the win. Several Dallas players unequivocally believe Adderley was *the* reason the Cowboys won it all in '71. For an ultra-control person like Landry, he may have felt the Super Bowl win was not really his, and without a Vince Lombardi player, he would not have been able to capture the crown.

Signs of trouble appeared immediately when the team reported to camp in Thousand Oaks. "I was appointed one of the captains in '71 and the first thing Landry did in training camp in '72 was demote me," Adderley said. "In front of the team he announced he was going back to the original captains and I was demoted and Lee Roy Jordan was promoted in my spot."

Why mess with a team chemistry that won it all?

Adderley believes Landry had a vendetta against him and a plan to do him in.

"The next morning the whole team had to go through a conditioning course that included ten stations of weight lifting," Adderley said. "At each one of those stations we had to do five repetitions of x-amount of weight over our heads, go to the next stop and repeat the same thing with the weight getting heavier each time. After completing the weight lifting, we had to run 100 yards up the field and 100 yards back. This had to be done under a time set by Landry."

Adderley said, "No one had a coach go from station to station to make sure there was no cheating on the number of repetitions. The guys who lived in Dallas had no problem making the time because they practiced the course during the off-season. The guys who didn't live there were not informed about the conditioning/weight lifting course, so none of us finished under the allotted time."

There was one little wrinkle for Adderley. "Landry came over to me before I started and said he was going to every station with me to make sure I did all of the repetitions. I struggled with the lifting because of the bad bicep and I didn't really know how to lift. I didn't finish within the set time, and we had to run four laps after practice every day until we made the laps in a certain amount of time."

Adderley doesn't back down from a fight, even when it's not fair. "I was in great shape and knew I could run the laps within the time, so the first two days I paced myself to see how fast I had to run to make the time. The third day I ran the course almost as fast as Bob Hayes, who ran the anchor leg on the 440 relay team in the '68 Olympics. I did it to prove to Landry and the guys that I was in as good a shape as anyone."

Adderley's trust for the head coach was shot. "Landry's motive was to justify demoting me as captain and showing the team I wasn't a good leader because I didn't report to camp in good shape." Coach Tom's tactics blew up in his face when Adderley showed everybody he was a leader who was in good physical condition. Adderley said, "In order to encourage the guys who were struggling with the laps, I continued to run with them every day until they met Landry's requirements."

The collision between Landry and Adderley as people and football men had begun, but the wreckage was far from over.

Of the Dallas coach, Pat Toomay said, "The schemes Tom devised to accomplish his task were labyrinthine. While Lombardi's defense might be described as 'Tackle the man with the ball,' Landry's Flex defense required recognition of offensive patterns, internalization of the probable outcomes of those patterns and a corresponding reaction. Locating the football came only after following the branches of his logic tree—a counterintuitive approach that could take years to master."

The complicated system came complete with a superior being armed with unchallenged control, power and a film projector to program his robots. Mark Washington said, "Tom was the person with the projector, the man with the clicker running the film back and forth. You were at his mercy. A lot of guys had problems with film because they were so afraid of what he was going to pick out."

Once a week Landry was a tour guide in hell.

"In Dallas, watching game films was a three-hour marathon, with all players and staff present, unlike other teams, who split off into position groups to watch films," Toomay explained. "During these sessions, Landry himself ran the projector, going over the performance of every player on every play. If you'd had a bad game, watching game films could be an excruciating experience. Some players, suspecting they were in for it, took barbiturates to get through the sessions. Their armpit sweat rings would meet across their chests."

Mark Washington said, "One of the things you figured out early in the program, when Tom was watching the film, he was like God. He would pick out anything he wanted."

The misplaced and indiscriminant Landry spotlight found Adderley in a '71 film session following a game against the Redskins. A running play went to the weak side, across the field from Adderley in the area of Cliff Harris. Like many defensive coaches, Landry emphasized stopping the play at the "point of attack." Harris was at the point of attack and got blindsided. "Charley Taylor was one of the best blockers ever and he came over and cracked back on Cliff Harris," Mark Washington said. "He caught Cliff in a (bad) situation that was just perfect. It was one of the worst shots I'd ever seen; I don't know how he didn't break Cliff's jaw. I would never want to be on the receiving end of something like that. Charlie Harraway goes for a touchdown on a fifty- or sixty-yard run and Tom is looking at Herb on the other side and saying Herb was not pursuing or something (to that effect). I'm thinking, 'Wait a minute, this is what happened here, why is Landry talking about that over there?' The guy went through a hole on the other side of the field away from Herb. That's when I first saw that something kind of strange was going on."

Cowboys head coach Tom Landry
Photo courtesy of *AP Images*

The problem for really bright people—and Landry was really bright—is that they sometimes fail to credit those around them for having at least some intelligence. Did Landry think no one would notice he didn't emphasize what happened to Cliff Harris at the "point of attack"?

"Landry did not get on the players on the side of the field where the action was," Adderley said. "He was trying everything he could to make me look bad during the film sessions even though he was making a fool of himself because of his vendetta against me."

Coach Tom's arbitrary brandishing of power went way back. Pat Summerall played for the Giants in the 1950s when Landry was an assistant and said, "You never knew where you stood with Landry." Pete Gent, who played for Dallas from 1964 through '68, agreed. "No, never; Landry didn't know. I quit the Cowboys. I got my five years in and quit. I couldn't deal with that shit anymore; it was crazy and it was making me crazy."

Landry had a code word for instincts: "clueing." It also meant "guessing" to the Dallas coach, and that is what he thought of Adderley's style of play.

Toomay said, "In one session during the '72 season, the refrain rang like a sour mantra: 'Herb, you're clueing again.' What he really meant to say was that Adderley, again, was guessing."

Zeroing in on Adderley, Landry repeated, "Herb, you're clueing again!" According to Pat Toomay, "The anger in Tom's voice, as the meeting progressed, escalated out of all proportion, and finally Herb rose to defend himself. It was an unprecedented moment for the team. No player had ever challenged the coach."

In Adderley's estimation, a double sin had been committed in Coach Tom's world. A player stood up to him and the player was black.

Renfro said, "We knew never to question Landry. Whether we knew he was right or wrong, we never questioned it; we just accepted it. Herb questioned him right there in the meeting. Landry got real tense and things just didn't seem to be the same after that."

The word "fair" is one of the most frequently used terms to describe Lombardi, and Adderley saw something very different from the head man in Dallas. By the time Adderley and Landry locked horns, the great cornerback had won six World Championships and five of them occurred when he was a Packer.

Lombardi wanted his players to be disciplined; Landry wanted them to be obedient.

"There was no on-the-field communication with the Cowboys because they were taught to play strictly by the book, a book that Landry put together," Adderley said. "Lombardi gave us the freedom to make on-the-field adjustments and the only way to do it was by communicating. That was one of our strongest assets on The Left Side in Green Bay."

Adderley occupies a unique position of having been a critical player on World Championship teams with both the Packers and Cowboys. "In Green Bay, I never worried about Dave Robinson or Ray Nitschke being where the defense called for them to be. It made my job easier," Adderley said. "The linebackers in Dallas made it tough on me because I had to cover my man short, deep, inside and outside, not knowing where my help was going to be."

In an apparent double standard, Landry accused Adderley of clueing and the white linebackers of doing something else.

"The white guys who made mistakes, Landry would ask them if they were 'false keying' and their answer was always yes. I was accused of clueing, but being in the right place. The white guys were out of position a lot of times and they got away with it," Adderley said. "The m\iddle linebacker and weak side guy false keyed many times during every game trying to make a big play. That shit happened so much until I never depended on them to get back in the hook or flat area to help me. I know the difference between what happened in Green Bay and Dallas. Landry used the word 'clueing' rather than 'intelligence.' There is a difference."

One Dallas linebacker paid a steep price for not heeding Adderley's on-field communication. "Charley Taylor of the Redskins was the best blocking wide receiver in the game along with the great Paul Warfield," Adderley said. "I told weak-side linebacker Chuck Howley before a game to listen to me for the devastating crack back block that Taylor was known for. He ignored my advice and Taylor ended Chuck Howley's career. Dave Robinson always listened to my advice, especially when we played against Taylor, Warfield or any other receiver cracking back on the linebacker."

Zeke Bratkowski ran more plays against Adderley than any quarterback because he directed Green Bay's scout team during preparation for the upcoming game. Green Bay's backup signal caller repeatedly saw a combination of athletic skill and football intelligence in Adderley's play. "From his cornerback position Herb could read the formation, and he was good at it," Bratkowski said. "Everything started from the formation and his ability to recognize it. So he anticipated certain routes. All of those things made him a great cornerback."

Adderley said, "When Landry made an example out of me, even though I was right, it scared the shit out of all the black players. They knew if they were right about something and were accused of being wrong, they had to accept it and keep their mouths shut. This caused guys to play scared because of the fear of making a mistake and getting benched."

A team playing tight and scared has a tendency to lose close games, and the '60s Cowboys wrote the book.

Inevitably, the edgy film session confrontation ran to its illogical conclusion. According to Toomay, "Not long afterwards, during a game with the Giants, Herb was benched after swatting down a potential touchdown pass. Out of position again, he had been reacting instinctively. Despite the positive outcome of the play, it was all Tom could take."

Or perhaps it was the time Landry chose to retaliate for Adderley challenging him during the film session in front of the team.

It was showdown at the not-so-OK Big D Corral when the top Cowboy and Adderley faced each other at halftime, and a peculiar assessment of the importance of stopping touchdown passes emerged.

Landry said, "Herb, you've got to play the defense like everybody else!"

"You mean I'm supposed to let a guy run by me and catch a touchdown pass?"

"Yes, if that's what your keys tell you to do!"

"No. I don't play that way."

Taking his verbal cowboy pistol and shooting himself squarely in the foot, Landry said, "Then you won't play at all."

What is the most bizarre thing that could have happened in the same half when Adderely batted down a would-be touchdown pass that resulted in him getting benched?

Try this.

"A touchdown pass was caught on the other side of the field," Adderley said. "At halftime Landry lost his cool and started yelling at me for knocking a potential TD pass down, screaming at me to play the defense. He never said one word to the D-back who gave up a scoring pass on the other side. It was without a doubt the loudest Landry ever spoke at halftime during my three years in Dallas. His bitterness towards me could not be controlled!"

In understandable terms, Adderley explained what happens when the quarterback throws a pass. "Once the ball is in the air, the called defense is off and it's time to go for the ball."

It's like a fumble. If there is a fumble, is the player supposed to try to recover the ball or keep reading keys? When a pass is thrown, it is literally up for grabs; a pass is like a fumble in the air.

When the going gets tough, the tough get weird.

"I was benched at halftime of the second game of the year against the Giants," Adderley said. "I started and played the entire games up to the ninth game. We were 6–2 when defensive backs coach Gene Stallings told me after practice that Tom wanted to see me in his office located in the city."

Stallings told Number 26 he needed to meet with Landry to go over mid-season grades. Adderley resents Stallings for being less than candid regarding the meeting's purpose. "I asked Brother 'Fro and Cornell if they had to see Landry concerning their grades," Adderley said. "They asked, 'What grades?' He had never done that to them. I knew the bad news would be Landry telling me I was benched for good in favor of Waters. By the way, Landry did not mention a word about my mid-term grades because my grades, if they kept them, were as high as or higher than any of the D-backs. I gave up one or two TD passes up until we were 6–2."

Lombardi used to say, "I will believe anything you tell me until I catch you in a lie. Then I will believe nothing." Like Lombardi, Adderley would talk, rationalize or argue with people and then move on. However, if dishonesty were involved, Adderley would have a strong reaction.

Herb Adderley spent three years with the Cowboys. "If Herb wouldn't have come to us when he did, we don't go to any Super Bowls, period. It's that simple," said Dallas defensive back Mark Washington. Adderley said, " The Cowboys were losers when I got there and losers when I left."

Photo courtesy of Scott Stroupe

"Because Landry didn't mention grades, I knew Stallings was lying," Adderley said. "When Landry finished telling me what he had to say, I got up and walked out of his office without saying a word. It did not surprise me, and I was prepared for it mentally. I lost total respect for Stallings after he lied to me and never talked to him again."

Mark Washington played in Dallas for nine years and said, "I never talked with anyone about grades."

Toomay said, "Whatever motivated Tom I think was absurd. I think it was so stupid and irrational."

Taking a trip into the psychological, Robinson said, "Landry probably looked at Herb and saw many of his own failures in big games."

The huffin' and puffin' by the big bad Cowboy sent a destructive wind through the Dallas secondary. Landry put Charlie Waters on the left corner and Adderley on the bench. For all practical purposes, Adderley's playing career ended that day. Adderley said, "I knew it was coming the first day of training camp when he demoted me from captain."

According to Pete Gent, "Landry never understood what it takes to be a great player. It's a step up from being a functionary and following the roles to that extra step that Herb had, which is actually magic. There were moments of just pure magic for Herb; you can call it instinctual play."

"Landry told me, 'Waters is the starter now. Stay or leave, I don't care.'"

The poor kid who fought his way out of P-Town was not going to quit and walk out on teammates and a paycheck. Later in the season, Landry went so far as to prohibit Adderley from actively being involved in practice, even as a member of the scout team. Adderley spent the rest of the season watching quietly from the sidelines.

As a youngster, Adderley was grateful for the broken donuts and pastry Hassis Bakery gave to the kids in P-Town. Now, years later, he had an omni-present head coach who wouldn't toss a crumb to the player who pushed the Cowboys to their first World Championship.

Tom Landry certainly went to great lengths to screw himself.

"They didn't treat him with any respect whatsoever and that's all Herb looks for in a relationship is mutual respect, and he certainly deserved that," Toomay said. "They made up a bunch of stuff about him; they did the same thing with me. Herb's a proud man and he wants to be accepted for who he is, and everybody deserves that, in my view."

Mel Renfro is neither an antagonist nor apologist for Tom Landry. When he was inducted into the Pro Football Hall of Fame in 1996, he chose Landry to be his presenter. However, Renfro knew the head coach blew it with Adderley.

Renfro said, "Landry put Herb on the bench and put Charlie Waters in there which, in everybody's opinion, was a big mistake."

Cornell Green agreed, "I think it should have been handled a *lot* differently than it was. The way Herb played and the way Mel and I played were entirely different. Herb guessed and 'clued' but, hell, he picked-off balls. He guessed a lot, but Herb guessed correctly."

According to Mark Washington, "Charlie was clearly out of position."

Toomay's analytical mind came up with two reasons the switch was made from Adderley to Waters. He said, "I think Tom liked Charlie quite a bit and Charlie reminded Tom of himself. You've got a white Southern kid and the black veteran from Lombardi."

Adderley believes Tom Landry had a racial agenda that cost the Cowboys championships as well as social progress. "Dallas had a quota of three black players on defense before I arrived. I was the fourth, Mark Washington was the fifth and there was no way Landry was going to let that happen."

It would have been an all-black defensive backfield if Adderley would have had his way. "Mark on the right corner, Brother 'Fro at free safety, Cornell at strong safety and me at the left corner should have been the starting secondary," said Adderley. "Landry didn't want four black players starting in the secondary and he did not want to add another black player to the defense. Mark was a better athlete than either Waters or Cliff Harris, and Mark could play all four positions in the secondary. Harris and Waters could only play safety. Neither Harris nor Waters would have made the Packers team because both Tom Brown and Doug Hart were better."

In a most stinging indictment of the Dallas head coach, Adderley said, "In my opinion, winning wasn't the most important thing to Landry. Playing the least amount of black players was at the top of his list. Landry had to have a white player in the secondary even though he wasn't as good as the black player. It was a perfect example of playing guys because of the color of their skin, rather than their talent. That tactic happened at other positions also, and that's why I said Landry did not put the best players on the field."

Adderley said, "Landry tried to make a corner out of Waters and it cost the team a shot to play in three straight Super Bowls." A solid argument can be made that Landry's coaching decisions cost his team a trip to Super Bowl VII.

During the 1972 NFC Championship game against the Redskins, Waters suffered an injury, making a bad situation even worse. Landry opened himself up to criticism with a couple of disastrous coaching gaffes.

"When Waters broke his arm, I ran on the field to replace him," Adderley said. "Landry yelled at me, 'Come off of the field' and he yelled for Mark Washington to replace Waters."

On the Redskins' sideline, Washington coach George Allen had a habit of licking his fingers and then putting his hands on his knees to watch the next play. You can bet he was licking his chops as he watched Tom Landry shuffle his defensive personnel. Adderley said, "Allen saw Mark Washington go on the field and called time out. He called his quarterback Billy Kilmer and Charley Taylor over to call a pass play to be thrown at Washington. The play was a fly-route turn-out that was executed perfectly for a 45-yard touchdown pass that won the game for the 'Skins. It was the first play against Mark Washington. Charley Taylor never caught a TD pass on me during my 12 years in the NFL."

Taylor knows he and the Redskins benefited by Landry's decision. "I'm glad that other kid came in," Taylor said. "If Herb would have been in there, it would have been a *whole* different story."

Mark Washington was a sitting duck out on the corner because he was just coming off knee surgery. His injured knee had not been properly rehabbed, he hadn't had sufficient practice time during the week leading up to the game and didn't have time to warm up before entering the game. "I thought Herb was going in, he was the backup; I was coming off an injury," Washington said. "I was surprised to get the call. They put me out there and I didn't even know what was going on. I had been practicing on the right side, not the left. I look back at the situation and there's no way that should have happened. I wasn't even in the mix. I don't know why Herb wasn't out there. To this day, I have no idea, I never asked about it. Obviously, I was disappointed for me personally, and I know Herb had to be disappointed for him. It made no sense. I think the world of Herb."

Adderley said, "After the game, I did not fly back to Dallas with the team. I stayed in D.C. overnight and drove to Philly the next day. I went back to Dallas a week later to shut my apartment down and flew right back to Philly. That 'etched-in-stone' hidden agenda of playing the least amount of blacks as possible was the main reason Landry benched me in favor of a white player who could not play the corner."

Adderley added, "Landry's cold-blooded treatment towards me cost the Cowboys a chance at making history. That history could have been made by appearing in three straight Super Bowls and winning two in a row. We would have played the same undefeated Miami team we beat 24–3 the previous year." The Dolphins defeated the Redskins 14–7 in Super Bowl VII.

"All of the guys on the team knew Landry's decision and stubbornness cost them a shot at winning back-to-back Super Bowls," Adderley said. "The guys were afraid to speak on the bad decisions made by Landry."

Other Dallas players and at least one coach have indicated Landry botched the Adderley experience.

Calvin Hill said, "Herb went to the Hall of Fame primarily for what he did in Green Bay, but if you look at the three years he was with the Cowboys, we went to three NFC Championship games and two Super Bowls. I would argue his charisma and leadership helped us get over the hump."

Even one longtime member of the Dallas coaching staff reached out to Adderley after the '72 season. Jerry Tubbs coached linebackers under Landry for 21 years. "He wrote me a letter after the season stating that he had nothing to do with Landry's decision to bench me and thanked me for what I contributed to the Cowboys' success, which was helping to get the *losers* to two Super Bowls," Adderley said. "Tubbs was the only coach who showed any feelings towards me. He knew that Landry was making a huge mistake, but he couldn't do a damn thing about it."

After Adderley was run off the team, Dallas didn't return to the Super Bowl for five years. Cornell Green firmly believes Adderley could have helped the club in the early and mid-'70s. "He was as capable of playing as anyone else was."

According to Adderley, Landry stuck it to him one last time with a trade to New England in '73. "During the offseason, Landry listed at the top of his agenda finding out where Phil Bengtson was coaching so that he could trade me back to the man who traded me to the Cowboys. To me, that was rubbing salt in the wounds," Adderley said. "If I had known, there is no way that I would have considered playing for Bengtson again. After one day of practice with the New England Patriots I got sick to my stomach because of being around Bengtson, and he knew it. They traded me to the Rams."

Adderley said, "Tom Landry had bitterness in his heart for me. After all I did for that team, I'll never understand it. The Cowboys were losers when I got there and losers when I left because of Landry's terrible decision to bench me for making a great play in the end zone. He said it was more important for me to play the defense called than play the ball when it's in the air. My answer to him was, 'I don't play that way.' I made adjustments all the time during the games because that is what I was taught to do in Green Bay. I made one adjustment too many in Yankee Stadium against the Giants and it resulted in me getting chewed out and benched."

Tom Landry ran the Cowboys' show and he got his way. Like a misguided physician, he believed it was possible to declare successful surgery even when the patient died. He had many successful surgeries in big games.

Adderley said, "The Cowboys lost two out of three title games; the Packers were undefeated in five title games."

Earlier in this chapter Mel Renfro was quoted as saying, "The Packers would always beat us and we were a better football team ..."

Perhaps the Cowboys had better players, but not a better team. Like a Texas oil gusher, talented players flowed from the Cowboys' personnel department into Landry's training camp every year and yet, they lost big games for years.

Lombardi's players were mentally tougher than Landry's. There was a roster full of tough guys in Green Bay; only a few in Big D.

"In Dallas, the training room would look like a scene from the program *M*A*S*H* after every game," Adderley said. "Guys were bandaged up from head to toe with ice pads or heat pads. In Green Bay you had to have a very serious injury to be in the training room on Mondays, like a broken bone or hardly be able to walk!"

Even the serious 1967 bicep injury did not put Adderley on the shelf. John Rowser said, "Herb lacerated his bicep muscle. He told Vince the doctor may have to operate and Vince told Herb they didn't have time to operate because they were going for the championship. Later on that year Herb had half a bicep."

And a Super Bowl ring.

Adderley played the rest of his career with half a bicep and the Cowboys' medical staff, Landry nor the players never knew about it.

"I had to struggle to lift weights twice a week in Dallas, but I did not complain," Adderley said. "I would bet my house none of the Cowboys knew about my arm during my three years there."

His closest friend and roommate, Mel Renfro, said, "I had no idea. He was a hard worker and a team player. He never said anything about any injury."

At some point, and the time is now, it must be stated that Tom Landry underachieved as head coach of the Dallas Cowboys. His own great players like Mel Renfro, Calvin Hill, Cornell Green, Pat Toomay, Mark Washington, Pete Gent and others indicated that Landry made *obvious* petty, stubborn, bad decisions that cost the team championships.

The top Cowboy also allowed a racial divide to split his team and locker room. No one in the organization could challenge Landry—not players, coaches, owners, fans or sports writers. It took a new owner to eventually fire Landry and that owner, Jerry Jones, caught seven kinds of hell when he did. Under the direction of Jones, Dallas won more world championships in the first eight years than Landry had in twenty-nine.

The question needs to be asked, how many championships would Lombardi have won with Landry's teams? The answer: a helleva lot more than

Landry, and the rednecks would have changed their ways or changed zip codes.

Lombardi had the power, will and desire to develop a culture of fairness, professionalism and respect that extended beyond the locker room. It was ingrained in his Green Bay Packers. "I met and knew the wives of all the guys in Green Bay with the exception of Jim Taylor's first wife, Dixie," Adderley said. From way down yonder in the land of cotton, Miss Dixie did not hide her racial beliefs. Adderley explained, "She made it known that she did not want to meet any of the black players."

For years in Green Bay, the home of defensive tackle Henry Jordan and his wife, Olive, served as sanctuary for the team after games. Olive said, "When the boys were winning so much, it was a little difficult to have a good time out in public. We would have everybody over to the house; we would go in the basement. A lot of times we were there 'til three, four, five in the morning."

Team unity in Green Bay was the polar opposite of what Adderley found when he attended a gathering at the home of Cowboys left guard John Niland. Adderley said, "I remember being at a party that I found out about at John Niland's house and two different wives came up to me and said, 'Why don't you go to the south side of Dallas where your people are?' No one wanted me there and that was the first and last time that I attended a party for white folks only. This was the type of racism that was happening with the wives of the white players. The black and white wives did not socialize in any way."

How 'bout them Cowgirls!

Adderley said, "During my three years in Dallas, I met one white wife and that was Margaret Lewis, wife of D.D. Lewis. We lived in the same apartment complex and that is the only reason I met Margaret."

Player after player from the 1970s Cowboys' teams has said Tom Landry's power was extensive. If he had wanted race relations to be different and better on his ball club, who or what would have gotten in his way?

Lombardi let no one stop him, while those with authority in Big D seemed intent to go forward to the past.

"During my nine years with the Packers, I was friends with all of my teammates and had conversations with them about football and current events" Adderley said. "I was also friends with all of the coaches and had conversations with them. In Green Bay we got together as a team after every home game either at someone's home or we would chip in and rent a room at the Downtowner Hotel. Even the assistant coaches would attend, and I felt warm positive feelings from all of my teammates."

"In Dallas I was friends with all of the black guys and we had conversations about what was happening with the team, including the racism. We also discussed current events of the times. I spoke to all of the white guys in Dallas and would start a conversation to see what type of vibes they were giving off. The guys I felt positive vibes from were Roger Staubach, Bob Lilly, D.D. Lewis, Steve Kinder, Pat Toomay, Dave Edwards and Dave Manders, who was a teammate at MSU. I had conversations every day with those, and the remainder of the white guys was nothing but, 'Hello.' They made it obvious that they wanted nothing to do with the black players by not speaking or opening up to any type of conversations. We never got together as a team after the games. I got cold, negative feelings from all of the white players except for the ones that I mentioned."

In his book, *Running Tough*, Hall of Fame running back Tony Dorsett said he was exposed to overt racism for the first time in his life when he began his professional career as a member of the Dallas Cowboys in 1977. Dorsett was a rookie five years after Adderley left the team and 19 years after the Lombardi Civil Rights Act was implemented in Green Bay.

Aside from race relations, the corporate cultures of the Packers and Cowboys were far from similar. Pat Toomay said, "Landry would mispronounce player's names. He would learn the names of starters but not anybody else and he would call the rest of us 'others.'"

It is easy, but wrong, to view Vince Lombardi as just a tyrannical, brutal, hard-ass football coach with little regard for people. He was not one dimensional and was hardly a man without respect for his players. He was a complicated creation, as his former director of public relations, Chuck Lane, said. "He was the facets of the diamond; that was all part of the Lombardi landscape. Lombardi had a tremendously gentle, compassionate side when it came to matters like deaths in families, etc."

In 1965, the Packers needed a backup tight end and coaxed veteran Bill Anderson out of retirement. Anderson had spent little time in his first Packers training camp when he learned of a family problem. It was still pre-season; Bill had not made the team and would only be a valuable reserve for Lombardi. Anderson would have been "other" in Dallas.

"I got word my dad had died, and he was just outside of Hendersonville, North Carolina," Bill explained. "I called (player personnel director) Pat Peppler and told him what my situation was, because I tried and tried and tried to get a flight down to the funeral. I couldn't find anything, so I got to the point where I told him about it and asked him if he could do anything.

He said, 'I'll see what I can do.' I was pretty down about everything because of dad.

"The next day I was in the locker room getting dressed, getting ready to go out to practice. Lombardi comes walking by and tapped me on the shoulder. I turned around and he said, 'Bill, I know how it is to lose your parent; that is one of the hardest times in life. Don't worry about anything. You come on and go to practice. I've got you a private plane. The pilot will stay with you until you're ready to come home.' I couldn't believe he did that."

A 74-year-old Bill Anderson, 45 years after the fact, choked back emotion as he described how his new team and teammates showed their concern. "When the funeral occurred, the players, coaching staff and everybody filled the place up with flowers. When I went back, I was ready to jump over the moon for him."

Bill hadn't even made the team when his coach and general manager arranged the chartered aircraft. Asked if Lombardi's gesture was the kindest thing that had been done for him, the grateful player said, "Yup."

The entire Adderley-Landry conflict clearly magnifies the difference between the two men who were head football coaches. If Coach Tom's decisions were defiant acts against Tex Schramm, a contrived power struggle with a great player based in racism or some psychological disorder regarding control, it indicates why Landry's teams lost so many big games. No question, his incessant control issues cost him championships.

While Lombardi was winning World Titles, Landry was programming androids.

Lombardi knew when preparation was over and got out of the way so his players, the human beings, could do their jobs. Boyd Dowler said Packer players had more latitude on game day than in practice. "It was easier to deal with him because he was on the sidelines and we were on the field. There were times when guys would turn around and say, 'Shut up' and stuff, you know. He didn't meddle much; he didn't call plays. We were on our own when we crossed that line and went out there, and he was over on the sidelines."

That wasn't happening in Dallas. Tom Landry was like the obsessive engineer who couldn't make a ball bearing round enough. At some point, the bearing needs to be put on the hub, the wheel needs to be put on the spindle and the car needs to be driven home. The parts work together on their own. At some point players need to feel free to play the game. Lombardi allowed it to happen in repeated championship fashion. Landry repeatedly prevented it in Big D, but he taught his boys to fetch.

"There was never any talking or making adjustments during the games in Dallas," Adderley said. "The guys would only discuss adjustments with the coaches and either it was 'yes' or 'no,' depending on what Landry said."

Margene Adkins said, "What I know about Tom Landry is this: Tom was a very knowledgeable man, but Tom did not let his coaches do their work. When we would come in on Tuesdays, Tom did the special teams, he did the offense and he did the defense. He did it all. He never did let his coaches coach; he did it all."

On many occasions Lombardi said other coaches may have known more about Xs and Os than he did, but he knew football players better than other coaches. If ever there was an example, it was Herb Adderley.

Lombardi only had a player's ass and pay check; Landry wanted their souls.

Wide receiver Lee Folkins played on Green Bay's 1961 World Championship team and spent the following three years in Dallas. Because he played for both, Folkins is one of a handful of players who can compare head coaches Vince Lombardi and Tom Landry and does so with crystal clarity. Lee says, "From my perspective, one was a terrific leader and the other was very cerebral, always trying to outsmart everybody. Lombardi wasn't outsmarting anyone, he was just gonna beat them. Lombardi, in my mind, was head and shoulders above Landry in terms of being a coach."

Lombardi was fully capable of intellectualizing his team into confusion and runner-up status. At the high school level he taught chemistry, physics and Latin.

With Landry's unchallenged stranglehold of power, and misuse thereof, it is little wonder Jerry Jones fired Tom two days after buying the team in 1989. In addition, the Cowboys were in decline during the final Landry years, going 7–9, 7–8 and 3–13. They missed the playoffs four of the final five years under "the only coach the Cowboys ever had."

Landry's coaching obituary appeared on the front page of *The Dallas Morning News* on February 26, 1989, a day after he was canned. In an article by Gary Myers, former Cowboys quarterback Roger Staubach was quoted as saying, "Tom Landry is the finest coach to ever coach in professional football ..."

Staubach's teammate, Pete Gent had another view of the coach who ruled the Dallas sideline. "The guy had a great system if he just didn't go to the games," Gent said. "Just keep him out of the stadium. He lost the first two games against Green Bay in the championship games."

Hardly a ringing endorsement for the game's finest coach.

Following Landry's death, *Sports Illustrated* offered comments from Mike

Ditka. "When you played for him, he's the boss," said Ditka, a tight end for four years and an assistant under Landry for nine. "When I coached for him he was the boss, too, but when you played for him there was a fear in there." Ditka said Landry was one of the most influential people in his life. "I love him very much," Ditka said. "He was always the epitome of fairness, honesty, integrity and all the virtues and values people talk about he had."

Toward the end of their coaching careers, Lombardi got to write his ticket to the Washington Redskins; Coach Tom got a ticket out of town.

There was no shortage of Texas-sized tears when Jerry Jones ran Landry off; however, some of those closest to the situation felt no sorrow. "When the firing came down on Tom like it did, it was inconceivable to me that he wasn't prepared, so I didn't have any sympathy for the situation," said Mark Washington. "Tom had been preaching that to us all the time. He talked about, 'You guys are under this umbrella. You're playing in this almost make believe world.' He would tell us from day one we better prepare for something else. He was under the same umbrella. What was a little shocking is that he was the one preaching it all the time, but I don't know if he was as prepared as some of the other people."

Robby To Washington

Meanwhile, for Dave Robinson in Green Bay, steps backward were taken throughout a once functional organization.

Robinson played three years for Phil Bengtson, who was in over his head as head coach and dreadful as general manager. Following three mediocre years under Bengtson, the Packer's Board of Directors hired as head coach and general manager Dan Devine from the University of Missouri.

He eventually left a legacy of bizarre behavior, distasteful incidents and paranoid comments in Green Bay.

In an effort to elicit sympathy for himself, Devine's manipulative and peculiar behavior included frequent references to his wife's multiple sclerosis. His disingenuous comments came at a time he was involved in an extramarital affair with one of the Packers' secretaries. The escapade was general knowledge throughout the Green Bay organization and helped render him a laughing stock before his dismal four-year masquerade ended.

Lombardi had established a Thanksgiving Day tradition with a family dinner gathering. The team traditionally played the Lions in Detroit and then returned to Green Bay where Vince and Marie Lombardi hosted the annual Thanksgiving dinner for players and their families.

Each adult was limited to two drinks, and games and baby sitters were available for the kids as the event was organized in Lombardi style. There was one iron-clad rule: The player and his family had to say "hi" to the Lombardis. Marie wanted to see each player's family, as a unit, each year. Ruth Pitts, wife of running back Elijah, said, "Marie would come by and see you, see how you were doing and always encourage you to keep your family together. That was always a good message for all of us. It wasn't just because I was a black wife; she said this to all of us. I always felt welcome; the Lombardis were warm and welcoming."

The tradition continued under Devine, who bastardized the event. In 1971, black defensive end Lionel Aldridge and his white wife, Vicky, attended the dinner, as they had for years. According to Vicky, "Devine stopped at every table to say hello to each person. When Dan Devine made the rounds at our table, he skipped saying hello to one person: me."

It was a blatant, racial slap in the face by a man much too small for the job of an NFL coach. He was especially unfit to represent the great Green Bay franchise.

Earlier that same autumn, Vicky's mother died and then, too, Devine found comfort on the underside of decency. Vicky said, "He would not let Lionel attend my mother's funeral. Lionel said he was going anyway and Dan called me and told me if I insisted that Lionel go, he would have Bob Brown be the starting defensive end from then on. So, Lionel was afraid to go."

Devine would not allow the organization to send flowers for Vicky's mother. Lionel ordered an arrangement and sent it on behalf of the Packers organization.

As further evidence of Devine's warped view of coaching in Green Bay, he had distaste for Lombardi Avenue. Robinson said, "Devine told us the worst part of his job was driving on a street named for another coach to get to work."

It was common for the collegiate coach to show film of his Missouri teams to a room full of pro players, many of whom had won Super Bowls. He was viewed as a buffoon who set himself up for scrutiny. In front of the entire Green Bay team, he was bragging about his 1969 college team and said, "You guys may not remember that team, but it was the best team I ever had." Robinson said, "I remember that team. Penn State beat 'em in the Orange Bowl." Robinson's teammates fell out with laughter when the Nittany Lion landed his zinger.

As part of Devine's purge of Lombardi players, Robinson was traded to Washington after the '72 season, where he played two years for George Allen's "Over the Hill Gang."

Robinson was a Lombardi man: professional, bright, confident, good and viewed as a threat rather than an asset by Devine. Robinson contemplated retiring after the 1972 season, and Devine made the decision easier by benching the star linebacker for game eight.

Milwaukee became home for the Robinsons when he went to work for the Joseph Schlitz Brewing Company in '69, and it was clear he had a bright future with the brewery. He invited his brothers to attend the 49ers game because it was probably going to be his final appearance at Milwaukee County Stadium.

During the week leading up to the game, Robinson told defensive coordinator "Hawg" Hanner that it seemed as though he, Robinson, would not be starting. Hanner dismissed such a foolish notion. Sure enough, in a spiteful move, Devine moved middle linebacker Jim Carter to the left side, an aging Ray Nitschke was given a rare start and Robinson had an uncommon view from the sidelines.

San Francisco quarterback John Brodie's eyes were as big as wagon wheels the first time he took his team to the line of scrimmage. He checked Green Bay's left defensive side and saw a welcome sight: no Number 89. The 49ers started running to Green Bay's left side and didn't stop.

In a stroke of coaching brilliance, Devine put Robinson in the game once Brodie had directed San Francisco to the Packers' 20-yard line. When

Robinson joined the huddle, defensive end Clarence Williams said, "Thank God you're here. We couldn't stop anything." The drive immediately stalled and Green Bay rolled up a 34–24 win. Robinson was voted a game ball by his teammates for his efforts.

Covering his petty posterior after the game, Devine told reporters he kept Robinson out of the starting lineup to motivate him.

"Devine knew my brothers were going to the game because of the special circumstances and he benched me out of spite," Robinson said. "That removed any doubt in my mind about retiring."

Robinson started the next week against the Bears and was awarded a second consecutive game ball, and that was enough for Devine. He told the team game balls were so important that a player would be allowed to win only one a year. "Good idea, Coach; I got mine," Robinson said.

With a strong defense and an offense directed by first year assistant coach Bart Starr, Green Bay made the playoffs, and the stage was set for Robinson to end his career in style.

During the off-season, a classy idea was formulated to hold a joint press conference with the Packers and Schlitz to announce the retirement of Green Bays' great linebacker and his appointment as Director of Minority Relations with the brewery. If Devine was anything, he was a political animal.

"When he heard about the proposed press conference, Devine told Schlitz he wanted to wait until after the draft to make the announcement so he could pick up someone to replace me. He said, 'If teams know Dave is retiring, it will cost me a lot to replace him.' I told the people at Schlitz I would not trust Devine as far as I could throw a locomotive, but they thought he was honest and genuine."

On draft day, Robinson was shipped to Washington and the personnel genius from the University of Missouri used a third-round pick to select a linebacker from Proctor, Minnesota, which just happened to be Devine's home town. The player who was supposed to replace Robinson lasted one year in Green Bay.

George Allen had been hoodwinked in the deal, but Robinson was put in a great position. According to Robinson, "George knew he had been outfoxed by Devine, and he also knew he had to make the best of the situation. He and I met several times and when we were together in D.C., he finally said, 'What will it take to get you?' I told him they printed it just down the street." Allen assured Robinson he could round up 81,000 "ones" from the place down the street, and they had a deal.

Robinson was a treasure trove for Allen. "He asked me to stop in his office after we made the deal," Robinson said. "He had a projector set up with film of the Packers' defenses and he picked my brain for hours. George was a defensive coach and was fascinated by talking defense."

Robinson joined the Redskins in '73, three years after Lombardi's death, and the racial problems had been addressed during the short stay of the Great Coach in Washington. Robinson said, "There wasn't much racism on the team, there were a couple guys, but not much." Not as good as Green Bay, but nowhere near as bad as Dallas.

Unlike Titletown, the nation's capital had a substantial African-American population. According to Robinson, "I went down to Washington, D. C., where the whole city was black, so off the field, I didn't have any trouble at all."

Robinson was part of Coach George Allen's "Over the Hill Gang" that included running back Duane Thomas. "Herb Adderley was my teammate in Dallas and Dave was my teammate in Washington," Thomas said. "There was a Vince Lombardi spirit in both of them that I could make a connection with." He added, "When I think of Dave Robinson, I always see this great big smile. He had wholesomeness about him. Dave's mom, there was something heart-warming from her." Following a game, Duane refused to sign an autograph for a little kid and Mrs. Robinson got on Duane's case and he signed. "It was like a letter from home. How can you refuse?" Thomas asked.

The Lombardi spirit within Robinson gave him trouble accepting what he saw as false pride in Washington.

He said, "When I walked into camp, everybody was talking about how happy they were that they went to the Super Bowl. It was the one they lost to Miami. I just couldn't fathom anybody being proud of losing a Super Bowl. It was a whole new way of thinking to me. It was a real, real, real, real change in my mind. George Allen took us to the playoffs, but we never won shit." Some would argue that's exactly what they did win.

The more Robinson thought about finishing second, the madder he got. "We were losers, we were losers and I can say it. They had a big ceremony when they got their losing rings. Vince Lombardi wouldn't have allowed it; he never would have wanted it. In Green Bay we sure wouldn't have gone around town showing it off. I just couldn't imagine Vince Lombardi or anybody on his teams showing off a loser's ring. I know he wouldn't have worn the ring and would have discouraged us from wearing the ring."

It was the Losers Bowl in 1964, Robinson's second year, that helped spur the Packers to three straight championships. At one time, the NFL held a runner-up game with the second place teams in each conference. The great Packers coach said it was a "rinky dink game, in a rinky dink town, played by two rinky dink teams. That's what second place is: rinky dink."

It is easy but wrong to view Vince Lombardi as just a hard-assed football coach. He certainly was that, but he was so much more. He passionately cared for the Packers organization while it was under his control. Player conduct off the field, organizational image, recognition of contributions made by player's families and front office personnel, expansion of stadium seating, construction of team offices, installation of locker room carpet, heating coils beneath the frozen tundra, toilet cleaning and anything else he could think of needed to work together at a high level for the benefit of the enterprise.

Under Vince Lombardi, the Green Bay Packers organization, in all facets, may have functioned better than any sports franchise in history.

As an enlightened tyrant, Lombardi expected perfection from himself as well as others. What Robinson saw in Washington provided him a comparison to Lombardi. "The big thing, going to a team that was good, from Vince Lombardi's teams that were great, was getting over the hump. We had a good team in Washington; we had a lot of solid ball players, but we never got over the hump.

"There was no doubt in my mind when I walked in the door in Washington that the difference was Vince Lombardi versus George Allen. They were both great coaches, but George Allen was like a salesman who sells and sells and sells but never asks for the order, he never closes the deal. We couldn't win.

"Vince was the type of guy who went in and sold and asked for the order right now; he closed the deal. He got us the championship." The sales pitch was given to his players who bought and delivered the order.

Robinson said, "Vince kept us mentally fresh. He would tell us the same thing a hundred times, a hundred different ways. George Allen would tell us the same thing a hundred times the same way."

Uniforms Under Glass

How nice it would be if dynasties would neatly come to an end.

Players would be given classy retirement tributes while they have a little left in the tank and fans would be protected from seeing their heroes decline or masquerade in another uniform. Business decisions and difficulty saying good-bye to the game ruin many fairytale endings.

Willie Davis was the only Lombardi Packer to leave having met the above-mentioned criteria. Bart Starr and Ray Nitschke were recognized with days in their honor but neither exit was completely clean. Starr fought the good fight for two years; however, his injured passing arm could not follow his brain's instructions at the end of his career.

In a Napoleonic effort to battle Lombardi's legend and his own psychological demons, Dan Devine attempted to embarrass Nitschke for two years before the great linebacker retired. Devine was more successful discrediting himself throughout the organization due to an ongoing affair with a member of his secretarial staff. He had no success humiliating a great player and fan favorite like Nitschke.

Forty-three years after the fact, we learned what happened to Herb Adderley.

He said, "The truth has never been told about my departure from the Packers because no one ever asked me my side of the story. There are two sides to every story, right?"

The Packers closed out the '69 season with a home contest on December 21, the day Willie Davis played his final game in the National Football League. It was his last game and he knew it. In a fitting tribute to his outstanding career, Green Bay honored its great defensive end with "Willie Davis Day."

It was also the day Adderley played his final game for the Packers. He just didn't know it at the time.

With high honors and tributes, the Packers respectfully held the door as Willie Davis made his exit to the business world.

On the same day, the same door slammed, hitting Adderley in the ass.

Adderley said, "After the final game in 1969, I walked up to the opposite end of our locker room where Willie's number 87 locker was located. I told him it was great being teammates for nine years and playing on The Left Side together. Bob Jeter's locker was about three lockers down and I heard

Bengtson tell Jeter, 'We nominated you for the Pro Bowl. We didn't nominate Herb, but don't tell him; we don't want him to know that.' So I asked him, 'Phil, I heard what you said. What's wrong, what did I do?' He started mumbling and grumbling and never did answer the question."

Members of the team's inner circle believe Bengtson harbored resentment toward Adderley for the incident at My Brother's Place. "Phil thought he had to stand up to Herb after what he (Bengtson) had done to Chuck Mercien," Robinson said. "Everybody knew about what happened at My Brother's Place, and Phil wanted to make sure the players knew he would come down on a great defensive player, too. It blew up in his face."

Adderley said, "Bengtson refused to talk to me about the situation, and it really pissed me off because I gave everything I had every time I stepped on the field, which was one hundred percent effort on every play. The best years of my life were during the '60s in Titletown, USA."

Associated Press writers selected Adderley to the 1969 All-Pro team, indicating he deserved to be nominated for the Pro Bowl. Adderley said, "I was upset about why Bengtson handled the situation the way he did, not because I didn't get selected to play in the game. I had played in five previous Pro Bowls, so it wasn't that important to me. I was happy for Jeter because it was his first Pro Bowl appearance. Bengtson let his personal feelings about the incident that happened at My Brother's Place influence him to be petty and not vote for me after I was selected to the AP All-Pro team."

With a lot of excellent football left in him, Adderley faced a tough decision on the eve of his tenth year in the National Football League. "Ten days before the 1970 season was scheduled to start, I received a call from Dallas General Manager Tex Schramm asking me if I would play for the Cowboys. I was shocked because I thought I would end up with one of the East Coast teams. I told Schramm I had to think about it and I would get back to him in a couple days."

"As much as I hated to play for the Cowboys, I had no choice, so I called the next day to inform Schramm I would play for the Cowboys."

An eerie and foreboding chain of events unfolded as Adderley joined his new team. "I flew to Dallas on September, 3, 1970, and read the headline in the Dallas newspaper that said Coach Lombardi had passed away in Washington, D.C., from colon cancer. I knew his chances of surviving were impossible, but I still cried."

What followed was one of the worst trips Adderley would ever make. "I called the Cowboys office from the airport in Dallas to let them know I was going to go back home to attend the funeral," Adderley said. "I was not offered a ride to New York with Landry on the Cowboys owner's private jet."

It was an awkward occasion inside St. Patrick's Cathedral when Adderley, perhaps Lombardi's biggest admirer, did not sit with the Packer contingent during the great man's funeral. "Even with the overflow crowd, I didn't have any problem getting into the church," Adderley said. "I noticed the entire Packers team and front office people enter and they had reserved seats near the front. I was seated in the middle row on the opposite side and after the funeral, I hurried outside to make sure my old teammates saw me. I waved at a few of the guys and was feeling bad about Lombardi and felt worse because I wasn't making the trip back to Green Bay with the guys."

On Monday, September 7, 1970, both Vince Lombardi's body and Adderley's Green Bay Packer career were interred for the ages.

A photo taken in May of 2011 shows retired police officer Gary Martin beside a dignified monument in Mount Olivet Cemetery in Middletown Township, New Jersey, which marks the final resting place of Vince Lombardi. The local Knights of Columbus and Martin volunteer to keep the site manicured. The drive from Gary's home in Parsippany, N.J., to the cemetery takes about three hours round trip, and for 26 years Gary has tried to visit once a month.

Photo courtesy of Gary Martin

With a heavy heart, Adderley joined his new team in Dallas just one week before the season opener. He played the second half of the final pre-season game against Joe Namath and the Jets, adjusting to the complicated Tom Landry defenses.

After three years in Dallas, Adderley was traded to the New England Patriots and guess who was running the defense? "When I reported to training camp, I found out Bengtson was the defensive coordinator, so I didn't even unpack my car," Adderley said. "If I had known Bengtson was one of the defensive coaches, I wouldn't have reported. Two days later, the Patriots traded me to the Rams and I reported to their camp in California."

Adderley's great career abruptly and unceremoniously ended. "When I started practicing with the team, head coach Chuck Knox had me playing every position in the secondary except left corner and I was being used as a backup to those positions," Adderley said. "After one week of the Rams camp I asked to be released. That was it, no announcement of retiring, being cut or released. There was no acknowledgement about a future Hall of Famer. Officially, on the record, the last team I was associated with was the Rams, not the Packers or Cowboys. It was a sad and terrible way to end my NFL career."

In the transaction section of the sports pages, five words appeared, "Adderley released by the Rams."

"No one contacted me for a final statement about my Hall of Fame career," Adderley said. "There are two sides to every story, and this is the first time I have ever told my side."

Eight years after retiring, the Pro Football Hall of Fame called Adderley, making him the fifth Lombardi Packer to be enshrined. He was one of the spicy ingredients that led to some uncomfortable moments for the HOF class of '80. Two former Dallas Cowboys, Adderley and Bob Lilly, were among the inductees.

"During the Hall of Fame festivities, every time I entered a room to be acknowledged, (some) lines from the famous hit song "My Way," by Frank Sinatra, were played," Adderley said. "I don't know who picked the great song for me, but I do know it fit me perfectly." Let the record show, both mentally and physically, "I took the blows, but did it my way in Dallas for three years," Adderley said.

Following his departure from Dallas, Adderley had no occasion to be around Coach Tom until the Hall of Fame events reunited them nearly a decade later. "The Hall classes get a free trip to Hawaii for one week during the Pro Bowl," said Adderley. "At the first cocktail party, I intentionally stayed away from Landry and his coaching staff because of the way I was treated by Landry." Except for courtesy extended by Dallas assistant coaches Mike Ditka and Jerry Tubbs, interaction between Adderley and the Dallas entourage was nonexistent. Adderley said, "Eventually, after a few drinks, Mike Ditka and Jerry Tubbs made it over to where I was socializing to speak and offered congratulations. Landry and the rest of his shaky staff never acknowledged me during the week of partying."

Being reunited in Hawaii was just like old times. I could still feel his bitterness and hatred towards me after not seeing him for eight years," Adderley said. "The color of my skin had a lot to do with Landry's bitter feelings towards me. I stared at him and smiled every time I caught him looking my way; the same thing happened in Canton during the weekend of the festivities."

On August 2, 1980, Adderley was presented for induction into the Pro Football Hall of Fame by friend and teammate Willie Davis. "He was known as the big-play man in Green Bay on defense," Davis said. Noting Adderley's kickoff and punt return skills, Willie added, "He was one of the most versatile players the Green Bay Packers ever had, but he truly made his mark on defense. I saw Herb make some of the greatest plays ever, and he always played well in the big games."

With pride, Green Bay's left defensive end said, "Herb was a competitor with unusual ability to make the big effort. His personal pride and dedication to high standards were a true inspiration to every Green Bay Packer. Along with our teammate Dave Robinson, we truly controlled the left side of the Packers defense."

In his opening comments, Adderley thanked his Packer defensive teammates and mentioned each of the other ten starters by name.

True to his beliefs, he said, "There is a beginning in everything. I have to go back to the beginning. In the beginning is God. I'd like to take time to acknowledge God and my spiritual beliefs because without God, I wouldn't be here. I wouldn't have been able to participate in football and I wouldn't be here. So I want to thank God number one for making everything possible.

"I'd like to thank my mother and father because without them, I wouldn't be here. Mom, I appreciate you taking care of me and leading me on the right road with your guidance.

"It takes the gift of self-guidance, parental guidance and it takes a certain spiritual guidance. And I had the three and it was difficult for me to miss. So Mama, I appreciate and I love you."

Adderley heaped praise on his two influential coaches, as well.

"I'd like to thank the two people responsible for my football career. My high school coach, Mr. Charles Martin, and I can honestly say if it wasn't for Mr. Charles Martin in 1955, there's no way I would be here because I thought I was a basketball player. But this man saw something I didn't realize and see in myself. I will always remember Mr. Charles Martin and his spirit. And his spirit will always live in me.

"I have to talk about Coach Vince Lombardi because Coach Lombardi reminded me so much of my high school coach. Those two people had more to do with me playing football and being successful than anybody in the world. I feel a certain sadness in my heart but I can still feel happiness that the spirit of my high school coach and Coach Vince Lombardi are within me. Coach Lombardi saw something in me also that I didn't realize."

In an effort to put the best face on a difficult situation, during his induction speech Adderley acknowledged his time in Dallas. He said, "I'd like to say to Coach Tom Landry, 'I appreciate the opportunity to have played in Dallas for those three years, and Mr. Gil Brandt, I appreciate your kindness when I was there.'"

No such reciprocal olive branch was offered by the other side. Adderley's childhood friend Al Chandler attended the induction ceremonies in Canton and noticed the snub. "Tom Landry ignored the fact that Herb was on that stage," Chandler said. "He had nothing to say about Herb. Unbelievable. He totally acted like Herb did not exist."

Adderley said, "Lilly and I were in the 1980 Class and Landry was Lilly's presenter. Landry felt I was raining on Lilly's parade because he often boasted about how great Lilly was and that he would be the first Cowboys player to be enshrined in the Hall. He was the first original Cowboy, but the team was listed on my info, too, as a member of the Cowboys. Landry was probably upset about me being in the same class with Lilly, especially after he boasted about Lilly and benched me even though I had Hall of Fame stats before playing for the Cowboys. I had nothing to say to Landry or anyone else representing the Cowboys the entire weekend."

Robinson played two full years, 1973 and '74, with the Washington Redskins as part of George Allen's "Over the Hill Gang." With an open checkbook from 'Skins owner Edward Bennett Williams, Allen signed a roster full of veterans. Other teams viewed them as some combination of overpriced cast-offs, has-beens and malcontents with a liberal number of them having been player reps.

"Williams had given Allen an unlimited budget, and by '75, George had exceeded it," Robinson said. The team owner tried to rein in spending and wanted something done with Robinson's $81,000-a-year contract. Robinson said, "Williams told George he could get three linebackers for what I was making but Allen said he needed me. I had a back-up who was making thirty-five thousand and Edward Bennett Williams liked the look of that salary better than mine."

A plan was hatched to have Robinson and his back-up each play a half in the final pre-season game, evaluate each player's performance and pick a starter. "I came out with the best grade and George told me I would be starting the next week, but I told him I didn't like the system of going in and out of games. I had been a starter and didn't want to do it another way."

Allen offered a couple of other solutions, including a trade to the Philadelphia Eagles. Robinson said, "I had a no-trade clause in my contract and I had to approve any trade. To me, there was a stigma attached to having four or five teams on your career record. I didn't want it said that Dave Robinson played for Green Bay, Washington, Philadelphia, Atlanta and so on."

There was another option. "George asked me if I wanted to come in as an assistant coach, come to practice every day to work out and stay in shape and be ready to play of needed. They could just activate me."

At age 35 with a wife and three children, Robinson put serious thought into his decision. "I went home and talked with Elaine about it. We decided she needed me at home a little more because the twins were thirteen years old and I had a job waiting at Schlitz. So that's what I did. In hindsight I should have gone to the Eagles because it was about ten minutes from where I was from. I could have played and started a business. But hindsight is always 20/20 and it worked out well anyway.

The congenial Robinson and George Allen parted on good terms. "He asked me if I wanted a press conference to announce my retirement and I told him no," Robinson said. "I retired in his office."

Standing for Your Brothers

Why does logic have to stand on its head and break our hearts?

It's not logic, of course, that breaks our hearts, it's people.

Beginning in the late 1950s, the National Football League experienced a trajectory of monumental growth, popularity and profitability. The game generated millions upon millions of dollars annually, creating many millionaires and making other millionaires richer still. Team owners, television network executives, agents and others were awash in money. Unfortunately, the very men who triggered the NFL's growth were betrayed by people who were authorized to stand for them. Players who started the National Football League Players Association (NFLPA), whose union dues and commitment gave birth and life support to the organization, were not represented by union leadership.

Two pioneering advocates for retired player pensions and benefits are shown at the exclusive Ray Nitschke Luncheon during a Hall of Fame weekend. John Mackey (l) served as president of the National Football League Players Association and Herb Adderley (r) sued the union after the old timers were abandoned at the negotiating table by Gene Upshaw.

In a 2007 class-action lawsuit, Adderley was the class representative on behalf of 2,062 retired players who sued the players union. Under the direction of Executive Director Gene Upshaw, the NFLPA decided to represent active players in the union, but not retired ones. The union was cheating its retirees out of a substantial amount of money generated by a video game.

"The main thing from the historic lawsuit is this," Adderley said, "it caught the National Football League Players Association and Executive Director Gene Upshaw stealing money from the retired guys by using our images, likenesses, etc., and not paying us."

In landmark litigation, retired players went after the NFLPA and Players Inc., the groups responsible for the negotiation of player compensation from EA Sports. The suit contended that images of players were being used by EA Sports without compensation from Upshaw's union to the retired players. Many old-timers were unaware of the injustice. Baltimore's great Lenny Moore asked, "What did we know? Many of us were being utilized, not knowing we were being utilized." Foolishness and greed on behalf of the union kept money away from retired players. Moore said, "It's so easy to be honest without playing games, especially when we're all in the same bag. I was very happy Herb was one of the 'front folks' keeping us informed it was a possibility we could win this suit. We got a check, thank the Lord."

As player salaries exploded in the late 1980s and beyond, players of the '50s, '60s and '70s were left behind with their increasing medical problems. A man of character, loyalty and principle took on the NFLPA with a class-action lawsuit. He was a man of God and a man of Lombardi: Herb Adderley.

The lawsuit split teammates, battered feelings, ruined friendships, opened suspicions and exposed a side of the game fans would generally prefer not to see. Vince Lombardi, a man of brutal honesty, would have been proud of his great cornerback for standing on principle. Adderley saw injustices and called them by name.

In the end, the entire experience was horrible for Adderley. Exploitation of the old-timers was not limited to the players union. The law firm that presented the class action suit made two huge tactical errors that cost the retirees millions of dollars. The same legal counsel grossly overcharged its clients and made false promises to Adderley. Presiding District Judge William Alsup slapped the law firm down on both issues. The judge reduced the law firm's reimbursement by $2,574,152.57.

Additionally, a lack of appreciation and support shown by scores of old-timers to Adderley for his efforts has left a lingering sting for him.

Logically, heroes of the game should have been cared for; instead, they were belittled, discounted and abandoned by Players Association Executive Director Gene Upshaw. Left with meager retirement income, little medical coverage and a multitude of physical and mental ailments, the players were denied income from an NFLPA agreement with Electronic Arts Inc. (EA Sports), the maker of "Madden NFL" video games. The historic class action lawsuit was filed against the National Football League Players Association, but during the discovery phase, an important e-mail surfaced that implicated EA Sports. Legal troubles may be just beginning for the video game giant, and the email was the smoking gun.

Adderley said, "Upshaw referred to us as dogs, stating that if we didn't eat the food that was thrown our way, he couldn't force us to eat it. Jeffery Kessler, the lead attorney for the NFLPA during the historic lawsuit often referred to us in front of the judge and jury the same way, adding that we were unmarketable and useless."

Dogs? Useless?

A rift developed between active and retired players as the NFLPA decided to represent only the active guys and left the old-timers to fend for themselves. Most unions are vitally concerned with the well-being of retirees, not so for the NFLPA under the leadership of Gene Upshaw.

Here is a very short list of distinguished retired players who were lumped in the category of dogs by Upshaw: Raymond Berry, John Mackey, Earl Campbell, Paul Warfield, Willie Davis, Frank Gifford, Don Meredith, Franco Harris, Sonny Jurgensen, Lenny Moore, Tommy McDonald, Bart Starr, John Elway, Bobby Bell, Nick Buoniconti, Abe Woodson, Darryl Stingley, Barry Sanders, Lance Alworth, Dennis Byrd, Ron Yary, Gale Sayers, Tom Dempsey, Eddie George, Rod Woodson, Art Donovan, Art Monk, Rosey Grier, Reggie McKenzie, Mike Utley, Steve Largent, Jan Stenerud, Mike Ditka, Gino Cappelletti, Dick LeBeau, Rocky Bleier, Earl Morrell, Randy Gradishar, Ronnie Lott, Chuck Howley and Chris Speilman.

That's one helluva fantasy dog pound.

During the trial, legal counsel for the retired players never established the market value of the men listed above. "A major mistake was made when Katz failed to bring in a marketing expert to prove that Kessler was wrong about the retired guys being unmarketable and should be thrown dog food," Adderley said. "If expert testimony would have shown our guys were marketable to many businesses, it would have proven Kessler wrong and could have convinced the jury to award us appropriate compensation. Expert testimony under oath would have been worth millions of dollars to us."

How could Gene Upshaw, a person who played the game, offer such an insulting portrayal to describe the great players and honored men of the game? Smart or dumb had nothing to do with it. Upshaw was making nearly $4 million a year, just from the union. Estimates of his annual income were in the $7 million range with side deals. Where did all that extra money come from?

Sadly, some of the most admirable qualities the old-time NFL players possess have damaged their cause. As a group, the men are proud, tough and competitive. They do not want to admit they need assistance and certainly don't like asking for help.

Adderley said, "Money that later turned to greed turned Upshaw against all of the retired guys except for the ones that he chose to put on the NFLPA's payroll. The list included some of his teammates with the Raiders that he turned against because of money and greed. He hijacked our union and had it changed to an association where he became a dictator."

It would have been one thing for a lawyer to call the old-timers "dogs," but Upshaw was a retired player who he turned on his own.

Thomas Jefferson said, "When a man assumes a trust, he must know he is bound to the goal of earnestly working in the best interests of the people he represents." Such integrity apparently did not take root in the heart of Gene Upshaw and his cronies.

Adderley was the class action representative in the 2007 lawsuit on behalf of 2,062 retired players against the NFLPA and Players Inc., the groups responsible for the negotiation of player compensation from EA Sports. The suit contended that images of players were being used by EA Sports without compensation from Upshaw's group to the retired players.

Upshaw and the NFLPA brought the lawsuit on themselves with their arrogant disregard for the retirees. Someone should have told Big Gene about the tenacious determination of Adderley.

Green Bay's great cornerback explained how he got involved with the litigation, "I received a call from Bernie Parrish, a former player for the Browns, requesting that I join him, Walter Roberts, Clifton McNeil, Bruce Laird and Walter Beach in a lawsuit against the NFLPA. Roberts and Beach both played for the Browns with Parrish, McNeil played for the 49ers and Laird played for the Colts. The lawsuit for breach of contract was filed against the NFLPA in New York on Feb 14, 2007." Bruce Laird has remained a prominent voice for retired players.

The actual court case was shifted to California, due, in part, to concern that a fair hearing would be difficult to obtain on the East Coast. Adderley said, "Our attorneys, Manatt, Phelps & Phillips, LLP, based in Palo Alto, California, filed legal documents for the case to be heard in California. The

NFLPA did the same thing requesting the case be heard in either Washington, D.C., or Virginia, their area. The union never lost a case in their area probably because of their connections with lawyers, union officials, judges and other people who could influence the verdict in their favor. The Judge overseeing the case *ordered* the case be tried in California."

Adderley said, "I signed an agreement with the NFLPA to be involved with an apparel promotion with Reebok. I wasn't paid as the agreement called for and I was ignored by Upshaw and the NFLPA every time I contacted them both via phone and e-mail. That's why I decided to join Parrish's lawsuit. I was ignored and placed on the blackball list because I was very outspoken about the below-poverty-level pension that I and two hundred other retired guys received at the time. The lead attorney for us was Ron Katz, a partner with the law firm Manatt, Phelps & Phillips."

Bernie Parrish was well-intentioned, but his conduct prior to litigation created enough baggage to get him tossed from the case. Adderley said, "He intended to be the class action representative for a few retired guys who signed agreements similar to the one that I signed. After an investigation into Parrish`s past personal history, Judge William Alsup dismissed him as the class rep, saying he was unfit."

Documents from the United States District Court for the Northern District of California explained why Bernie Parish needed to be eliminated: "Certification of this class was denied, however, on the grounds that Parrish was an inadequate class representative. This finding was explained with reference to numerous examples of Parrish's conduct that illustrated a racist prejudice and personal vendetta against Gene Upshaw, the then executive director of the NFLPA (for example, comparing him to "Caesar, Napoleon, Idi Amin, Hitler, Stalin, Milosevic, [and] Saddam"), and had invoked black racial stereotypes in analyzing Upshaw's motivations for his professional acts (e.g., "I'm sure that Upshaw hip hop/gangsta rap fraternity will keep [Coach Bill Parcells] busy sorting through a quality pool of dog fighting, gun toting, dui driving, strip club shooting, ass showing team, that only gambles on dog fights and don't take steroids or HGH"). Parrish had made extreme remarks directed at Upshaw. Moreover, Parrish had indicated that he would be unwilling to make any settlement in the case, even if it were ultimately beneficial to any certified class."

After the court threw Parrish out, the lawsuit was left looking for a leader. Adderley explained, "The lead attorney requested that I be the class rep and I said *no,* because the only thing I wanted to be was a plaintiff and not the class rep. The lead attorney began to beg me to be the rep for a few days because I was qualified to be the rep and he knew it. I didn't want to let the retired guys down, so I decided to be the rep. *After* I agreed, the lead attorney informed me that I would receive an 'incentive fee' in the amount of $100,000 if we won the case and that helped me feel better about being the rep." The promise should never have been made, and the judge made sure no such payment occurred.

The lawsuit stumbled out of the gate and seemed destined to die.

Adderley said, "A few weeks after the case started, it was dismissed by Judge Alsup because there weren't enough guys to form a class action complaint. The Judge's order to dismiss the case was appealed and re-filed; once again, the case was dismissed."

A surprising development put the case back on track as the judge, not the lawyers, found a way to put the case back in court.

According to Adderley, "About two weeks after the case was dismissed, I received a call from the lead attorney telling me that Judge Alsup gave us a road map to sue the NFLPA. Judge Alsup noticed in the discovery received from the NFLPA that there were 2,074 retired guys who signed a Group Licensing Agreement [GLA] to share the revenue from any promotions that included six or more people. It could be all retired guys or a mixture of active and retired guys. The active players were being paid and the retired guys were not being paid. This was a new theory to sue the NFLPA. The paperwork was presented to Judge Alsup and he accepted it as a new theory and the defendants had to try to get it dismissed. They did everything possible during the next two-and-a-half years of trading thousands of documents for the judge to view.

"Finally, Judge Alsup agreed with us, and we had a legitimate case against the NFLPA. The Judge ordered jury selection to start, and the case began after selection of jurors. The case was heard by a federal jury in San Francisco that started in late October of 2008."

A jury comprised of eight women and two men listened to three weeks of detailed testimony regarding the operations of the NFLPA and Players Inc.

Dignified, wearing his gold Pro Football Hall of Fame blazer every day, Adderley attended the trial in U.S. District Court. He said, "I believe it was around November 7, 2009, when the jury agreed with us and awarded the retired guys $28.1 million in damages. This happened because the Judge came up with the new theory, not the attorneys."

The union apparently conspired with EA Sports to create a monopoly for interactive video football games. Another company, Take Two, had attempted to enter the business but encountered stiff competition, thanks, in part, to the

NFLPA, which was working against Take Two and the old-timers while working on behalf of EA Sports.

Players Inc. Senior Vice-President Clay Walke, admitted as much in the following e-mail, published by gamepolitics.com.

"Take Two went after retired players to create an 'NFL-style' video game after we gave the exclusive to EA. I was able to forge this deal with [the Pro Football Hall of Fame] that provides them with $400K per year (which is significantly below market rate) in exchange for the HOF player rights. EA owes me a huge favor because that threat was enough to persuade Take Two to back off its plans, leaving EA as the only professional football videogame manufacturer out there."

Former Buffalo Bills Safety Jeff Nixon said, "Discovery information also shows that the NFLPA and Players Inc. unilaterally made a decision to take eight-million dollars of the gross licensing revenue that should have been shared with retired players and reallocate it to the administration of the NFLPA and Players Inc."

The union siphoned off money that should have gone to the old-timers and put it in leadership's pockets. In some places, a union taking from its members would be frowned upon. Some NFLPA officers stole from their members and no heads rolled.

Two prominent members of the Oakland Raiders were front-and-center in the controversy: Gene Upshaw and his old head coach John Madden. Like it or not, the popular Madden is squarely in the middle of the squabble because he is the face of the popular video football game. The iconic Madden has remained silent about his role, if any, in the conspiracy. He has said or done little publicly to help get money to the old-timers.

On April 3, 2011, a news story surfaced that John Madden wanted the video game Madden 12 to reflect concern for players with concussions. In the 2011 version of the game, those players were not allowed back in the video version. In *real* life, the *real* old-time players who suffered *real* head injuries were given a *real* screwing because their images were used in EA Sports video games at grossly below market value.

It must be gluttony that compels a major company to believe it can make a politically correct gesture and everything is magically fine. As if somehow a politically correct tactic, pulling injured players out of a video game, makes up for anything. The old-timers, many of whom were in rough shape physically, mentally and financially, felt swindled.

Regardless of how sophisticated or realistic electronic games have become, the figures are still a series of dots on a screen. So a concussed series of dots is not allowed to re-appear in a make-believe game, but the *real* men who were cheated have not been given the respect of a voluntary monetary amount as a genuine gesture. Even now, an apology would be nice. According to Reuters, the Madden video games sold more than 85 million copies over a 20-year period and made more than $4 billion.

Adderley sees EA Sports as a co-conspirator with the NFLPA. He does not think the video game giant is likely to voluntarily pony up money to the old-timers. Adderley said, "The only way EA will pay the retired guys what we deserve will take place in a federal court room with a jury and judge. They are being sued at the present time by a group of retired guys representing a class action suit similar to the one that I was the class rep for. The evidence will favor us, and EA will end up paying us millions."

The tactic of "scrambling" is detailed in the class action suit filed by Tony Davis on behalf of 6,000 players against EA Sports. "The only significant detail that EA changes from the real-life retired NFL players is their jersey number," the suit says. "Despite EA's 'scrambling' of the retired NFL players' numbers, the games are designed so that consumers of the Madden NFL video game franchise will have no difficulty identifying who the 'historic' players are."

John Madden has repeatedly voiced his great admiration for Vince Lombardi the football coach. He would do well to study Lombardi the man. How do you think Lombardi would have responded if a video game bearing his name were engulfed in such a controversy? Adderley said, "If Lombardi's name was being used on anything that made money involving the players, he would make sure we all received an equal amount for the use of our names, images, etc."

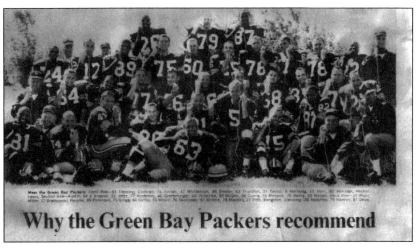

In a 1964 endorsement for Norelco electric shavers, Lombardi made sure everyone was treated fairly, from superstar to groundskeeper. The picture is old and wrinkled, but fairness never gets old.

Adderley's comments are not revisionist history; Lombardi made sure people in the Packers organization were rewarded when championships were won. Shares of money were distributed based on a vote taken by the players— sort of. Tight end Ron Kramer said, "Some of the guys were trying to vote out guys like Dad Braisher, who was our equipment manager. Lombardi went bonkers. He said, 'We don't forget anybody.' And everybody got a part in the championships. That was the most important thing to him, that everybody in the *organization* was part of the team ..."

Adderley echoed the sentiment, "Lombardi made sure that important people working for the Packers would receive a fair amount of the championship money when we voted on how much they would receive. Some of the people were the equipment man, trainers, scouts and John Proski, the man who took care of our practice fields and Lambeau Field." People like a groundskeeper and equipment man were important to Lombardi. There were no little people and there were no dogs.

The player's voting process in Green Bay was not completely representative of a democracy, but it was fair. Adderley said, "After we voted shares to different people, Lombardi checked out the results and if he didn't think the amount was fair, he ordered us to vote again and give the people more money. He was more than fair because he believed in doing the right thing. I don't believe Lombardi would have been involved in any type of political correctness stuff because it was all about the Packers, your family and God."

In 1964, the Packers endorsed Norelco electric razors and Lombardi's fairness was evident. Adderley said, "You will notice that all of the assistant coaches, the trainer and the equipment man were involved in the promotion for Norelco. We all received the same amount and a Norelco electric shaver."

Lombardi even tried to share championship money with his front office staff, but NFL Commissioner Pete Rozelle shot it down. Longtime Lombardi secretary Lori Keck said, "There was one year that I actually typed the list of names of people in the office who were to receive it, my name included, and I was excited. Lombardi decided he was going to take one championship share and split it between the girls in the office and, I think, Al Treml (film director, photographer). It was submitted to the Commissioner's office in New York and the Commissioner turned it down. He said, 'Absolutely not. It's for the players.' It was one of the very few times Lombardi did not get his way, but he fought for his people."

There are several things in life that are futile, like trying to find a one-ended stick or attempting to compare Vince Lombardi the coach and man to other coaches. Lombardi was the real deal. He didn't cheat and he didn't screw people over.

Adderley said, "Someone should ask John Madden why he didn't speak up to EA when he knew damn well that the retired guys in the vintage Madden video game weren't getting paid and the active guys were all being paid."

Adderley added, "The evidence presented at our historic trial proved there was corruption and *greed* involved by the NFLPA and EA. The main thing from the historic lawsuit is this: it caught the National Football League Players Association and Gene Upshaw stealing money from the retired guys by using our images, likeness, etc., and not paying us."

Documents offered during Adderley's lawsuit explained what constituted scrambling and confirmed collaboration between the NFLPA and EA Sports. In an e-mail sent by Players Inc. Vice President of Multimedia LaShun Lawson to Madden NFL Game producer Jeremy Strauser, with a copy going to Doug Allen, then-president of Players Inc., Lawson said: "For all retired players that are not listed ... their identity must be altered so that it cannot be recognized. Regarding paragraph 2 of the License Agreement between Electronic Arts and Players Inc., a player's identity is defined as his name, likeness (including without limitation, number), picture, photograph, voice, facsimile signature and/or biographical information. Hence, any and all players not listed ... cannot be represented in Madden 2002 with the number that player actually wore, and must be scrambled."

As damning as the "smoking gun" e-mail was, the legal team for Adderley's group mishandled it. Adderley said, "The e-mail stated the retired players will be 'scrambled' in the Madden vintage videos to avoid paying us. Katz failed to establish a platform to present the crucial info to the court and jury. When he attempted to present the e-mail to the jury, Judge Alsup stopped him, saying it was not admissible because he had not established a platform. The inexcusable mistake cost us millions of dollars."

Since his abrupt retirement from broadcasting April 16, 2009, little has been seen or heard from John Madden. We can only speculate how Madden's hero, Vince Lombardi, would have stood up for the players and against those who have exploited them, especially if Lombardi's name would have been on the video game.

The fairness, conscience and greatness of Lombardi have never been replaced in the National Football League.

If Lombardi's name were on the game, Mel Renfro says, "He would do what made him a successful coach; he would do the right thing. Just like Mike Ditka, just do the right thing."

Jeff Nixon is willing to cut Madden some slack but thinks the former coach and game analyst should play a role now. Nixon said, "I don't think

John knew what was happening with the whole thing at the time. But now, I think it would do him and his legacy some good if he would come out and say, 'This is ridiculous that this happened. I wasn't part of the internal mechanics of what was going on. Now that I know what happened, I think they need to do something for these guys.' It will be a black mark on his legacy if he doesn't come out and say something; if he doesn't come out and say EA Sports needs to rectify this."

Bruce Laird agrees, "Madden is listening to his advisors. John Madden, the person, should stand up for the players he coached for and against. But he is just another suit doing what his lawyers tell him. I wonder how he sleeps at night."

Retired player advocate and Hall of Fame member Joe DeLamielleure said of Madden, "Don't give me 'my business agent said this or that.' Do the right thing. It's obvious what you should do."

There is more trouble looming for EA Sports and John Madden. Approximately six thousand former players, headed by Tony Davis, have filed a class action suit against the video giant and its namesake. There are growing questions involving the timing of John Madden's sudden broadcasting retirement announcement. Some people speculate he wanted out of the spotlight when word leaked that six thousand players were going to sue the video game sporting his name. It was the 2007 class action suit against the NFLPA that opened the gates for litigation that will put John Madden and others in the news for years to come.

Ultimately, the federal jury's verdict in Adderley's case included two awards: $7.1 million in actual damages plus an additional sum of $21 million for punitive damages. The website Duhaime.org defines punitive damages as: "Special and highly exceptional damages ordered by a court against a defendant where the act or omission which caused the suit, was of a particularly heinous, malicious or highhanded nature." Other definitions of punitive include such words as "egregious," "reckless" and "insidious." The 10-member jury found that the NFLPA breached its duty to represent the interest of retired players. In legal terms, Gene Upshaw and his union suffered a substantial defeat. In football talk, it was a complete and justified ass-kicking.

Despite the smashing victory, which was not appealed by the union, several retired players believed the monetary awards were too small. More ill feelings resulted.

Part of Adderley's bitterness stems from actions taken by Parrish following the trial. Adderley said, "A few days after the historic verdict awarding us the money, Bernie Parrish made it known through the Internet that I sided with the lawyers to accept the $28.1 million and we should have received more than $100 million. I believe he made up fictitious stories about me with intentions of turning as many retired guys against me as possible."

Retired player advocate Bruce Laird said, "Parrish is like the old warrior who comes out of the hills twenty years after the war is over and still wants to fight the same fight."

According to Jeff Nixon, "It seems that 'Bernie's Next Big Thing' is to try and discredit any other group of players or lawyers who want to sue the NFL or the NFLPA. He did everything in his power to discredit the retired players and the lawyers involved in the class action against the NFLPA."

Parrish and several other players filed a malpractice suit against Manatt, Phelps & Phillips, LLP. The effort had a short life and little authenticity. It was dismissed on December 13, 2010, when Judge Alsup wrote in a court order: "Parrish organized a letter-writing campaign that accounted for the majority of comments received and submitted multiple letters himself. Again, various orders directed class counsel to investigate and address concerns voiced in these letters, and at the fairness hearing the concerns were revisited and deemed resolved (see Adderley Dkt. Nos. 650, 657, 664, 665, 670). There is little doubt Parrish is the moving and organizing force behind this sequel lawsuit."

Judge Alsup also wrote, "In fact, 41 of the 53 letters received were copies of a standardized objection letter that Parrish had drafted, posted on the Internet, and encouraged other former NFL players to sign and submit."

Adderley said, "Judge Alsup issued an order regarding attorney fees, cost and incentive payment for the class rep. In the order, Judge Alsup criticized the way that the lawyers put on the case."

The plight of many former NFL players is more apparent now, thanks to Adderley's lawsuit. An excruciating number of old-timers suffer dementia in numbers far exceeding the national average. The league has taken action to reduce concussions with the imposition of new rules, fines, suspensions, improved equipment and playing surfaces. Inherent in the changes is an admission that players had been at risk in previous years. If not true, why change rules to disallow head-to-head contact and tackles made by players launching themselves and leading with the crown of the helmet? Why improve the concrete-hard original AstroTurf?

In the final analysis, the jury awarded $28.1 million, and $26.25 million remained to be divided after legal fees and expenses. Some of the game's greatest players, like Hall of Fame cornerback Mel Renfro, received a check from the settlement. Renfro said, "I got about nine-thousand dollars compensation, which was dearly needed at the time. My pension was like a hundred and sixty bucks." That's per month for a man who played 14 years and went to the Pro Bowl 10 times.

Adderley was falsely accused of conspiring with attorneys to line his pockets at the expense of his fellow retired players. The allegations were unfair as well as inaccurate.

Laird said of Adderley, "Can you imagine what it took to stand up to the NFLPA? Adderley did it with dignity and grace." When Laird was asked if Adderley was the Rosa Parks of the retired player's movement, Bruce said, "That's about right."

Much good came out of Adderley v. National Football League Players Inc., No. C 07-00943 WHA. For the man who served as class representative, though, the experience was awful for many reasons.

For starters, Adderley feels a lack of gratitude from his fellow retirees. He said, "Of the 2,062 guys in the class action suit, less than fifteen have said 'thanks.' There were seventeen Hall of Famers who received a check and zero have thanked me."

There was one player who was not part of the lawsuit and who received no money from the verdict, yet supported Adderley with a special gesture. It was the night before closing arguments in the case when a surprise visitor showed up.

"I was in bed when Ron Katz called my room and said there was a Packers teammate in the lobby who had flown in to see me," Adderley said. "I had no idea who it was until I made it down to the lobby and was pleasantly surprised to see Bart Starr. His support meant a lot to me personally, and I told him that." Starr had flown from his native Alabama to San Francisco that day in order to fortify his fellow Green Bay Packer. The next day Bart caught a flight back to Birmingham.

Adderley added, "They billed us twice for some things, there were two law firms and there should have been only one. They had twice as many lawyers than they should have, making $700-$800 an hour. They had three times as many legal assistants from both firms on the payroll. I agree 100 percent with Judge Alsup's criticism of the way they put on the case. They failed to present crucial information that would have gotten us more money; greed was their number-one goal. It should have been getting as much money for the retired guys as possible."

In conclusion, Adderley said, "I have had no contact with Katz since Judge Alsup's final settlement order, which is public domain."

Adderley stood for the players who millions of fans fell in love with in the 1950s, '60s and '70s. During those times, names of great NFL stars found their way into conversations at dinner tables, local bars, barber shops, playgrounds and hunting shacks. Johnny "U," "Crazy Legs," "The Grey Ghost," Nitschke, Butkus, Y.A., Alan "The Horse," Broadway Joe, "Dandy" Don and others were being talked about in addition to baseball's Mickey, Willie and The Duke. We got to know the football guys; we liked them and the way they played the game. They were not supposed to get old and need help, but they did, and very little assistance was available for them. Adderley, a Hall of Famer, put himself on the line against a powerful union for the greats, and not-so-greats, in a lawsuit that exposed exploitation of former players.

A man who knows a thing or two about standing up courageously against injustice, Ernie Green of the Little Rock Nine, believes Adderley has transcended the game. Adderley's efforts to improve the lives of the old-timers have earned a special place in Green's mind. "I really think he should have gotten a lot more recognition for what he has contributed to modern football, more so than just being a member of the Pro Football Hall of Fame," said Green. "Herb Adderely is a class act and deserves as much positive exposure as the world can give him. I really applaud that Herb is getting his due. I'm a Herb Adderley fan for life."

With the exception of a very few, notably Mike Ditka, Carl Eller and Joe DeLamielleure, Hall of Fame players have stood mostly mute regarding the state of affairs of NFL retirees. Adderley continues to speak out against those who, by design and with intent, commit acts to exploit retired players while putting money in their own bank accounts.

In time, the historic class action lawsuit will be viewed as the event that opened the door for retired players to get relief from a league and union that have not acted in the best interest of the men who built the game. Major litigation has been filed against EA Sports, NFL Films and the National Football League in the aftermath of Adderley's smashing victory.

Emlen Tunnell is still held in the highest regard by students of the game. By his own description, he was "the first black everything" in the National Football League and earned legions of fans for his excellence as a player and person. One of Emlen's greatest admirers is Herb Adderley.

As a player, Green Bay's great Number 26 believes his finest achievements are 1) election to the Pro Football Hall of Fame and 2) selection as one of the game's 100 greatest players.

History may view it differently. When he "stood for his brothers" in the landmark legal case, Herb solidified his place with Tunnell and those *Chosen* few who step outside themselves for the betterment of others.

Herb Adderley is a hero.

The Genie Got Loose

Herb Adderley's lawsuit opened a bitter battle between some of the game's great players and Upshaw's union over one issue: payments for use of images in a video game.

It may have been just the opening salvo of many legal battles to be waged by former players, including a showdown over health problems caused by the game.

Reasonable people would conclude the injuries and associated health problems plaguing former NFL players were caused, in large part, from collisions during games and practice. It is logical to conclude their dementia, Alzheimer's, Lou Gehrig's Disease, damaged joints and other maladies were not caused by film study, bus rides to stadiums or flights to away games.

On December 20, 2009, the Associated Press reported, "The NFL is partnering with Boston University brain researchers who have been critical of the league's stance on concussions." The league has been encouraging current and former NFL players to agree to donate their brains to the Boston University Center for the Study of Traumatic Encephalopathy. A member of Lombardi's Left Side, Dave Robinson, has agreed to participate in the program. As of this writing, Robinson is concerned he may be in the early stages of dementia. Boston University reportedly has found links between repeated head trauma and brain damage in boxers, football players and a former NHL player.

Two years to the day following the AP announcement regarding the NFL-Boston University partnership, another historic development was reported by ESPN's Chris Mortensen. The NFL took another step in its attempt to deal with head trauma. "… effective this week, an independently certified athletics trainer will be assigned to monitor all suspected concussion-related injuries, a league official confirmed Tuesday," Mortensen wrote on December 20, 2011.

Just before Christmas of 2011, two separate suits were filed against the NFL by former players who claimed they were suffering post-concussion symptoms. Several additional suits were filed in early 2012 and it is reasonable to assume the NFL will be dealing with the issue for the foreseeable future.

Players and their legal counsels will be seeking answers in order to determine if the best possible equipment and medical treatment was provided by the league and its teams. In the aftermath of Adderley's litigation, hard questions are going to be asked of a professional sports league that is bathing in money.

Cowboy's Hall of Famer Mel Renfro said, "The lawsuit has opened the door for players to get their just due. Hopefully, we won't all die off before we can make that happen. My main beef is they've got the money and they will figure out a way not to give it to the old guys."

Former Buffalo Bills player Jeff Nixon said, "Absolutely, Herb really *did* open the door to questions about other things that are happening with the union and the NFL too. It's amazing; I think he's the face of the retired player's concerns. He's not the kind of guy who goes out and attacks people; he's a real gentleman. Herb set the stage for guys finally getting paid for their image."

Tony Davis said, "Herb opened a book. No one could ever get into the NFL Players Association book so to speak."

According to Davis, it was Adderley who brought attention to the business side of the game for the old-timers. Tony said, "Frankly, the NFL retired player is too proud for his own good. They have thought it was just a sport, a sport they chose. Herb stood up and said, 'You know what, it's a little bit more than that.' There is now awareness we were employees of a business that has left us in pretty bad shape physically. That damage has transferred and transformed into an inability to handle a lot of things mentally in later life."

Ramifications of a suit filed July 19, 2011, could eventually send seismic tremors through the structure of the National Football League. Seventy-five former players sued the NFL, claiming the league intentionally withheld knowledge of the damaging effects of concussions for 90 years. If any doubt remained, the gloves came off August 19, 2011, as retired players took extreme measures to force the NFL to provide medical coverage for injuries suffered during competition. Other similar suits have since been filed.

More and more, retired players realize they were entertainers and want to be treated in like fashion as other performers. They also know their retirement benefits are inferior when compared to other sports.

Six former NFL players have filed a class action against NFL Films, and thus the NFL, for using names, images, and likenesses of those players to promote the league. Plaintiffs and proposed class representatives are Hall of Fame defensive end Elvin Bethea, former quarterback Dan Pastorini, defensive end Jim Marshall, tight end Joe Senser, guard Ed White and defensive end Fred Dryer. Following his playing days, Dryer was a successful actor whose credits include playing the lead on *Hunter*, a police drama television series that ran on NBC from 1984 to 1991. He knows the value of entertainment.

Similar to an actor getting residuals for a TV series in syndication or a movie released on DVD, the players would like a piece of the revenue that has been generated by NFL Films, both in the past and future. Ramifications of such a lawsuit, if it goes to court, could have monumental consequences.

Jeff Nixon said, "For me to even get my own films, I have to pay fifty dollars a pop. I think the NFL is going to have to do something to compensate the players."

The suit, if approved, will represent "persons who played professional football for any NFL member team, who are retired or no longer active, and whose name, voice, image, likeness, or other indicia of identity has been used by the NFL to promote the NFL or any of its member teams, sell products or services, otherwise to increase the brand awareness or obtain revenue for the NFL or any of its member teams." That's lawyer talk that means any player who has appeared in NFL Films video.

In another legal case spearheaded by former player Tony Davis, class action papers on behalf of approximately 6,000 players were filed against EA Sports on July 29, 2010. In part, the charges claim, "EA's commercial exploitation of retired NFL players is both blatant and prolific as the 2009 edition of the NFL Madden video game contained over 140 'historic teams' containing likenesses of thousands of retired NFL players."

In some ways, the Adderley and Tony Davis suits are closely related because EA Sports is the union's top licensee and a central figure in both class actions. A major question needs a definitive answer: Did the NFLPA and EA Sports conspire to cheat retired players? Another question is being asked: Where is the face for the Madden game? Does John Madden give a damn about the physical and mental condition of the men whose images have been used in the Madden electronic games?

At the time this book was being written, neither Davis nor EA Sports offered substantive comments because the case was pending.

Adderley presented a few thoughts about the Davis/EA Sports suit. He said, "The retired guys who were 'scrambled' in the vintage videos were paid nothing; it has cost EA Sports millions of dollars. EA Sports and the NFLPA made the decision to shut down the videos and lose millions of dollars instead of paying us for using our images. It was a very bad decision because the lawsuit Tony Davis filed against EA will cost them more than they would have paid us."

Adderley believes evidence from his litigation against the players association will be important in the Tony Davis proceedings. "The historic lawsuit, along with the e-mail messages from the NFLPA to EA stating that they should scramble us will be key evidence that will influence the jury to award us millions of dollars," Adderley said. "My gut feelings are EA will make an out-of-court settlement because they are in a no-win situation because of greed and disrespect. The truth will prevail in the court room and they will be exposed again!"

The video Goliath is facing another significant legal and public relations battle. On April 1, 2011, EA was hit with a huge lawsuit from Robin Antonick, the original creator of the game. According to Reuters news service, Antonick has filed suit for "tens of millions" of dollars in royalties, plus a portion of the enormous profits EA has made on the series. Antonick reportedly has not been paid royalties since 1992.

Aside from the entertainment litigation against the NFLPA, EA Sports and NFL Films, another monster issue is etched on the mangled faces, bodies and minds of old men who used to play professional football. In so many ways, the NFL old-timers are second-class citizens when compared to other sports. Publicity generated by Adderley's litigation let the genie out of the bottle and brought attention to the plight of damaged people who had played in the National Football League. Individuals and groups are now emboldened to seek legal remedies when negotiations fail.

The retired players want their pensions brought up to active players' levels. As Mel Renfro said, "they've got the money …"

Hope was rekindled when DeMaurice Smith succeeded Gene Upshaw as Executive Director of the NFLPA. Maybe the new guy, in conjunction with the NFL, would do for their old-timers what baseball had done years for its retirees years before.

No one could have envisioned the numerous health problems that plague many retired NFL players. From 1974–82, Lou Piccone played with the New York Jets and Buffalo Bills. His boyhood love affair with football has left him perplexed in his senior years. Piccone said, "I never thought something I did as a kid, that was advocated and promoted so much systematically throughout our youth and young adult life, could be so deceiving. For those of us who met the challenge to play at the pro level, how could this be? Risk life and limb and have former players acting as player representatives flip for the money. The owners, the NFLPA and the sanctioned player agents all participated in the systematic fleecing of innocence."

At one time Piccone believed he suffered seventeen concussions as a player. In 2010, the league changed base line criteria for what constituted a concussion, prompting Lou to say, "I would have had too many to count."

An alarming frequency in the incidences of dementia and Alzheimer's has spurred conversation about retirement conditions of former professional football players and a listening audience is gathering.

Many retired NFL players cannot afford the health care they need and receive. Who is paying for the medical expenses of these guys? If you are a taxpayer, you are.

Evan Weiner, in an article entitled "NFL's Billion-Dollar Healthcare Question," shed light on the issue of the general public paying health care costs of retired players.

While the Collective Bargaining Agreement was being negotiated in 2011, Weiner wrote, "There is a major question that the American People should be asking in the ongoing labor dispute between National Football League owners and the National Football League Players Association as the two sides head to a March 4th lockout. Are the players association's negotiators asking for a change in post career health benefits or are the reps asking for status quo? Status quo means that qualified former pros get health care for just five years following their last game. That is important for the American People to know because the American People are picking up the cost of taking care of broken-down former pros who cannot get health insurance and, instead, are living on Social Security Disability and Medicare."

Weiner asked, "The cost to the American taxpayer? Higher than a billion dollars."

Is there at least one major national politician who sees the value in trying to get money from somewhere besides taxpayers to pay for the medical costs of retired NFL players?

Where are the politicians who can get medical expenses of retired NFL players off the backs of America's taxpayers? Are they sitting in luxury boxes at NFL games?

Are there principled owners, agents, active players or union leaders with a conscience to stand for the old guys?

Nobility, where have you gone? Did you ever exist?

These types of questions are being asked partly because Adderley had the courage to take on corruption.

What does the future hold for cage fighters and participants in other such sports who beat each other senseless? Who will pay their medical bills when they are broke and need help? You and other American tax payers will get the tab. Where are the politicians now who can save us money later? Why are the politicians waiting until these cage fighters don't know if they should go another round or pop out of a cuckoo clock?

It seems some money may be available for the retired players based on a significant element of the 2011 labor agreement. Loads of money is wasted every year on first-round draft picks who bomb. An Associated Press report, cited by the *Detroit Free Press*, April 14, 2011, stated, "Overall, NFL teams have paid nearly $2 billion to top-10 selections since 2000." Much of the money went to guys who flopped as pro football players. Each year multiple millions of dollars are guaranteed to unproven players who have never been involved in a single professional play.

A rookie salary cap was included in the 2011 labor agreement, indicating that sanity made an appearance at the negotiations. Everybody knew it was crazy to guarantee millions of dollars to unproven players. The fans knew it, veteran players knew it, sportswriters and broadcasters knew it, owners knew it and agents knew the system assured they would get paid a lot of money first.

Here is the "elephant-in-the-room" question that nobody wants to ask publicly: Did agents buy off the NFLPA's leadership to keep the rookie cap from being *significantly* lowered for all those years?

Hall of Fame offensive tackle Joe DeLamielleure of the Buffalo Bills said, "In my opinion, DeMaurice Smith is a puppet for Tom Condon, Dick Berthelsen and the other agents. The agents run that league."

Adderley said, "Mr. Smith, Upshaw's replacement, has continued to implement Upshaw's policies the past two years. He told me during the press conference announcing the settlement of our lawsuit that his main goal was to bring all of the guys, past and present, together under one roof and the NFLPA represent all of us. That statement has been proven to be false because Mr. Smith has refused to meet with George Martin, the president of the NFL Alumni, without a room full of his cronies."

If a portion of the extravagant money wasted on first-round drafts were to be put toward an adequate pension plan, the controversy would probably end.

Piccone said, "They could slay the dragon right now and shut us up. They could pay for a period of time and then we're gonna be dead. They could pay the debt back to those who built the game up to where it is. And it should be so."

The dialogue is on. Where are the supposedly responsible people who can help the old-timers?

Increasingly, the players association is coming under scrutiny and criticism. Their fiduciary, primary trust relationship with retired players is being questioned and, in some circles, being viewed as a farce.

Tony Davis said, "My father was a union man. He told me this about the NFLPA: 'This is not a union, it's a social club. They don't look out for you people. Unions are not supposed to exist to make their officers wealthy. Unions exist so all the workers can share in the wealth and benefits of the industry they work in.' That is not the case with the NFL Players Association. The size of the money Gene Upshaw was making was off the charts. Quite frankly, DeMaurice Smith is doing the same thing. We trust them with our benefits plans, to run these plans and do things for the benefit of us as retired players. They were caught cheating and stealing from their members. That's almost unforgiveable and that's what Herb exposed."

On several fronts, the old-timers may prove to have lots of fight left. Like Adderley, many of them believe it is possible to break the grip of inequity.

Gene Upshaw was empowered to neglect retired players, but he was wrong in doing so. A look at what he *didn't* do for many retired players is a pitiful epitaph for his regime.

Among the saddest stories of retired players is that of Pittsburgh Steelers center Mike Webster and the help he did not receive from his union. The great "Iron Mike" anchored Pittsburgh's offensive line, played on four Super Bowl winners, appeared in nine Pro Bowls, but ended up living out of his car and died at age 50. Joe DeLamielleure said, "Mike Webster was a good friend of mine and he took 'em to court. Mike is the guy who took 'em to the Supreme Court and won 1.18 million dollars. He played in the league for seventeen years and took the union to court. Shouldn't the union be taking the NFL to court on our behalf?"

Joe D's question deserves an answer.

Webster's settlement of $1.18 million was awarded by a federal court in April of 2005. He died three years earlier, broke and broken. It was not until after he died that Webster was diagnosed as having had chronic traumatica encephalopathy, a neurodegenerative disease.

On January 4, 2010, Dr. Bennet Omalu, a founding member of the Brain Injury Research institute testified before a House Judiciary Committee saying, "I discovered the first case of footballer's dementia in Pittsburgh Steelers Hall of Famer Mike Webster. I performed an autopsy on Mike Webster in 2002 when he died suddenly at the age of 50. Mike Webster's life after retirement from football was marred by progressive symptoms of dementia, major depression, mood disorders, drug abuse and violent/criminal tendencies."

Dr. Omalu added, "I classified it in fact as Chronic Traumatic Encephalopathy [CTE]." Mike Webster is considered the father of CTE.

It has been speculated that Webster's ailments were due to wear and tear sustained during his playing career, and physicians who examined him for disability benefits estimated "Iron Mike" had been involved in the equivalent of 25,000 violent collisions while playing high school, college and professional football over a 25 year span.

The head trauma issue is close to the heart of Adderley

Packers' Hall of Fame free safety Willie Wood (front) entered an assisted living facility in November 2006. Green Bay's surest tackler, Wood is afflicted with dementia. Fellow Hall of Famers Jim Taylor (l) and Herb Adderley (r) are shown with Wood in 2008.
Photo courtesy of Scott Stroupe

and Robinson because two former teammates, Willie Wood and Bill "Bubba" Forester, were both afflicted by dementia.

On November 20, 2006, Adderley's good friend Andre Waters, who played for the Eagles, committed suicide. ESPN's Jeremy Schapp reported in May of 2012 the findings of the doctors who examined Waters' brain post mortem. The Emmy-Award-winning Schapp said the tissue appeared like that of an "85-year-old Alzheimer's patient."

Compare NFL retirement benefits to those of Major League Baseball and it becomes very clear, very quickly: there is no comparison. Baseball's labor negotiations produced far superior packages for their guys. The Boys of Summer get more money and are not asked to donate their brains for research studies in order to determine damage caused by the game they played.

Robert D. Manfred Jr., executive vice president, Labor Relations & Human Resources for Major League Baseball, said, "We are very proud of what we do for our former players. We are the only employer I'm aware of in all of the United States that has ever gone back and given benefits to Negro League players who never worked for us and pre-1947 players who played when there was no pension plan. We used to have a four-year rule in order to get a pension. Working with the players association, we just went and provided benefits to those players who didn't qualify." How about that for getting it done?

Major League Baseball players begin accruing pension benefits imme-diately, according to Manfred, "They vest after one day. They have to work a quarter of a year, sixty days, to get a meaningful benefit, but they literally vest after one day."

Would it make sense for a pro football player to have the same plan? After all, football is an ultimately more violent game where the participants suffer more injuries than their baseball counterparts. The NFL plan kicks in all at once, after four years. A lot of football players suffer lots of injuries and never last four years.

Manfred explained, "When the union was formed, the pension plan was a contentious issue back in the '40s and '50s. Since I've been around, which has been since '87, pensions have been relatively noncontroversial." When asked if the tranquility is a result of all sides knowing they should do the right thing, Manfred said, "That's right."

Retirement pensions for baseball players put the NFL to shame. Manfred said, "Any player with a significant career, like five years, really ends up with a pension equivalent to the IRS maximum, which is a hundred and eighty-five thousand dollars ($185,000) a year." Again, Renfro played 14 years in the

NFL, went to 10 Pro Bowls and said, "My pension was like a hundred and sixty bucks per month." The NFL labor agreement of 2011 boosted Adderley's retirement from $176 per month to about $2,000. It is a nice increase, but a far cry from the benefits of his contemporaries in baseball. When compared to an MLB player with similar years of service, Adderley's pension is about 15 percent of his MLB counterpart.

In the area of health care, Major League Baseball's retirement benefit package is proof positive that MLB values its former players. Manfred said, "We subsidize retiree health care from the time they leave the game through their death."

Baseball Commissioner Allen "H." Bud Selig's tenure has brought labor peace to the national pastime, in part because the retired guys were cared for. Especially in the realm of labor harmony, Mr. Selig stands apart from his fellow commissioners. Perhaps it matters that Commissioner Selig has been a dedicated, lifelong baseball fan. It may also be significant that he is not a lawyer and has not operated a sport for the benefit of other lawyers. He genuinely loves the game, players and fans. In his senior years, as the most powerful figure in his game, he held dear the dignity of heroes who enriched his youth and the game's tradition. In thoughts and deeds, Joe DiMaggio, Hank Aaron, Jackie Robinson and hundreds of other players of much lesser stature have been respected and treated as treasures by Commissioner Selig and Major League Baseball. In addition to superstars, Bud Selig cares about guys like Puddin' Head Jones.

When Major League Baseball and the MLB Players Association reached agreement on a new Collective Bargaining Agreement in November of 2011, it guaranteed labor peace through 2016. The deal meant 21 consecutive years without a work stoppage for our national pastime.

Not one complaint was heard from retired baseball players because their union sold them out.

Adderley said, "In my opinion, the NFLPA will not be embarrassed into coming close to doing for the retired guys what baseball has done for their guys."

When football's Collective Bargaining Agreement was reached in August of 2011, a portion was left as an afterthought. Predictably, pension benefits for the old-timers were left to be resolved after the active players had a new deal. How is that for losing bargaining leverage?

During the 2011 NFL labor negotiations, contempt for the retirees and a callous refusal to help them were personified by one of the player's most visible and vocal leaders, New Orleans quarterback Drew Brees. He said, "There's some guys out there who have made bad business decisions. They took their pensions early because they never went out and got a job. They've had a couple of divorces and they're making payments to this place and that place. And that's why they don't have money. And they're coming to us to basically say, 'Please make up for my bad judgment.'"

News flash, Drew, some of the old guys have so much brain damage that they can't form those or any other audible words. They have such high levels of neurological impairment, suffered while playing football, that they don't know where they are and cannot care for themselves.

Speaking of bad judgment, Brees' comments became even more egregious and reflected the institutional arrogance of the New Orleans Saints in March of 2012. The National Football League announced unprecedented sanctions against the Saints for a "bounty system" that paid defensive players to injure members of opposing teams, especially quarterbacks. Saints defensive coordinator at the time of the program, Gregg Williams, admitted his participation in the system that was in place from 2009-2011, at a time Brees was the team's signal caller. The NFL banned Williams from the game indefinitely, and head coach Sean Payton was given the boot for a year. The unprecedented discipline for Payton was administered in part because he lied to the Commissioner.

Player representative, quarterback, team leader and community icon Drew Brees said he knew nothing of the program that was in place for three years.

Head and other serious injuries suffered by the old-timers are precisely the reason rule changes were made to protect quarterbacks, especially undersized ones, like Drew Brees. Hopefully, Brees will live a long and healthy life, remembering forever the beautiful image of him holding his little boy, Baylen, after Super Bowl XLIV. Telling, isn't it? Baylen was wearing big earmuffs to protect his hearing during the post-game celebration. Someone cared about his health.

Perhaps one day Drew Brees will be grateful for the men who gave their health to help protect him so he could break Dan Marino's single-season passing record December 26, 2011.

Bernie Parrish uses the phrase, "Delay, deny and hope they die." He and many retired players believe the NFL, the NFLPA, EA Sports, John Madden, agents and others are playing a waiting game as the old-timers die off. Every time one of the retired guys is buried, another potential lawsuit, an increase in benefits or a reminder of the neglect vanishes six feet under.

A society says a lot about itself by the way it treats the elderly, the infirm, and those without power. If the same is said about the way unions care for their retirees, the National Football League Players Association under Gene Upshaw was a ruthless autocracy. To his credit, players' salaries increased enormously, but many vulnerable old-timers were left out of negotiations by Upshaw. Rookie salaries, specifically for first-rounders, skyrocketed.

A comparison can be made between retired NFL players and other beleaguered groups in America's history. The retirees were without power because they had virtually no representation through the union, agents, owners or active players at the negotiating tables. Among the most despicable aspects of America's history has been the abuse of power. Similar to other groups struggling for equality, oppressed retired NFL players found the deck stacked against them and are fighting back. In the bad old days of our nation, laws were on the books denying women, blacks and others of their fundamental constitutional rights. Laws and procedures are not right and just, solely because they exist. The road to fairness, complicated by the unethical, seems to be endless.

In 2007, Gene Upshaw told the *Charlotte Observer,* "the bottom line is I don't work for the retired players. They don't hire me, and they don't fire me," he said. "They can complain about me all day long." Later Upshaw said the remark wasn't to be taken literally, but DeLamielleure said his family was frightened. "He is the head of a union. He has the wherewithal to do it," DeLamielleure said, adding that Upshaw should be fired. Upshaw's outburst was in startlingly poor taste. It was also consistent with his public dealings with retirees. Last year he brushed off the old-timers by pointing out that "they don't pay his salary."

One of America's greatest leaders said, "Force is all-conquering, but its victories are short-lived." The words of Abraham Lincoln clearly describe how temporary battles won with power can be challenged and corrected by honorable people with appropriate remedies. Lawsuits and conflicts seem to be measures designed to correct the union's negligence.

Contrast that with the words of Thomas Jefferson: "The greatest honor of a man is in doing good to his fellow men, not in destroying them." Jefferson also said, "I have never been able to conceive how any rational being could propose happiness to himself from the exercise of power over others."

Reflections on Greatness

Too often claimed and misidentified, greatness is not overrated.

With the inevitable demise of the Lombardi Dynasty, greatness in Green Bay was both lost and captured eternally. True greatness, coupled with class, endures. True greatness *requires* class.

There are no split loyalties for either Adderley or Robinson, even though both played for other teams in addition to Green Bay. "I am a lifetime Packer," Adderley said. So much so he has never even put on his finger the Super Bowl VI ring he won while playing for Dallas. "I was going to put it up for sale on eBay a few years ago, but my daughter asked me not to do that," he added. "I have never worn it because wearing rings from both teams didn't feel right."

Robinson said, "Once a Packer, always a Packer." Tom Murphy, a director with the Packers Hall of Fame said, "Dave is one of the most enthusiastic guys you could hope to find. He attends our annual Hall of Fame Golf Classic, the Alumni weekends, and basically does anything we ask him to do. He is a great Green Bay Packer."

Great friends and great linebackers Ray Nitschke (l) and Dave Robinson (r). NFL Films selected Green Bay's linebacking trio of Nitschke, Robinson and Lee Roy Caffey as the sixth best in the history of football.

When Lombardi, Adderley, Robinson and the rest of the Packers dominated football in the 1960s, it was a period when television brought the game into our homes on a consistent basis for the first time. Week after week and year after year, we saw the same players on the same team win NFL championships. America saw pro football's first dynasty of the television era from cradle to grave and that can never be duplicated. The explosion in popularity of the National Football League happened in large part because of the Green Bay Packers. The viewing public became familiar with a team that dominated for a decade.

It has been a beautiful dynasty from then until now, and the magnitude of the Glory Years has only grown with the passage of time.

Adderley and Robinson are part of one of the most charming and romantic stories in sports history, as Steve Sabol of NFL Films has accurately stated. Romance, nostalgia and charm, however, are easily distorted when viewed through the prism of hindsight, and it matters who is looking back.

"I agree with Steve Sabol's comments about the '60s time period being a romantic one," Adderley said. "He failed to mention who was involved with the romance and why."

Just as Adderley has no split loyalties regarding the teams for which he played, he is clear about his allegiance to the players of his era and how they have been treated.

Adderley said, "Without question, Green Bay had the best fans in the NFL during that time. The owners didn't have a 'romantic thing' going on with the fans; it was all about the dollars. I guess you can say it was a romantic thing between the fans in Green Bay and the team, and we helped to get it started in the '60s, before it was called Titletown."

He said, "Yes, it was a good time for me to play even though I had to have two jobs to make ends meet. It was the players' love for the game and self-pride that brought out the best in us. It wasn't for the money, because we didn't make very much. Can you imagine only making fifty dollars for an exhibition game? The romance was displayed by the owners, with their love for money and they did not share it fairly with the players like they are forced to do now. They paid us the lowest salaries possible, including fifty bucks for exhibition games, while they hired Brinks trucks to haul their millions to the bank. There was a big difference about who loved what and why."

As it was being played out, the Lombardi Dynasty appeared radically different when viewed by a white teenager in Wisconsin Rapids, Wisconsin, or black athletes from Philadelphia and New Jersey. Adderley and Robinson's observation deck was a pair of cleats in stadiums across America. Adderley said, "Playing in the '60s alerted me to the fact that I was included in the

Chosen few because there were only a few black players on NFL teams, and some of the teams did not have one. It alerted me also to the fact that Jim Crow law had something to do with some of the NFL owner's decisions concerning the color of a man's skin. In some cases, the black players had to be twice as good as the white players to make the squad. For me to be a number-one draft choice of an NFL team with a no-cut contract, I felt blessed and like one of the *Chosen*."

Given the circumstances, Green Bay was the best place for Adderley. "There is no way that I could have had better teammates or a better coach or be with a better team," he said. "We all didn't love each other, but we liked and respected each other both on and off of the field. Lombardi had a lot to do with that fact."

Once physically swift with mechanical precision, members of Lombardi's Left Side experienced the inevitable effects of aging. Longevity requires payment. These days Adderley and Robinson walk a little slower, sometimes on a cane, occasionally not at all. One pacemaker, a few replacement parts and some surgeries have been divided between the two and both have battled the disease that killed Lombardi.

Adderley said, "I had a herniated disc, a bulging disc, spinal stenosis, you name it. I had surgery a couple years ago to fuse the L4 and L5 vertebrae." The great cornerback suffers pain when he stands or walks. The pain is on the left side, just like he was for so many opponents.

Adderley's family physician, Dr. Kevin Fleming, said, "He did have a herniated disc. Normally you'd try to do everything other than surgery because I've had a number of people who had surgery and they were worse off after than before. Scar tissue develops and that impinges on the nerve. In Adderley's case, he was having chronic pain and didn't want to take any narcotics for the pain, and so I sent him to one of my neurosurgical buddies in south Jersey. We tried everything. We tried physical therapy; we tried epidurals, steroids; we tried all of the things to try to avoid surgery but it just wasn't working. I would say the surgery was successful as far as having him be able to walk without a whole lot of discomfort. He is absolutely the best patient. If he ever has a question, he never hesitates to ask me and I give him whatever answer I can. If I don't have the answer, I'll find out for him. He's a pleasure to take care of from that standpoint, and he's not your typical superstar athlete. He's down-to-earth and he's a real person. He's not one of those guys who thinks he's bulletproof."

Vince Lombardi taught his players about life and may have contributed to extending the lives of Adderley and Robinson. Both men have been afflicted with the same disease, colon cancer, that claimed the great coach's life.

Adderley's was detected in a routine physical examination and dealt with in short order. "In January 1991, Dr. William Morris removed the tumor and about six inches of large intestine on each side of the affected area," Adderley said. "If I wouldn't have had the physical, I would not be here today. Thank God for making me one of the chosen few."

Robinson received a new lease on life when a pacemaker was installed during the summer of 2009.

Two additional medical problems were discovered in May 2011 while he was undergoing a physical examination. Results led his medical team to believe Robinson had pancreatic cancer and, therefore, a 2-percent chance of survival. A biopsy revealed his pancreatic cancer was benign, but evidence of the colon cancer and an 80-percent blockage of a major artery to the heart were detected.

Fortunately for Robinson and football fans who root for their legends, both issues were addressed with positive outcomes.

Colon cancer claimed Coach Lombardi's life, due in part because he would not submit to the rudimentary testing available in the mid 1960s. Robinson's intestinal cancer was detected in the very early stages, and a June 2011 surgery removed a small area of damaged tissue. So successful was the procedure that no follow-up radiation or chemotherapy was needed.

Coronary issues have been a frequent and unwelcome visitor to the Robinson family. Robinson's father lost his life to heart problems at age 52, and Robinson's 42-year-old son, Richard, suffered a fatal heart attack in 2007.

Robinson received blood thinners and a stent that have restored him to cardiac well-being.

Adderley has a lot to live for, including the good-luck-charm baby girl who was born six weeks after the Ice Bowl. She is now a confident and accomplished woman, Dr. Toni Adderley. With a dental practice in Washington, D. C., and two athletic children, she is a dedicated and busy mother. Dr. Toni graduated dental school in 1994 and is a self-professed "football fanatic."

The transition from superstar to father and grandpa is complete for Adderley. Toni Adderley, DDS, said, "He is just "dad" to me, but I do regret I didn't see him play and wish I could have. I've seen the film footage and people's reaction when they find out who he is. But he's just dad to me and papop to my kids." Justice Page, Adderley's granddaughter, is 11, and Joshua Satchel Page is 14; both are gifted young athletes. The two kids are the center of Adderley's universe, although Josh will require a lot of work. Dr. Toni said, "My dad lives for his grandchildren and the Green Bay Packers, but my son is a humongous Cowboys fan and they go at it during the season."

Adderley took on the world's best wide receivers, battled the NFLPA and survived Vince Lombardi, but this grandson business is trouble to the second power. "It's very difficult because his dad raised him to be a Cowboys *and* Ohio State fan!" Adderley said. "He will make the switch somewhere down the road to be a Packers and Spartan fan."

Dear Dr. Toni:
Mamas, don't let your babies grow up to be Cowboys. Please.

Pride flows from father to daughter and vice versa. Adderley takes great satisfaction in the professional achievements of his daughter, but is even more pleased with the quality person and mother Toni has become.

She wasn't old enough to see her dad compete on the field, but Dr. Toni watched him battle with the NFL Players Association in the historic lawsuit. She said, "I am extremely proud of him for that. He pretty much stood alone in the end, and that was huge. I think he did it totally unselfishly. He ended up doing well with his life and he didn't have to put himself out there that way."

In the spirit of helping others, father and daughter are heavily involved in Metro Warriors Youth Organization (www.metrowarriors.org). In addition to her duties as a mom and dentist, Dr. Toni has established a non-profit 501(c) in order to deliver a multitude of programs and services to Washington, D.C., youngsters. Herb, his good friend Dr. Kevin Fleming, and others are enthusiastic volunteers in the program that was started by Dr. Toni's high school friend, Tami Goode. Like Toni, Ms. Goode devoted herself to a career in medical care, and today her proper name is Dr. Tamara Goode, veterinarian.

The infectious passion of Metro Warriors founder Patrick "Tommy" Johnson to help kids soon found a place in the heart of Dr. Goode and her special friend.

Metro Warriors has teamed with Bo Kimble, a basketball player who started at Philadelphia's Dobbins Technical High School, to screen young athletes for cardiac conditions. National attention was focused on the issue in March 1990 when a 23 year-old who played with Kimble in both high school and college collapsed and died during a game.

Dr. Kevin Fleming said, "There is a medical condition called prolonged QT. It's the condition that killed Bo Kimble's teammate Hank Gathers at Loyola Marymount University. When you see these high school athletes dying on the field, it's usually of prolonged QT. The heart just stops, and if you don't have a defibrillator around, you can't get it going. Herb, Toni and a lot of Toni's friends became involved and we've got a bunch of defibrillators placed in various facilities in the Philadelphia area. That is thanks in large part to Herb pushing for it; defibrillators being available are absolutely essential."

In addition to helping a lot of kids, Dr. Fleming says the project has been great for Adderley and his daughter. "He and Toni get along tremendously well together; he has a great relationship with his daughter. He absolutely adores Toni."

Robinson is truly one of the most likeable people and he thoroughly enjoys his fellow human beings. He had a successful business career with a beer distributorship and other various ventures after retiring, but he has suffered a father and husband's worst pain.

His youngest son, Robert, began having kidney problems at age 28 and spent three years on dialysis before receiving a cadaver kidney transplant. "Rob was the baby, and after he got his kidney and it was working, Dave and Rob played golf together a lot and enjoyed the new lease on life," Robinson's sister Retta said. Unfortunately, the donor was somewhat older and the replacement kidney also began to fail. On October 21, 2001, Robinson and Elaine Robinson lost their youngest while he was waiting for another transplant.

"It's way too simplistic to say, 'A parent should never have to bury one of their children.' The experience is devastating," Robinson said. Within a short time, one or two days, another father who had lost a son reached out to his friend and teammate. "Bart Starr called me and we talked for a long while. Because Bart and Cherry had lost their son, we were able to just talk father-to-father," Robinson said. "I'm not sure if I could have gotten through it without Bart. There is just something that another father understands. He gave me some advice that I followed and it made a big difference in my life. It is not uncommon for couples to experience marital problems after the loss of a child. Bart may have saved our marriage."

Before joining the Packers in '63, Robinson looked at the roster and saw: Jim Taylor, Baton Rouge, Louisiana; Paul Hornung, Louisville, Kentucky; Bart Starr, Mobile, Alabama …

After his Gator Bowl experience, Robinson was not sure what to expect from a team with a large number of Southern whites. Many years before the comforting call from Starr, Robinson learned he could count on his teammates, on and off the field.

A black linebacker from New Jersey and a white quarterback from Alabama opening their hearts, and sharing tears in a private phone call may say more about the Lombardi Dynasty than any book, documentary or movie ever will.

In 2007, Robinson found Elaine on the couple's kitchen floor, where she had suffered a debilitating stroke. Robinson shut down the rest of his life and spent as much time as possible with her during the following three months before she passed.

Robinson's sister Retta said, "You might as well say Dave and Elaine grew up together. They went together in high school, through Dave's college years and were married for 44 years. They were meant to be together; it was preordained."

The cruel reality of death struck a third blow three months and four days later. Upon entering the den of his Akron, Ohio, home Robinson found his 42-year-old son, Richard, dead on the floor from a massive heart attack.

"That void he has suffered with the loss of Robert, Elaine and Richard will never be filled," Retta said. "Dave is very strong and I am sure he and I are alike in that way. I'll put on a brave face; I'll smile and be sociable, but when I go home and close that door and I am by myself, that's when I let it go. Dave will do the same thing."

Robinson's sister added, "We have been taught and we have learned that God does not make mistakes. We don't understand it now and maybe we never will on this planet, but He will never abandon you. I have depended on that for a long time and I know Dave has, too. You have to accept God's will. Especially with Elaine and Richard being so close together, if he would have wound up being an alcoholic or something like that, people would say, 'Oh, he couldn't take it.' Mom and Dad didn't raise us that way. He's a Robinson; he's got strength and character. We were lucky we had good parents."

Partly because of how he was raised, Robinson is one of us. "He was always Dave, Lefty," Retta said. "When the nieces and nephews got older and started playing little league and things like that, when the other kids' fathers found out, they would say, 'Oh, Lefty Robinson. That's your uncle who plays football.' The kids were dumbstruck and would say, 'That's Uncle Dave.' To them, he was Uncle Dave. There was no big to-do about it.

"He never came off like 'I am the big celebrity.' It wouldn't have worked anyhow. When he's here and he needs a glass of water, he gets up and gets it himself," she said.

Herb Adderley and Dave Robinson: Lombardi's Left Side.

Time has taken a toll on the two men, but dignity and greatness remain completely intact because those qualities cannot be taken, only surrendered. These two never learned how to give up.

They have been blessed with long lives and we have been fortunate to have had them. If only the Great Lombardi could have seen them live his lessons on into their senior years.

Adderley and Robinson came from the opposite end of privilege. Both were truly great football players. Better still, they are excellent human beings who know the difference between right and wrong and made a positive difference to those they touched. Today, whether they enter the Packers' offices, walk onto Lambeau Field or roam the team's Hall of Fame, they add to the prodigious history of the fabled franchise.

From the original Acme Packers through the glory and struggles of the Curly Lambeau years and the dismal seasons between Lambeau and Lombardi, the little city with an NFL franchise built a tradition in search of more greatness. Adderley said, "Looking at the history posted around Lambeau Field helped us make history while setting the standard for those who followed."

There are so many things to like about the Lombardi teams. The players were good guys on and off the field and the coaching staff didn't resort to cheating tactics like illegal filming or bounty systems. Who knows what kind of shenanigans go on these days with technology?

Since leaving the game as players, Lombardi's men have conducted themselves in the same upstanding fashion with which they played. The image of the Lombardi Years is even greater because the players have not sullied the greatness with damaging conduct during their post playing days. Adderley, Robinson and their teammates have been solid citizens and tremendous ambassadors of the Packers through the years. There is no expiration date on greatness.

Oh, and one more thing: they won championships like no NFL team before or since.

Shown on the floor of Lambeau Field during a 1997 reunion are members of Lombardi's defense. Left to right: Doug Hart (43), Herb Adderley (26), Bob Jeter (21), Lee Roy Caffey (60), Ray Nitschke (66), Tommy Joe Crutcher (56), Jim Weatherwax (73), Willie Wood (24), Dave Robinson (89) and Willie Davis (87).

Beginning in 1989 when Bob Harlan was appointed President and CEO of the Packers, he returned the franchise to excellence while cherishing the team's rich heritage. Much like Lombardi thirty years earlier, Harlan took the helm of a franchise in disarray and returned it to glory. Lesser men would have been intimidated by such greatness, knowing the Dynasty would probably never be matched. Harlan stepped from the huge shadow of Lombardi to aggressively nurture the rich history of the organization, rather than be swallowed by the ghost of greatness past. The Harlan Era honored the greatness of the 1960s by embracing the legacy of professional football's most fascinating franchise.

"I have a keen appreciation for the resurrection of the Packers franchise under the direction of Vince Lombardi because we faced many of the same challenges," Harlan said. "Herb Adderley, Dave Robinson and other players of similar character were important contributors to the team's success under Coach Lombardi. We can all be proud of how they have represented the Green Bay franchise through the years."

Lombardi's teams seized the moment and seemed to have won every time it mattered. Adderley, Robinson and their teammates, never shortchanged themselves, each other or the fans with a lack of effort. The games were as serious as life itself.

Adderley said, "I always make the comparison between how styles change, for instance, clothing, hair styles and music, to name a few. However, class never goes out of style. All sports change for different reasons. Mainly, the athletes get bigger and stronger with each generation, but the basic fundamentals of all sports remain the same. My natural athletic ability was a major factor to my success. I was born with that."

Adderley can click off an impressive list of events in his life. "Competing against the great Wilt Chamberlain will always rate in the top sporting events of my athletic career. The others are listening to my high school football coach, Mr. Charles Martin, when he convinced me to play football." Adderley's journey out of the inner-city was laden with accomplishment, and he points with pride to highlights on his road to greatness. "Earning a full football scholarship at MSU, being drafted number-one, playing for Coach Lombardi and the World Champion Green Bay Packers, playing against the great Jim Brown and Johnny Unitas are cherished events in my life. Also, playing in four Super Bowl games, returning an interception for sixty yards in Super Bowl II, and being elected to the Pro Football Hall of Fame in 1980."

Adderley is always mindful that he did not succeed alone. "Without the guidance and help from all of the people who helped me at the club in the neighborhood, I wouldn't have made it," he said. "So, I owe a huge thanks to all of those who lent a helping hand to me. The only way I could repay all of the people was to do what I was taught and to treat everyone with respect. Reverend Adolphus Hobbs at Enon Baptist Church always preached about treating people the way you want to be treated. I never forgot that and still treat people that way."

Adderley and Robinson are big fans of today's Packers and the solid foundation built by Bob Harlan and General Manager Ron Wolf. Robinson made the trip to Dallas for Super Bowl XLV, and Adderley took out a congratulatory advertisement in the *Green Bay Press-Gazette* following the club's win February 6, 2011. They root for Mark Murphy, Mike McCarthy, Ted Thompson as the franchise continues a pursuit of greatness. Pure class.

Lombardi's Left Side shut down the left side of the field and opened the right side of our minds.

Profound, fundamental changes. Only a few *Chosen* people make them.

Acknowledgements:

We would like to thank Vince Lombardi for touching our lives with his greatness and giving us a story to tell. In time, we hope the Great Man is appreciated for his historic efforts to move our country and the National Football League forward in matters of racial equality.

A special thanks to an American treasure, Bill Cosby, for writing our Foreword and providing additional comments. Mary Finberg of the William Morris Endeavor Agency was especially helpful regarding communication with Dr. Cosby.

A good friend and knowledgeable Packer fan, Scott DeLaurelle, contributed his time, talent and writing skills. It's amazing how a person so young can know so much about the Packers. Thanks, Scott.

Packers' Hall of Famer Willie Davis, the great left defensive end, supported his teammates once again with his unique insights of the Lombardi Years. Thanks, Number 87.

Boyd Dowler has been a tremendous friend, teammate and resource who holds a unique place of admiration for all three of us. Our book is much better because the fine flanker opened his mind for Lombardi's Left Side.

Thanks also to former Packers and judges Ken Bowman and Nelson Toburen for their comments on our behalf. Bow was as rugged as he is bright and Nelson is a miraculous man who deserves our admiration. You can find the reasons in Chapter Nine.

Members of the Lombardi Packer family, Jimmy Taylor, Paul Hornung, Olive Jordan Frey, Vicky Aldridge Nelson, Pat Peppler, Chuck Lane, Lori Keck, Jesse Whittenton, Ron Kramer, Zeke Bratkowski, Tom Brown, Donny Anderson, Jim Grabowski, John Rowser, Phil VanderSea, Marv Fleming, Bill Austin, Bill Anderson and Pat Cochran, offered valuable comments to our book.

We extend our gratitude to Bob Harlan, chairman emeritus of the Green Bay Packers, and Director Dennis Tattum, Archivist Tom Murphy and Office Manager Gwen Borga of the Packers Hall of Fame.

Pat Richter, Bruce Laird, Jeff Nixon, Tony Davis, Joe DeLamielleure, Mel Renfro, Mark Washington, Calvin Hill, Cornell Green, Pat Toomay, Duane Thomas, Margene Adkins, Gail Cogdill, Jim Gibbons, John Brodie, Bill Wade, Lenny Moore, Charley Taylor, Lem Barney and other former players offered insightful comments. We especially appreciate the courage of the Dallas players who confirmed the unbelievable events that occurred in Cowboyland.

The highly respected Ernie Green, member of the Little Rock Nine, offered support and reassurance regarding our direction on racial matters. Mr. Green and other "kids" from the grill at Michigan State University helped us capture the flavor of the times for African-Americans. Carolyn Rush Robinson-El John Young and Gregory Eaton have been Herb's cherished friends for half a century.

Herb's lifelong friend and mentor, Leonard "Bunky" Rhodes, provided useful comments and the cherished photo of the Mr. Airy Badgers basketball team.

Another of Pulaski Town's finest, Al Chandler, joined our team and put his decades of experience behind us. Thanks, Al. We could not have done it without you.

Herb's friend and physician, Dr. Kevin Fleming, has been a source of trust before and during the compilation of *Lombardi's Left Side*. Thanks, Doc.

Scott Stroup of Yesterday's Heroes was exceedingly helpful locating photos and putting them in a useable format.

Sam Speigel of Partners Book Distributors introduced the parties from Lombardi's Left Side and Ascend Books to enable the project to take flight.

Heartfelt thanks to the staff at Ascend Books, who were helpful, supportive and professional during every step of the process: Publisher Bob Snodgrass; Editor Cindy Ratcliff; Publication Coordinator Christine Drummond; Lenny Cohen, sales & marketing; Bob Ibach, publicity; and Cheryl Johnson, designer.

We also offer a special "thank you" to Green Bay Packer and football fans around the world who care about the game and the men who play it.

Herb Adderley

Dave Robinson

Royce Boyles

Herb Adderley

Herb Adderley played for the Green Bay Packers from 1961–69 and ended his career with a three-year stay in Dallas. Adderley is one of the NFL's all-time greats.

He is a member of the Pro Football Hall of Fame and the 1960's All-Decade team. He was selected as one of the NFL's 100 greatest players and was a five-time Pro-Bowl member. Adderley has been enshrined in six halls of fame.

Herb is one of three players to be a member of six world championship teams, and played in a record seven College All-Star games. He and Green Bay teammate Bob Jeter were selected as the 4th best tandem of cornerbacks in league history.

Adderley scored the first defensive touchdown in Super Bowl history with a 60-yard return of an interception in Super Bowl II.

In his 12 NFL seasons, Adderley recorded 48 interceptions, 7 touchdowns, and averaged 21.8 yards per return.

Herb served as lead plaintiff in a class action suit on behalf of more than two thousand retired players who claimed the National Football League Players Union breached licensing and marketing terms for use of their images in video games, sports trading cards and other dealings. A clear-cut victory resulted in a $28.1 settlement in favor of the players.

DAVE ROBINSON

Dave Robinson played outside linebacker for the Green Bay Packers from 1963–72 and was a member of Vince Lombardi's three consecutive World Championship teams in '65, '66 and '67.

The Packers won Super Bowls I and II as a crowning achievement to the great dynasty.

He was Green Bay's first-round draft choice for the '63 season after being selected as a consensus All-American at Penn State as a tight end. Dave also played defensive end for the Nittany Lions.

In their "greatest series," NFL Films selected Dave, Ray Nitschke and Lee Roy Caffey as the sixth greatest group of linebackers to ever play the game.

Robinson is a member of the Packers Hall of Fame, the 1960's NFL All-Decade team, and the College Football Hall of Fame. He serves on the Board of Directors of the Pro Football Hall of Fame.

He played in the Pro Bowl in '67, '68 and '70, earning Most Valuable Player honors for the game in 1968. He was traded to the Washington Redskins in 1973 and concluded his career after two years in the nation's capital.

A co-author of the acclaimed books *The Lombardi Legacy*, and *The Lombardi Impact*, Robinson is now semi-retired in Akron, Ohio.

ROYCE BOYLES

Wisconsin native Royce Boyles is a lifelong sports fan with a distinct curiosity regarding Vince Lombardi and the Green Bay Packers. Co-author of *The Lombardi Legacy* with Green Bay's great linebacker Dave Robinson, Royce continues to explore the personal dimensions of Green Bay's legendary coach and general manager.

His first book, *The Lombardi Legacy,* was used and credited as a resource for *HBO*'s 2010 Emmy award-winning documentary, "Lombardi."

Boyles also authored *The Lombardi Impact*, a unique look at Vince Lombardi's leadership style. Vince Lombardi Jr. told Royce, "I leaned things about my father I didn't know by reading your books."

Recognized as one of the foremost authorities of the Lombardi Era, Royce resides in rural Rock Springs, Wisconsin, near the tourist area of Wisconsin Dells.

Visit www.ascendbooks.com for more great titles
on your favorite teams and athletes.

www.ascendbooks.com